Sir Henry Wrixon

Socialism

Being Notes on a Political Tour

Sir Henry Wrixon

Socialism
Being Notes on a Political Tour

ISBN/EAN: 9783337132774

Printed in Europe, USA, Canada, Australia, Japan

Cover: Foto ©Suzi / pixelio.de

More available books at **www.hansebooks.com**

SOCIALISM

SOCIALISM

BEING

NOTES ON A POLITICAL TOUR

BY

SIR HENRY WRIXON

Late Attorney-General of Victoria, Australia, and Commissioner for Inquiry from that Province

London
MACMILLAN AND CO., Ltd.
NEW YORK: THE MACMILLAN CO.
1896

CONTENTS.

CHAPTER I.
SYDNEY . . . . PAGE 1

CHAPTER II.
THE PACIFIC, FIJI, AND HONOLULU 23

CHAPTER III.
CANADA 48

CHAPTER IV.
ENGLAND 65

CHAPTER V.
SOCIALISM IN ENGLAND 79

CHAPTER VI.
MEETINGS 96

CHAPTER VII.
SOCIALISTS I HAVE MET 128

CONTENTS.

CHAPTER VIII.
	PAGE
THE UNITED STATES	158

CHAPTER IX.
THE UNITED STATES (*continued*)	195

CHAPTER X.
SOCIALIST LITERATURE	232

CHAPTER XI.
THOUGHTS OF THE MAN IN THE STREET	260

CHAPTER XII.
RELIGION AND THE FAMILY UNDER SOCIALISM	280

PREFACE.

In the year 1894 I was appointed by the Government of Victoria to be one of its delegates at the Colonial Conference that was about to be held in Canada; and at the same time a commission was given to me to inquire into some public questions that interested and concerned us colonists in common with all the more progressive communities of the world. Socialism was the subject that under this authority mainly occupied my attention during my visit to Canada, England, and the United States; though, as I am following the incidents of a tour, I also deal with other kindred topics as they came in my way. There have been a great number of able and ingenious books written upon the Socialist movement, and my object was rather to learn from the workers themselves what they thought of it, and how it is presented by the literature of the bookstall to the man in the street. While I express—I hope clearly—my own conclusions, my mission was, and this record of it is, rather that of an observer and a reporter than an instructor.

A French writer remarks that nothing misleads

some men more than the aversion that they feel for those whose manners are unpolished. No such feeling dwelt in me. I sought out the obscure toilers, and felt for them that sympathy that a man naturally has for his own people. At the same time I availed myself of the information that was to be obtained from higher authorities, and I am indebted for ready assistance to several gentlemen of position in the Socialist world, or who take an interest in social questions in England and the United States. Among many I might mention Mr. Sidney Webb, of London, and Mr. Carrol Wright, of Washington. I have also to acknowledge my obligation to the Earl of Kimberley, then Secretary of State for Foreign Affairs, for giving me letters to the English Consuls in the United States, and to Mr. Walter, of *The Times*, for an introduction to one of the representatives of that paper. Personally I was no stranger to the subject, and my political experience in our Australian provinces, where Socialist views (though not those of the most advanced type) are often advocated, and have been to some extent adopted, gave me at least that useful condition of truth-seeking which consists in knowing what questions to ask. I would add that I felt it to be a duty no less imposed upon me by my commission than agreeable to my own feelings, to inquire impartially into all aspects of the subject, and to gather knowledge from every quarter where it could be obtained. It certainly is of the last importance, whether we approve of Socialism or condemn it, or are in doubt about it, that we should know what it is, what it proposes, and what it leads to. It need scarcely be said that neither the Ministry of Victoria that advised my appointment, nor any subsequent Government, are responsible for or identified with my opinions.

The Premier who submitted my name to the Governor, the late Sir James Patterson, acquiesced in the request that I made that I should not be expected to present an official Report of my experiences, so as to leave me greater freedom; and I have thought it better to throw them into a more popular form. I found a general readiness to give me information; but, as many of those with whom I conversed were in dependent positions, either in industry or in the humbler walks of politics, I have thought it better not to give the names of those whose views I record.

It must be borne in mind that my main object was to inquire into Socialism, and therefore these pages are chiefly occupied with the views of that portion of the working classes who adopt that principle. The number who do this to its full extent is small in both England and the United States, though many have leanings that way, while in public and municipal affairs many things are done in the name of Socialism that are not Socialist in the true sense; and, on the other hand, many things that are directed by Socialist motives are justified upon quite different grounds. Great expectations and great dread have equally been excited by the march of Socialism. The Paris Correspondent of *The Times*, writing in September, 1894, says that the real victor at a recent important election in France was Socialism. "It pervades the artisans, it will next pervade the peasants, and will not be long in claiming the mastery. It is less deep-rooted here than in Germany, but it covers more ground. Nothing can be done to check it." The only outcome, he considers, is a military despotism that will at least give men peace. Similar reports from other Continental countries appeared. Since that time, however, the Socialist party have received a marked check by their political weakness being exposed at the General Election in England, and by the successful but by no means unanimous, nor apparently very intelligent, revolt of the Old Unionists at Cardiff. The victors there would, according to their declared principles, have been classed a short time ago as thorough Socialists. They have also suffered defeats during the year at the polls throughout the Continent, and the Populist party in America shows little sign of being able to assert itself as a distinct political power. It would be a great mistake, however, to conclude from all this that the principle of Socialism was disposed of. It has still to be reckoned with, and political parties will still court it. The problem that it presents lies deep in the industrial conditions, joined to the political conditions of our time. Its solution, as it is wise or foolish, will lead to the vastly expanded prosperity of nations or to their premature decay. Its votaries, in common with many others who are not Socialists, are quite right in demanding a great improvement in our social conditions; and so far they no more can be checked than they ought to be. Their scheme, carried to its full extent, means an influence before which civilisation would wane. I shall be amply compensated for a good deal of labour—and no work is more laborious than interviewing—if in these pages anything can be found that will help towards the solution of the question of our age—how to better distribute wealth, but without impairing energy; to mitigate the struggle of life, yet maintain its progress; and, while making the people more happy, still to keep them free.

SOCIALISM

BEING NOTES ON A POLITICAL TOUR

CHAPTER I.

SYDNEY.

On the 5th of February, 1894, the Government of Canada passed an Order in Council inviting the Governments of the Australian colonies, of the Cape of Good Hope, of New Zealand and Fiji to send delegates to a Conference which it was proposed to hold at Ottawa in June that year, " for the purpose of considering the trade relations existing between Canada and their respective countries, and the best means of extending the same, and of securing the construction of a direct telegraphic cable between the Australian colonies and the Dominion of Canada." The Imperial Government was also asked to send a representative. The invitation was readily accepted, and representatives from Canada, New South Wales, Victoria, Queensland, Tasmania, South Australia, New Zealand, and the Cape of Good Hope met together, to hold the opening meeting of the Conference in the Senate Chamber at Ottawa, on the 28th of June in that year. The Earl of Jersey was present to represent the Government of Her Majesty. The sittings were continued till the 9th of July, when the proceedings terminated after some important business had been transacted, and much useful interchange of opinion had taken place upon matters that were of common interest to Britain and to her dependencies. It may be safely said that no other country in the world could have shown such a national family gathering of free communities. The delegates from Victoria were the Honourable Nicholas Fitzgerald and the Honourable Simon Fraser, both members of the Upper House, the Legislative Council, and myself, a member of the Legislative Assembly. We arrived in Sydney, whence we were to embark for Vancouver, British Columbia, in the middle of May, 1894. In passing I may pay a tribute to the merits of my brother delegates. We worked together with perfect cordiality and successfully carried out the objects of our mission.

Before we arrived, there had been a split in the Labour party in the New South Wales Parliament. This party had gone in somewhat upon the lines of Mr. Parnell's Irish party in the House of Commons. Their platform was to serve Labour as their sole mistress, rather than to fulfil the duties of general representatives of the country, and for this purpose to vote together as one man. After a while they found causes, partly political, partly personal, to divide them. In truth, the position of a representative who says that he will only act for one interest is, under our Parliamentary system, an unsound one, and is generally found to be impracticable, unless, perhaps, they represent a distinct province such as Ireland, so intertwined are all the varying elements that make up the social state. One of the leading Labour politicians told me that in his opinion it was a fatal mistake for them to go into Parliament at all. When they do so, jealousies and distracting influences at once arise. In all countries they should, he thought, wait outside, perfect their organisation, and direct other men whose return they can control. Speaking of Socialism, he said that he did not know what to say of it till he knew what it included. The answer of the plain-spoken Socialist on this point is not doubtful: he will take as much of the new social system as he can get now, and the whole when he is able to take it. There is no uncertainty as to their objects, though intelligent thinkers admit that a long time must elapse before their ideal can be reached. Another prominent leader, who has since risen in the political world, was more explicit. He said that at present what his party wanted was to nationalize the land in New South Wales. That was the great reform, wanted first of all and wanted now.

I.—How will you get it?

He.—Tax the value away gradually to the vanishing point.

I.—Would that be fair to men who, under your laws, and, indeed, at the invitation of the State, have given their money for it and generally given it to the Government directly as the great seller of land for the past fifty years? One man puts his earnings into land, another into a ship. The one is sacred, the other is confiscated.

He.—There can be no property in land; no Government can give it away from the people. The people themselves never gave it. Besides, it would all be done gradually, and there would ensue such general prosperity from the tax that they would not feel it.

I had many opportunities of conversing with Labour leaders and Single Taxers, both in England and the United States, as well as here in Australia, upon land nationalisation, and found their views and arguments always identical. The same remark applies to all the many phases of Socialism. Printer's ink makes the whole world kin. At headquarters, whether by a Henry George or a Fabian Essayist, certain views are propounded and supported by appropriate arguments. These at once spread to the remotest parts of the earth, and the humblest believer, wherever he be, faces you with them at once. But it is a curious fact that this drastic measure is so urgently demanded in a vast unpeopled territory like New South Wales, which contains over 310,000 square miles and only some twelve hundred thousand people—a country thus nearly four times as large as Great Britain, with about a thirtieth of its population; yet this party believe that their salvation depends upon seizing the lands that a few hundred of their population have taken up. They justify it by saying that all the good lands near the centres of population are gone into private hands. The object of the "Single Tax League of New South Wales" is declared to be: "To abolish from time to time existing systems of taxation and to gradually substitute for the manifold taxes now in operation a *single tax* levied upon the bare value of land, exempting from taxation all improvements, until the annual value which attaches to the land from the needs and growth of the population is ultimately absorbed by the Public Treasury to be administered for general public purposes." Their organ is a well-printed paper of eight pages, published monthly, and full of facts and figures, such as Single Taxers love to set forth all the world over. I shall afterwards have something to say as to the awkward position that this party finds itself in, when summoned to join the advance of the whole line Socialistic.

Both Houses of Parliament were sitting while we were there. The Assembly, or lower house, is elected by manhood suffrage, while the Council, or upper house, consists of members nominated by the Ministry in power and appointed by the Governor. The Secretary of State for the Colonies has laid down the rule, as a general one, that in accepting these nominations, the Governor simply acts upon the advice of his Ministers, as in the usual course of constitutional government. Being a nominated chamber, it has little direct popular power in the country, but it presents what has been described by a high political authority "as the physiognomy and aspect of a grave legislative body" even more completely than does the ruling chamber. The Legislative Assembly of New South Wales may be taken as a fair type of the Australian Legislatures. If they cannot lay claim to the culture that used to mark the House of Commons, they are free from many of the conditions that enfeeble the local Legislatures of America. Perhaps I may be allowed here to take the opportunity of giving some account of them.

The House of Commons is described as being composed of bankers, merchants, shipowners, brewers, railway directors, men known in literature and science, lawyers, doctors, country gentlemen, colonial governors, soldiers, sailors, and working men. Our small communities could not supply this variety; but we have lawyers, doctors, journalists, storekeepers, farmers, business men, mining managers, and working men. Lawyers have generally been numerous in popular assemblies, notwithstanding the prejudice against them. In the States-General of France that struck the keynote of modern democracy in 1789, there were 374 lawyers! In the United States they predominate in several lines of political life; but they are not so numerous in our Legislatures. Briefly, our Assemblies may be described as middle-class bodies. The poorest are represented there, but do not dominate. The other end of the social scale can scarcely be said to be directly represented at all, though indirectly they may have influence. We can lay no claim to the culture or polish of aristocratic Parliaments. You cannot combine the political advantages of a past age with those of the present, nor join in one assembly the merits of both aristocracy and democracy. This is not peculiar to politics; it applies to other phases of life, public and private. The political is only one aspect of the social state—perhaps the liveliest and most prominent; also, the closest scanned. In all, equality and the inrush of members gives breadth and vigour rather than elevation. But if our legislators are plain men, they need not fear comparison with aristocratic bodies in the matter of personal honesty, while they naturally feel more concern for the wants of the people with whom they are identified.

The many functions undertaken by our Governments, and the large measure of assistance that they render to districts out of the general revenue, enfeeble the position of the representative, and impair the public spirit of the constituencies. Each locality naturally seeks to get as much as it can, and for this purpose wants rather an agent to look after its interests than a statesman to take care of those of the country at large. The representative is harassed by a divided duty. This I take to be the greatest impediment to statesmanship in our ranks, and the more Socialistic Governments become the greater is the danger that Burke's prophetic fear may be realized, and "national representation degraded into a confused and scuffling bustle of local agency." The forbearance of many constituencies towards a member whom they respect upon public grounds, and the sense of duty to the State of members, have so far done something to mitigate the worst results of this principle. Many years ago, when in the Victorian Legislature, I had the difficulty that I speak of brought home to me practically. I—perhaps with more zeal than knowledge—actually proposed to do away with local representation altogether and to adopt Hare's system of proportional representation applied to wide divisions of the colony. My resolution ran thus: "That the representation of localities is foreign to the principle of manhood suffrage, and moreover, by the special duties and obligations to each locality that it imposes upon members, taken in conjunction with the power of the Government over the expenditure from the general revenue for local purposes, has a tendency to impair the position of the representative and to endanger the true character of Parliamentary representation."

The House gave a very fair hearing to the proposal, but considered it to be outside the range of practical politics. Yet we all feel the burthen of local work, and how, at times, it conflicts with public duty.

This position of our Governments naturally promotes the formation of small parties in the Legislatures to secure what they consider justice for the interests they represent. Thus we have amongst us country parties, mining parties, and all the interests that look to State protection of industries; while our powerful Public Service associations have often made their weight felt both inside and outside the Parliament. The cities are always and naturally combined, and able to conserve their own interests. They return the members of the Labour Party. Our Parliaments are sometimes blamed for their hasty and varying legislation, and it is not to be denied that all popular legislation is experimental, changeful, harking back upon itself. Look at the Imperial legislation on bankruptcy. The State of Maine amended its liquor law forty-six times, and then it did not answer its purpose. But the legislation is experimental, only because it actually reflects from time to time the varying feelings of the community, as they are prompted by impulse or warned by experience. With us, as with all democracies, there is impatience under any inconvenience, a disinclination to submit to any evil, or supposed evil, for ever so short a time, joined to a simple belief that you have only to get an Act of Parliament to set it right, whatever it is. Are the hours of labour too long, or the shops open too late; is there too much gambling, drinking, or general immorality; are the banks obstructive in business, or the sharebrokers too sharp, or the lawyers too free with their tongue; nay, does that most ancient of wants—the want of money—make itself again generally felt, the first cry is to Parliament, Right this wrong! And some new law is accordingly made, sometimes with good effect. But as it is the most difficult thing in the world to frame the principles of a law wisely, and then to express them accurately, frequent alterations are required; while at times, the object to be attained being really impracticable, the Act quietly becomes inoperative. For laws, with us, to be real laws, must commend themselves "all the time," as the Americans say, to the people. If unsuitable they are tacitly ignored. Experience is picked up quickly. Hence looking back to the legislation of even a few years ago is like walking through an old armoury full of curious weapons and quaint shields quite unsuited to to-day. But in all this the Legislature can only be blamed for too faithfully reflecting the popular will.

Looking at this Parliament in Macquarie Street, Sydney, one finds carefully reproduced the practice and procedure of Westminster. It is the same in all the Australian provinces. We are as observant of precedent as the English themselves. The Speaker is in gold-embroidered silk and full-bottomed wig upon great occasions; in silk and wig at all times in the chair. A silver-gilt mace, richly ornamented, an exact copy of that at Home, lies upon the table when the House is sitting, but is hurried underneath when the Speaker leaves the chair and Committee begins. A few years ago ours in Victoria was stolen from the Parliament building, under the belief, it is supposed, that it was gold; and it now having gone to the thieves' melting-pot, we have to content ourselves with a small wooden one, which, however, proves equally potent as a symbol of authority. The useful rule of referring to members by the place they represent is observed. Any title that can be given to a member is carefully given. Any one connected with the militia is termed the "hon. and gallant member;" any one with the law in any of its branches, "hon. and learned member;" any one connected with medicine is "the learned doctor;" if there is a Baronet among us, he is always "the hon. Baronet." We have never got to the length of calling one "the hon. and rev. member," as Lord Palmerston did John Bright, though we have some gentlemen in our Parliaments who occasionally preach to bush congregations that might be otherwise untaught. With all our love of equality, we relish these little distinctions; like the Americans, who began by a resolution to allow no title to their President, but to send papers to "George Washington" simply, and have ended by having "Honourables" and "Colonels" innumerable.

In matters of procedure we follow as closely as we can Imperial precedent. Hatsell, May, Todd are our authorities. Ever since Lord Cowper, on the 9th of February, 1721, in the House of Lords, asked the Government whether one, Knight, whom the House wished to proceed against, had been arrested, which is said to be the earliest recorded instance of a question asked in Parliament, the privilege of questioning the Government has been a favourite one with members of Parliament; though with us, as also in older lands, the actual practice at times differs widely from the theory that you ask only for some specific information and get a reply containing that information, both question and answer being without comment or argument.

When we enter the House we bow respectfully to the Speaker; but probably few of us, or few even of the House of Commons itself, remember that in so doing they are only repeating what had its origin in the old English Parliament, not as a reverence to the person of the Speaker, but a clerical obeisance to the east.

The rules of the House of Commons against personalities, disorder, irrelevancy in debate, are our rules too. In extremity I have heard a Speaker threaten to "name" a member, and the threat had effect, though none knew its import or consequence. Imputing motives, not necessarily of a base kind, but indirect motives for any political conduct, is a favourite form of what strictly is disorder, but which, if skilfully done, it is hard for any Speaker to stop. The leader of the Government and the leader of the Opposition confer with one another as to the course of business, as at Westminster, and the whips upon both sides look up votes, arrange pairs, confer with members, persuade and remonstrate, just as if the affairs of an empire were being transacted. The friendly co-operation of the in and out law officers which distinguishes the House of Commons is fully sustained among us.

In nothing is adherence to ancient English usage more shown than in our retaining the old forms relating to voting the public money. Still in theory the Crown demands supply, which we reluctantly grant. If any motion is made for a "charge upon the people, the consideration thereof may not be presently entered upon." If any report of a resolution from a Committee of Supply comes up, it must be received on a future day. The Appropriation Bill is jealously retained by the Assembly till the prorogation, and then handed by the Speaker to the Governor. The old and once so vital principle of redress of grievances before supply is still recognised by our Standing Orders; though, in order to prevent intolerable abuse, its exercise has been limited in Victoria to specified days. And all the while some of us are only anxious to grant as much money as possible to the Crown, and have had positively to be prevented by Act of Parliament from voting it except upon the invitation of the Crown. Not only so, but we obviate the effect of this law by, in any case of supposed need, addressing the Governor with a request that he will recommend us to vote the desired money. The position of old times is reversed. The people are really voting money to themselves, not away to the Sovereign; but all the old forms of unwillingness are scrupulously preserved.

Another ancient right of the House of Commons that our Parliaments have, in past times, claimed and exercised—as vested in them by the Constitution Act and subsequent legislation—is that of treating offences against them committed outside Parliament as breaches of privilege, and punishable summarily by them at their discretion. On one occasion, during the period of demoralisation caused by the land lottery system in Victoria, the Assembly there sent two gentlemen to gaol for the alleged bribing of members. The Chief Justice, after consultation with the other judges, and, as he stated, "without hesitation," discharged the prisoners, upon the ground that the Speaker's warrant of commitment should have specified the contempt for which they were committed, whereas it simply stated that the Assembly had adjudged them to be guilty of contempt. But the Privy Council, presided over by Earl Cairns, promptly overruled this decision, and held that the Assembly had in this respect all the rights of the House of Commons.

Lord Brougham, in his speech on the second reading of the Reform Bill of 1832, said that if he ever felt confident in making a prediction it was that, when the people were properly represented, the Press would become subordinate to Parliament. In fact it is just the other way. The more the suffrage is extended the stronger the Press becomes relatively, till, in the most advanced democracies, it overshadows Parliament altogether. It is the readiest, and also the most constant of all organs of public opinion. The Australian Legislatures have had for some years past the good sense to refuse all proposals to enforce the obsolete right to deal with alleged libels upon them as a breach of privilege. The public would not support them if they did desire to exercise it. More than once, when a member is aggrieved by some unusually bitter criticism, he has moved to bring the printer to the Bar; but after indignant self-defence, followed by appropriate deprecation of offensive written remarks all round, the matter is let drop, the injured man being left to his remedy at law.

A trifling instance of our adherence to Imperial precedent, but one which concerns the general impression that we make upon a sight-seer, may be added. Hats are worn in the House as at Westminster, but of all descriptions, from the stately tall silk to the pliable wide-awake, of various shapes and many colours. If a question of order arises while the House is dividing, a member can only call attention to it with his hat on. To put a crushed wide-awake on in order to challenge the notice of the chair seems an undignified proceeding to onlookers. Sometimes this is done with an air of defiance, however awkward the hat. Sometimes a diffident man will borrow a tall hat from a neighbour to serve the turn. Thus do the instincts of the Saxon remain conservative, while all else has changed.

The Australian natives are, in the Legislatures of the younger provinces, a new element rather than a party. They are divided among all parties, but chiefly belong to the advanced and progressive side. They labour under two obvious disadvantages: their country has had no political experience—and the course of no country is determined by the experience of another; and she has had none of the struggles that give nations grit and leave inspiring memories to coming generations. But the impression that they leave on an observer is distinctly hopeful. They show freshness of thought and spirit, with a contempt for the old hackneyed methods of the political stage. Indeed, some of them do not hesitate to say that the local Parliaments are not worthy of the energies of an able man, and that they would leave politics altogether were it not for the hope of Federation and a national Legislature. They often favour new and sweeping modes of dealing with abuses, and will not be debarred by any old world maxims from effecting thorough reforms; but they do not fall in readily with the class cries imported from Europe, which are unsuited to our young countries. The native-born members show a spirit of respect to order in Parliament, and display more deference for senior members than they are at times credited with. But all such feelings are founded upon reason, as being proper and becoming, not upon authority or custom. None have more freely denounced obstruction and senseless waste of time. It is not merely that it is wrong; it seems to them so absurd. We would be more useful to the country and to ourselves, say they, if we stayed at home, at work, at the office or the farm. Their tone of discussion is always fearless—at times original, not always profound.

As mere oratory is going out of fashion in even the Imperial Parliament, it cannot be expected to survive in our small assemblies. One thing alone would suffice to forbid it—namely, that every member speaks on every prominent subject. This was not always so—with us in Victoria, at least At one time only selected leaders from each side made the second reading speeches, and then each upon subjects with which they were conversant. Members generally expressed their views, where necessary, in committee. Until late years such was the example set us by the House of Commons. A man of even the universal knowledge of Macaulay, when he addressed the House upon the second reading of the Sugar Duties Bill, apologized for doing so, and, admitting that it would be out of place for him to speak upon a financial or commercial question, contended that much more than commerce or finance was involved in the sugar duties. The more there are who do speak, the more remain who must speak. The constituents like to see their member to the fore: it is better to be heard of some way than no way. Repetition and diffusiveness, however, kills oratory, of which earnestness is the soul; and who can be earnest under such conditions? Then there is not time to think out each subject, and loose thinking makes long speeches. To prepare a speech properly is one of the most difficult of intellectual tasks, as you have to study and think sufficiently to be quite conversant with your subject, but not so as to deaden the freshness and spontaneity of delivery. Many and many a speech that would have been good has been spoiled by too much trouble being taken about it.

Further, no man, however industrious, can be well informed upon all subjects. He who really has mastered any one has done well—whether it be trade, finance, constitutional questions, social science, or practical matters connected with the people's daily work. Yet upon all of these, at times, the member is expected to say something. Generally, too, the current of public opinion or public feeling runs in regard to any of them all one way at a given time, and unless a man has full information and conviction in himself, which can only come from previous thought, he is apt, in any assembly, to follow the tide and repeat rather than originate.

But our speaking is what might be expected from the conditions—plain, ready, at times forcible. Even in the best assemblies of the old world nothing tells better for ordinary work than a plain conversational style. In our grandfathers' times, incredible as it may seem, it is yet true that when Burke rose in the House of Commons members ran out to avoid being bored with his eloquence. Romilly mentions that he was once in this way deprived of Burke's assistance with one of his bills. Burke stood up to speak in its support, but there was such a stampede that he became disgusted and sat down. Canning's brilliant rhetoric was enjoyed by the House, but he took care to keep in close sympathy with his hearers by going round when intending to speak and interchanging ideas with as many men as possible, so as to keep his idea upon their level. Gladstone's wonderful powers of speech have had effect mainly in giving enthusiastic voice to whatever was the prevailing sentiment of the day. On the rare occasions that he was in opposition to this, as for example upon the Divorce Bill, his eloquence was not so effective. Certainly, each generation the speaking in the senate and the forum—though not perhaps in the pulpit, where rhetoric sometimes still lingers—becomes less finished in style.

But marked natural powers at times come to the front in our debates. The course is free to all. No artificial disqualification exists, no deadening influence of social position or proscription. If a man has any idea in him to express, he is not overawed by the fear that he may not give it with authority or put it in classical language, or that it may be considered odd. I have known in the Victorian Assembly several self-made men who, if they could have had the training and the opportunity, would by sheer force of ability have secured a high place in even the House of Commons, which, I suppose, may still claim to be the most intellectual as well as the most critical assembly in the world. And it need not be said that when a ray of true eloquence penetrates our debates, as sometimes it does, all own its touch. Its influence is mesmeric wherever it falls, be it Old Bailey Court full of roughs, crowd in the market place, Salvation Army gathering, poor South Sea Islander gesticulating about the wrongs of the labour traffic. Like the shoot of the sunbeam, it strikes bright and vivifying, into the murkiest atmosphere.

In all popular assemblies there will at times be rough speaking, and ours are no exception to the rule. Demosthenes used to describe his opponent as "an accursed scribbler," "a traitor," "a monster of wickedness and malignity." He also reflects upon his birth and bringing up, and asperses the character of his mother! Personal topics are the natural weapons of men in the wordy war, and are only a step removed from the blow of manual fight. As late as 1680 personal violence threatened to break out in the House of Lords during the exciting debates on the Exclusion Bill. Yet the members of our Parliaments who exceed the limits of debate are few. Why "scenes" sometimes loom large to the public eye, is because they are always fully reported, while other matter is generally compressed. Thus the few minutes' work of but one man among seventy or eighty will appear in print as if it were the main business of the evening. Nevertheless, it is not to be denied that parts of the *Hansards* of all Parliaments, from the House of Commons downwards, will make queer reading for the political bookworm a hundred years hence, when our institutions may perhaps have grown into some new form. I fear that, as with people at a distance now, they will give him an exaggerated impression, unless he remembers that it is the empty bodies that float upon the surface and obscure the substance of the stream.

For our Parliaments may be claimed a sense of

justice and rough spirit of fair play. I have been a member of various bodies, lay and clerical, and though our methods are less refined in the political assemblies, I have found the spirit of justice to opponents and to views that are really distasteful to the majority, stronger in the rougher body than in the more select ones. This I attribute not so much to any superior virtue upon our part, as to the fact that we are so much in the blaze of publicity; and also that we are taught, and indeed compelled, by the hard experience of political life, to hearken to and make allowances for opponents.

Of all our Australian Legislatures it may at least be said that they reflect the community. If the elected have defects it is because the electors have them too. It is true—though an old truism—that every people is as well represented as it deserves to be. If you want perfect assemblies you must look out for perfect peoples. I am no believer in the creed that ascribes perfection to the masses, and charges all the ills of the political world to the politicians whom the masses appoint and control.

I could not end these few notes on Australian Parliaments without paying my tribute of homage to some whom I have known as members. These men combined the soul of honour with a sense of duty that would have put to shame not a few of the successful politicians of the world. They simply and fixedly did what they believed to be right, often in contradiction, at times to their own loss, and without even that infirmity, which besets many good men, of a craving to get the recognition of the public for their services. This reward has not been wholly denied to them. Yet our Legislatures have not got such good repute from their merits as they have incurred disrepute from the defects of those who fall below the standard. The account of Parliament in the national ledger is often not evenly balanced.

It was towards the end of a long session, when Parliaments get demoralised and unfit for work, like schools at breaking-up time, that we visited the Sydney House of Assembly. It, however, gave the observer the impression of plenty of vigour. Some leading men told me that the *personnel* of the House was altering, and going into the hands of men who followed the occupation of politics alone. The long hours of the sittings now as compared with those of even a few years ago are held to be accountable for this. While we were there Mr. J. H. Want, a leading barrister, and Mr. Bruce Smith, a prominent shipowner, announced their retirement from politics, and wrote letters to the papers to explain it. Mr. Want in his letter says that by an analysis of the records of the House he finds that in 1883 the days of meeting in the year came to 59, while in 1893 they were 116, and the hours of sitting were 419 in the former year, and 1,096 in the latter, while less work, he maintains, was done in the longer hours. He declares that he has awakened to the fact that not only is he "burning the candle of life at both ends, but that he is doing so in vain." One notices how identical the conditions of political life in democratic countries become. A leading American mentioned to me much the same facts as one cause of the absence from their Legislatures of men who held positions in the world of learning, the professions, or in business; while in at least the provincial Legislatures of Canada the same evil is observed and is explained in the same way. This explanation is, however, only partial; the problem is many-sided. You cannot combine the advantages of two opposing systems—the aristocratic, with its select and skilled representatives, marred as it has been by neglect of the masses; and the democratic, with its imperfect exponents, but all devoted to the service of the people from whom they spring. This question of the decline of legislative power will be again met with in my notes upon the United States, where it is more forcibly presented by the fuller development of the political conditions of our time, and when it will ask for further consideration.

A general election was in prospect in New South Wales, and the community appeared to be much exercised, and also a good deal divided in opinion, upon the question of free-trade. The policy of protection adopted in the United States and most of our colonies is supported by arguments and considerations, some of which appeal to the interests of the wage-earner and some to those of the capitalist.

It is not mere argument, however, that determines public opinion on questions upon which men's feelings and inclinations are strong. In most countries the wage-earners have a natural leaning to protection. The very idea of protection is pleasant to many. Each man is apt to look to the immediate result promised in his own calling, and is not disturbed by the more distant difficulty of the undue stimulation of the trade and the want of a market. But in Sydney I found that the workers were by no means agreed upon the question. Some of those who were most democratic in feeling were for free-trade. The great mercantile interests of their city, and its position now as the shipping centre of Australia, have much to do with this feeling.

As Sydney was the headquarters of the "New Australia Co-operative Association," which started on Socialist principles to settle a large tract in Paraguay, something may be said of it here, though I did not meet the settler whose views I record till a later period in my travels. In 1892-3, when depression began to overshadow Australia, it occurred to a number of persons who had still something to lose that it would be a good idea to combine their means in a brotherly way, leave the country, and settle all by themselves in another clime, where they could get plenty of good land, and arrange their affairs and industry as they pleased. The climate of the country they proposed to go to was healthy, the land excellent, two acres being sufficient to support a native family. Leaders appeared, offices were opened in Sydney, a prospectus issued, and a newspaper published to disseminate their views. The object was stated in the prospectus to be: "To put into practice, on a voluntary basis, and under the most favourable conditions available, that form of industrial association which will secure justice to all." The preamble of another document runs thus: "Whereas it is desirable that good actual proof shall be given that, under conditions which render it impossible for one to tyrannize over another . . . men can live in comfort, happiness, and orderliness unknown" in the present state of society, therefore this new venture was founded. The rules provided ownership by the community of all the instruments of production and exchange, and maintenance of all children by the State. "Division of wealth-production among all adult members without regard to sex, age, office, or physical or mental capacity." The little commonwealth was to be governed by a director and superintendents; regulations (or laws) to be annually submitted for reconsideration. "Religion not to be officially recognised by the community." Among the conditions of membership was the following: "Every member to agree to subscribe to the common fund of the association all he possesses, except personal effects, and to migrate to the land selected by the association, there to devote all his energies to the success of the settlement, and to showing the world that, under fair conditions, even workers can live a life worth living." "Each for all, all for each" was the motto on the cards of membership. Hopeful accounts of the new venture appeared in the London press.

Some six hundred persons joined, from all the colonies, and two shiploads were despatched to South America. All were necessarily persons of a little means —£60 at least had to be paid down—and were also possessed of energy; and not a few were, as far as I could learn, impelled by enthusiasm for the social ideals now scattered, both by novels and by graver works, throughout the world, and fully believed that those ideals were sound and capable of being readily realized. They hoped to demonstrate their value in practice, and to enjoy the promised ease and plenty in a new land and under new social conditions. The leaders of the movement were practically self-appointed, but each squad of workers elected their foreman. As is known, dissensions soon broke out, and the Sydney Government was appealed to to bring the people back. I met one of the members as he was returning to Australia. He was an intelligent man, with an evident bent towards enthusiasm, at least that sort of enthusiasm which expends so much fervour upon public matters that it has little left for home use. He stated that he had lost in cash £143, together with all his effects, and he was full of grievances concerning the management of the venture. He had told them they might take his tent for the general use, but no other things of his stock; but they seized everything. Also he brought more serious accusations against the probity of the management, which subsequent information led me to think unjust. But, notwithstanding all, he still declared his faith in the principle of such a social settlement to be unshaken. Had he money, he would join another.

1.—How would you arrange as to the sort of work and the hours for each?

He.—Quite easily. Every little group would elect its foreman, every man and every woman voting, and he would appoint the job to each. If we did not like him we would change him. And we would not be like a lot of loafers; we all had something to lose.

While listening to his narrative I had recalled to my mind the remarks upon this subject of one of the ancient masters of the political science—if I may be excused for invoking an old authority upon what many consider as novelties peculiar to our age. He says that the evils we complain of "arise not from properties being private, but from the imperfection of mankind; for we see those who live in one community and have all things in common disputing with each other oftener than those who have their property separate."

I mention this venture only as one more instance added to many previous ones, of the difficulty of voluntary Socialism, and particularly in communities such as ours, where all enjoy so high a standard of personal freedom. In such communities people are taken with fancy sketches of the co-operative commonwealth, but when it comes down to fact, they realize that there are none who love liberty so much that they don't want to impose their will upon others; they find restraints by their fellows more irksome than if fixed by a power high above them all, and at once their love of independence asserts itself. It must not be supposed that I cite this instance as a proof that the complete "scientific" Socialism advocated now would also break up when tried. That Socialism is avowedly based upon force of law. The true Socialist looks with contempt upon these voluntary efforts. He gives them no countenance, because they discredit his ideal, which is a state of things to be established by law, and to which people must submit. In 1893, in England, some Socialists propounded a scheme not unlike that of "New Australia," to be tried in England itself, as "the easiest way to Socialism," hoping that, if once it were started, it "would attract continuously a larger and ever larger proportion of the nation and more and more skilled workers, until well-nigh all the industry and commerce of the country were absorbed into it." But the leaders of the cause knew well where voluntaryism would land them, and accordingly scouted the proposal; one of the most thoughtful of them (Mr. Sidney Webb) truly declaring, in a lecture which he gave upon the subject, that "To suppose that the industrial affairs of a complicated industrial state can be run without strict subordination and discipline, without obedience to orders and without definite allowances for maintenance, is to dream, not of Socialism, but of Anarchism." Discontent still would doubtless be there; that is only human nature under any system, but not the freedom to indulge it that the settlers in New Australia claimed.

I mention this because many whom I subsequently met on my journeys appeared to assume that they could have the Socialist State and also the personal freedom that they now enjoy. So far no outcome has been found for the difficulty of industrial government under it. If the workers elect their master, there will be no discipline; if he is imposed upon them by authority, there is no freedom.

CHAPTER II.

THE PACIFIC, FIJI, AND HONOLULU.

WE left Sydney by the steamer *Arewa*, Captain Stewart, on our way to Vancouver. We were to call at Suva, the capital of Fiji, and at Honolulu, that of the Sandwich Islands, and would thus see some quite new forms of human life and social state, which, savage or half-civilised though they be, yet give the political traveller subject for thought. Nothing can be pleasanter than voyaging in the Pacific at this season. Sea, sky, atmosphere, have all the clearness and brightness of the best days in the Mediterranean.

We were fortunate in having on board a well-informed gentleman who had long been resident in New Zealand, and whose opinions upon social matters possessed the more interest, as, though a close observer of all social questions, he was not himself a politician. I had many interesting discussions with him. As the reader may possibly be aware, New Zealand is the community that has distanced all others over the world in the race towards State Socialism. This has not been brought to pass by the presence in their midst of that sordid poverty that in older lands makes, and indeed excusably makes, humanity long for any change. On the contrary, their country was equally blessed by the bounty of nature and in having a good sound stock of early settlers. Jay Goulds, Fisks, Vanderbilts, were unknown among them, while the middle class was so large and powerful that they might have claimed the benediction of the ancient who exclaimed: "Happy is that State where the middle is strong, and the extremes weak." Yet, for some years back, the tide of political feeling has run with an irresistible flow towards State Socialism. The feeling seems to be that the old social system is so bad that any change must be for the better. Later on, while in England, I had the advantage of discussing this subject with Sir Westley Percival, then the Agent-General for the colony, who gave me many official papers dealing with it. The Socialists point with pride to what has been done in New Zealand and to its results; while opponents declare that personal energy and initiative is being sapped in the community. Whatever view we may be disposed to take, it must be remembered that a young community, with plenty of fertile land, and a good stock of settlers, cannot go very far wrong; and also that there has been no time yet to test by experience much that at the outset looks well.

Certainly in New Zealand it may be fairly said that the people rule. The Assembly is elected by universal suffrage, men and women voting alike. The Premier lately told a deputation of ladies, who came to demand the right to sit in Parliament, that the justice of their claim was undoubted, the only objection was that they had not sufficient political experience. Unquestionably, if women are entitled to the franchise, they are also entitled to sit in Parliament, and in the Executive. You can say that politics are no more their sphere than war, or navigation, or enforcing the criminal law would be, without conveying the least disparagement of the sex. But if you admit that they ought to enter the political arena, to refuse them any more direct share in government than voting, is to assign them a position of inferiority such as Roman Catholics were in before Catholic Emancipation.

Most of the Ministers of the Crown come from the

class of wage-earners. The Upper House is nominated, but several of the nominations have included working men. The principle that their leading men announce is, that their struggle is to put an end to the struggle for existence. Lord Onslow, in the paper that he read before the Colonial Institute upon his return to England after his retirement from the office of Governor, quotes the words of one of their ablest men, Sir Robert Stout: "We have a noble opportunity. . . . We are not encumbered by privileges; we are not encumbered by prejudices, and we are, therefore, free to make experiments. I ask the House to make those experiments. I ask the House to believe that these experiments may be made. I ask the House to think that even if these experiments fail, still it is our duty to make them." Workers generally, and especially settlers upon the land, are generously helped by the State, land being leased upon easy terms and money advanced. Large estates are denounced and discouraged by taxation. A Labour Depôt, presided over by a Minister, endeavours to find work for the wage-earners, and generally to promote their interests. Government work on railways and public undertakings is given to the men direct, so as to eliminate what one Minister termed "the absurdity of the middleman being kept to make a profit from both the Government and the workmen." Their objection to contractors appears to be as strong as that of the great Napoleon, who used to term them "a curse and a leprosy to nations." The manner in which the wages paid is arrived at, is thus explained: Ascertain first what it would cost to do the work at per day's wage, current in the locality, for a similar class of work. Add to this the percentage of profits which a contractor would require. "The earnings of the men should, with all first-class men in a party, be ten per cent. higher than the current rate of wages for similar work." The official report also describes how the supervision is managed. "The Government Engineer, in fact, has practically to take the position of the contractor, whilst the overseers have to act not only as overseers for the Government, but also as a foreman of works for the contracting parties." The Minister adds, "The work has cost no more than it would have cost if it had been done under the contract system, and at the same time a better class of work has been done." It was stated in the press that in some cases the men who were intrusted with a job, themselves employed a contractor who, with good plant and machinery, was able to do the work with a profit to all parties.

Provision is made by law for the Government to buy up estates near populous centres, and to lease them out in small blocks to the people. In the Budget of 1894 the Government asked for £250,000 to purchase private lands, and another £250,000 to improve them for settlement by the people; and also for authority to borrow in London a million and a half, which was to be advanced to settlers at cheap rates, the Minister declaring, "The country must have a plentiful supply of money. It must not be dependent upon the whims of investors." This money was subsequently raised with ease in London. The State carries on a vast Insurance business, and is able, by its superior position, to cripple the advances of any private undertakings. The hours of labour and the manner of work in all shops and factories are strictly supervised, and the employer required under a penalty to give his *employés* one half-holiday a week. Most employers do this readily; but there have been some prosecutions in the police court for failures to comply with the law. It need not be said that protection against foreign goods, and as far as possible against the immigration of foreign labour, is an essential feature of this self-contained community. The obedience of the representative to his constituents is so absolute that he is their delegate rather than their representative. New Zealand is twice the size of England and Wales, and its population is about equal to that of Manchester. Yet with all this, as late as June, 1895, the Wellington correspondent of the Melbourne *Age*, which has always been favourable to the progressive policy in New Zealand, says that it is deplorable to see the number of unemployed clamouring to the Government for work in Dunedin; and that the Knights of Labour there had resolved that all incomes of £200 a year and over should be reduced, and the savings employed for a fund to provide work for the people. A month later the Melbourne *Argus* correspondent from the same city wrote that the demands for employment were more clamorous than ever.

Life on shipboard gives ample time for conversations, and sailing over the bright Pacific, of whose islands it may be truly said, as it was of Greece, "pure the air and light the soil," I often talked with our New Zealand passenger upon *the* problem of social life, with which his community was grappling. He approved of all that had been done, and was an advocate for the State doing a great deal more. He quite agreed with Sir Robert Stout's views, though both he and Sir Robert disclaimed being Socialists. They were regulators of unrestrained individualism. He would have the State own all the instruments of production and employ the people; but this must be done gradually; some branches of industry, such as shipping, would not be taken over for a long time. The fact was that they could not renew, in their social state, the condition that had in the past prevailed in Europe—the poor wallowing in squalor, misery, and crime. They must be helped out. This appeared to be the bed-rock of his views, as it is of so many other thinking and humane men; yet it does not prove the conclusion that their remedy is the true one. But with several Socialists that I subsequently met that was the real argument. "Are these horrors to continue? No. Then adopt our plan to end them." He said that he and his friends held that the struggle of life was yearly increasing in intensity—that the prospect of a fair chance for an individual was getting less and less—that in the absence of State control they would have corporation despotism. Let the Government employ the people and treat them fairly. I asked him if he did not anticipate difficulty as time went on from the political representatives advancing claims upon behalf of their workers, that industrial conditions could not stand, and mentioned that, in one of the Australian provinces, just on the eve of a general election, a motion was made and quickly carried in the Assembly to give an increase in pay to the railway labourers, against the opinion of the commissioners, whose duty it was, under the law, to arrange the wages of *employés*. The members who voted against it were all men marked by the powerful Labour interest at the coming election. And truly, was such a motion or such a consequence to be wondered at, every little addition to the wages of the worker seems to be so reasonable, and opposition to it so heartless? Yet could you combine this political control with business management that would be fair to the outside workers and to the whole community that had to pay for it? He said that he feared no difficulty of that kind with his people, and that the people must everywhere be trusted, particularly now, when every woman had, or soon would have, a vote as well as every man.

I.—Having done so much, you have still the poor among you; in what direction will you now move?

He.—Well, I would not allow the accumulation of very large properties. When a man had made a good fair competence, tax away the rest and employ the people with it. We must put an end to the horrors of the old civilisation. Under a proper system, a few hours' work a day would do for all, and the people could live happily.

I.—Is there not a fear that men would degenerate if in life there were no effort, no struggle—like those South Sea Islanders, some of whom we shall soon see at Fiji. You leave no incentive to enterprise and the large operations of the able man. From what you say, I confess that if I were a young man, and were conscious of ability to make a career, I would not start in New Zealand, when your full programme is carried out.

He.—Well, perhaps neither would I. But institutions must provide for the average man, who has so far been neglected.

With this oblique compliment to ourselves that conversation closed.

No country in the world has a greater future before it than New Zealand, with its water supply, fertile soil, and grand climate. It is, as has been said, the Britain of the South. It is making experiments, and it can afford to do so. It can also afford to make mistakes.

FIJI.

After a week's sail we arrived at the Fiji Islands, which are some 1,900 miles distant from Sydney, and, consist of over 200 islands, islets, and rocks, the superficial area of which is about equal to that of Wales. The two considerable islands are Viti Levu, which is about 30 miles in length by 55 in breadth, and Vanna Levu, literally "Great Land," which is 96 miles long by about 25 broad. "Levu" means "great," so Viti Levu means "Great Figi," "Viti" being properly Figi. This little community is one of the smallest of the Crown colonies of England, but it is worthy of the attention of the political observer as an instance of the colonizing power of our country and its aptitude for governing dependencies in circumstances however new or difficult. These island savages, for such they were, with the "blazing air of freedom and defiance" which old novels ascribe to the "Fegee chief," are now ruled in peace and content, and their ferocious habits suppressed, by an Englishman who has given his life to understanding them, assisted by a few intelligent officials. He has no armed force at his command. The districts have small native police corps of their own. His influence is mainly a moral one, assisted by diplomatic control of the antagonistic feelings of rival tribes. The administration of the public revenue and public works, of justice, trade, and charity is carried on in as exact a manner as it would be at Westminster; while the supervision over the labour engagements of the natives is vigilant, and, as far as a stranger could judge, while just to both master and servant, was particularly careful of the interests of the latter. I will refer to this again later on. "The Fiji Blue Book for the Year 1894, Published by Authority, and Printed by Edward John March, Government Printer, Suva," adopts in its statements of public accounts and the returns of its supplies, all the fulness and precision that we expect from such State compilations in England. It is drawn up from the records of the Colonial Secretary's Office, and I am indebted to it for many useful statistics.

As long ago as 1858, Thakombau, then king, offered to cede the sovereignty of the whole group of islands to England; but Colonel Smythe, R.A., who was sent out the next year to report, declared that it was not worth having. Possibly in itself it was not, but looking at the valuable possessions that England had on both sides of the Pacific, with the Dominion of Canada at one end and Australia at the other, and between them only a few islets for the Empire, whereon to rest the foot, an Imperial policy would certainly dictate the securing of more than one point of influence on the route across the ocean. This policy at last prevailed, and Fiji was, under the advice of the then Mr. Thurston, now Sir John, the Governor, ceded to the Queen. The islands were not conquered or forcibly annexed by England, but were ceded by the native King Thakombau, for a consideration, which was, that the Imperial Government would secure to the islanders their rights, public and private, and protect them against the undue aggressiveness of the white man, of which they already had some experience. Thakombau sent to Her Majesty his favourite war-club, in token that thenceforth he renounced club-law. This is now, I believe, in the British Museum. The result has been beneficial to the natives so far as the action of the Queen's Government has been concerned; though they have not escaped all those ill results that appear ever to follow the advent of the white man among half-savage tribes. Sir John Thurston has been thirty years among them, and joins a profound knowledge of their character and customs to a deep sympathy with them, while at the same time his rule is marked by firmness.

He had difficult material at first to work upon. It is a slow and delicate process engrafting upon the savage nature so much of the higher civilisation as is fit for it. When he began, cannibalism was rife among them, and the premature destruction of life in the case of sickness, old age, or for the sake of the most absurd caprices or customs, was a common practice. When a chief demanded "long pig," his wish was at once gratified by slaying one of his people and presenting the body. "May you club some one," was a common form of friendly salutation, founded upon general usage. Thakombau, their king, however, who long had been a confirmed cannibal, became converted; Christianity was spread among them, partly by the missionaries, but mainly by the sword of the invading Tongan Tribes, who had been Christianized, and who, as did Mohammed with the Koran, presented themselves with the Bible in one hand and the spear in the other. The Wesleyan Mission stands first among those of all the religious bodies, having 941 churches, and 379 other preaching places, 31,000 church members, 36,000 day school scholars, all of whom are enrolled upon the Sunday school lists, and 98,000 adherents. Though the Christianity of the natives is not the noblest type of our faith, it yet lifts them above their old barbarous and debasing habits. Mr. Allardyce, in a lecture that throws much light upon Fijian life, gives an amusing example of the simple form that their theological ideas take. At a service of native Christians that he attended the preacher was praying for a spirit of thankfulness to the Creator, and suddenly exclaimed, "Oh, that we were dogs, and could show our thankfulness by wagging our tails!" One is apt to be shocked at the recital of the savage practices that used to prevail among the islanders. Yet it chastens our indignation and contempt for these dark men and brethren, to bear in mind that in the last century cannibalism was not unknown in some Russian corps when they were hard pressed for food, and that certainly in the middle of this, the nineteenth century, the mob of Messina roasted and ate sixty Neapolitans. Nay, some men who figured in the French Revolution justified cannibalism; and akin to it was the savage industry carried on at the Tannery at Meudon, where the skins of the victims of the guillotine were tanned into good material for breeches; and it was recorded that the skin of the male was tougher and more serviceable in the manufacture than that of the female!

With all the savagery buried within them, the Fijians are not an unpleasant looking people. They have an air of independence about them. They have a regular gradation in their own social state—chiefs, warriors, common people, slaves. The native proper names appear to consist of sounds that to the European are hard to spell and impossible to pronounce. In the list of Government officers we find names such as these: Saleri Kinikinilau, Jovesa Korovulavula (who holds the office of the Governor's assistant Matanivanua), Opetaia Kuruvakadua, Timoce Roqereqeretabua, Wawabalavu Naivariga, Nemani Vakacakaudrove; with many others equally inexplicable to the stranger, but which have a meaning no doubt for those who know the language. One notices a number of Christian names that appear to be taken or adapted from the Bible, such as Osea

Tuinairai, Samuela Naulu, Elaija Radovu, Mosese Volavola, Jeremaia Kalokalo, Solomoni Mariwawa. The natives are affectionate in their family relations, and love their children; but the regard of children for parents is weak, and what we term "filial reverence" is unknown. They love to celebrate the important events of life with feastings and shows. They work better when away from their own district or their native island. We saw in Suva some Solomon Islanders, who were working steadily, and we were told that they would not work that way in their own islands.

The chiefs are a real power among them, and are in fact true captains, leaders, able men, and have been so from time immemorial, because they are bred from selected parents. The chief always marries from a special tribe. This is the simple secret of their success. The Governor told me that he knew a chief the moment he saw him, though he was without any special garb, or at least knew him when he spoke. His policy is to govern the people as far as possible through their chiefs and native councils, carefully respecting all their old customs as far as it is possible to do so. Thus the Native Tax is assessed in a lump sum for each district, and the local native authority arranges the details as to how it is to be raised. It is paid in produce, which the Government take at a good market price. There is a native Parliament, or gathering of the chiefs, which is formally opened by the Governor. They regard Sir John Thurston as something more than a mere human ruler, for Thakombau "Tammared" to him, and thus devolved his authority upon him. This consists in bowing the head to the person to be honoured, and making a sort of grunt or exclamation. It is what the common man always does to his chief. The Queen's peace is well maintained throughout the whole island. You can travel everywhere in perfect safety. White children are sometimes sent up to the hills to escape the heat.

The Governor is assisted by an Executive Council, consisting of the Attorney-General, the Receiver-

General, the Colonial Secretary, and the Native Commissioner. Laws, termed "Ordinances," are made by the Legislative Council, which is composed of the Governor and the Executive Council, with seven unofficial members who are nominated by the Crown. Executive and legislative functions are thus mingled together, and practically the Government may be said to rest upon the personality and the mastery over the natives of Sir John Thurston. The salaries of the officials are, as might have been expected, small, but they retain the principle of rewarding long service by a pension. A Native Stipendiary Magistrate will get £1 a month for his services, or in some cases only ten shillings a month; a Provincial Scribe, £6, £10, or £15 a year. In the Pension list we read that Ananaiasa Solevu, an armed Native Constable, who was wounded in action, enjoys a pension of £3 a year. This may seem small, but it is really handsome, being twelve shillings a year more than his pay when in active service. Another native, who was wounded fighting for the Queen, gets as much as £10 a year.

The population consists mainly of Fijians, with a few Europeans, Indians, and Polynesians. Latterly, the introduction of Japanese as labourers was tried, but it has not been so far a success. In 1894 the population was estimated to consist of 2,666 Europeans, 103,750 Fijians, 9,130 Indians, 2,333 Polynesians, making up, with a few other islanders and half-castes, a total of nearly 122,000 people. The population of the Islands has decreased. In 1875 the measles swept away a quarter of the whole people, and left the rest much weakened in stamina. It will take a generation, at least, for the race to recover. Foreign diseases, too, among the natives, mark the advent of the stranger, and undermine the simple and, to them, healthful conditions of savage life. The area of the colony is put down at 4,953,920 acres, of which some 39,000 are cultivated. Bananas, pine-apples, copra, cocoa-nuts, maize, sugar-cane, yams, are the chief products. The public revenue amounts to £80,000 yearly, and the expenditure to £72,000; thus showing a surplus equal to one-tenth of the revenue. But they have a public debt of £224,000, £100,000 of which is lent by the Imperial Government without interest. Their immigration charges come to nearly £6,000 a year, and they pay a small subsidy to the Canadian Australian Steam Service. The value of all the imports for 1894 was £285,000, and that of the exports, £581,000, showing that the yearly trade of this small community is, as the returns grow yearly, now worth not far from one million sterling a year. Sugar to the value of £328,000 was exported in that year. There are nine sugar mills and two tea factories. Planters hope to be able to grow tobacco successfully. Some 350,000 letters, 282,000 newspapers, and 31,000 books and parcels passed through the post office in the year, which, unlike similar institutions in older lands, not only clears all its expenses, but pays a surplus into the general revenue. There is a Chief Justice who presides over Her Majesty's Courts, with a numerous Bar, including one Queen's Counsel. The law provides the necessary machinery for all the usual jurisdictions, from Common Law to Admiralty and Divorce, and the Rules of Court specify all details much as they do in England. Thus they stipulate that Counsel in the Admiralty jurisdiction may be allowed one guinea for a retaining fee, ten guineas on his brief, from one to two guineas for a consultation, and from two to five guineas for a refresher after the first day. The fees for writing attorney's letters are set out, but it is provided that they must be "*necessary* letters to the adverse party." All the old writs, so familiar to the English lawyer, are specified with their appropriate fee, Injunction, Prohibition, Scire Facias, Quo Warranto, Mandamus, and the noblest of them all, Habeas Corpus. Under English law the black man can thus claim his writ of personal liberty against the Governor, successor to Thakombau though he be. They also have the ancient institution of the Grand Jury, and "Bills" accusing Her Majesty's dusky subjects of crimes are duly "thrown out," if the evidence does not satisfy the Grand Jury that there is a *primâ facie* case.

The Labour Laws that have been enacted by the Local Government show a real desire to ensure fair play and prevent abuses. The Labour Ordinance of 1895, which deals with the case of the Fijian natives, may be referred to as an example of the care that is taken. An employer wishing to engage Fijians must get a permit from the Native Commissioner, who is the head of the Department of Native Affairs. At present this office is filled by Mr. William Allardyce, the value of whose public service, both to Europeans and Natives, is well known to the settlers. The native who desires to enter into a labour contract has first to get the consent of the *Turaga ni Koro*, and also that of the *Buli* of his district, which must be given in writing. A form of this consent is given in a Schedule to the Ordinance, and as the reader might like to see a Fijian official document, I give a copy of it here :—

Kivei koya 189
    Na Turaga ni Lewa ni Vavalagi
        I saka
            Au sa volavola yani oqo me'u tukuna vei kemuni ni'u sa vakadonuya na nodra la'ki cakacaka ki   ko ira ka volai tu oqo era.

A yacadra.	Sa vakawati se segai.	A gauna ni nona la'ki cakacaka.

            Au sa loloma yani
              Koi au
                Ko
Ai Vakadinadina   Buli

The contract of service must be ratified by a magistrate, and if the terms are "manifestly unfair," he is to refuse to sanction it, however much the native may desire it. The labourer is to get a Fijian copy of the contract, and may be paid £1 in cash as a *yagona* or customary payment preliminary to a contract, but no more; apparently lest the natives might be bribed by gifts to enter into unwise agreements. Fraud or coercion exercised to induce a Fijian to enter into a labour contract is punishable with fine or six months' imprisonment. Time work is to consist of nine hours a day for five days in the week and five hours on Saturday. If an employer ill-uses his servant, he can be fined and imprisoned, and the Native Commissioner can cancel his contract. If there are over fifty labourers on any plantation, a certified hospital must be provided. There are special directions as to the food that is to be supplied to the men. In addition to the native fruits, meat or fish is to be given, and so much tobacco, soap, and salt weekly. No married man can be engaged for a longer period than three months, and no woman, or child under fourteen. The employer must return all labourers to their homes at the termination of the contract.

On the other hand, punishment is provided for the labourer who is idle or who misbehaves. If he absents himself from or neglects his work, he may be imprisoned for a month. He is not allowed to sell any of his rations. He is forbidden to organise a "strike." If the labourers want to lay a complaint against their master, not more than five are allowed to leave the plantation together, and they must not carry sticks or weapons with them. Using threatening or insulting language to the employer is punishable by imprisonment.

The protection that the natives have always got from Sir John Thurston's Government, leads them to look to it as their guardian, and quite apart from the rights that the Labour Ordinance gives them, they depend upon it, in case of any dispute with an employer, to see that justice is done to them.

As we steamed along the coast we could see how well adapted much of the country was for growing tropical produce. Considerable mountains furnish a good water supply, and rich flats and valleys are available for growing sugar, cotton, tobacco, maize. The harbour of Suva is beautiful, and the view from the high land surrounding it most picturesque. The town itself is interesting, with its busy little shipping port, prosperous-looking shops, and dark natives from many islands clustering about, interspersed with white men who also come from different lands. Going into a shop to make a purchase, the shopkeeper told me that he came from Victoria, and that he retained a lively interest in the doings of that province. It is like Colombo on a small scale, and without its heathen temples; for all the natives profess Christianity, and there are three churches here, and three also at Levuka, the old capital of the colony. There is more than one good hotel, the usual Mechanics' Institute, a Hospital and Lunatic Asylum supported by the Government, but which accommodate also paying patients, and a gaol which contained 457 convicted prisoners. The returns for the hospital and gaol give very full information as to all arrangements for the health, cleanliness, food, and employment of the inmates, who almost all belong to the native race, or are Indians or Polynesians. We are told that in the lunatic asylum the patients are amused by cards, draughts, dominoes, music, and illustrated papers. Suva has its English newspaper, the *Fiji Times*, and its Fijian organ, styled *Na Mata*, and also the *Fiji Royal Gazette*. Levuka has a paper of its own. The gaol at Suva costs some £2,500 a year to support, but the prisoners earn, or do outside work, to the computed value of £2,191, so that it is nearly self-supporting. The Government House is a handsome wooden building, situated upon the side of one of the hills that rise around the Bay, and having before it a lovely prospect of tropical beauty. The reception-rooms are large and airy, and the wide verandah all round enables one to enjoy the evening breeze, as it may come from the Bay on the one side or the Ocean on the other. The Governor did the delegates the honour of entertaining them at lunch. We were waited upon by natives. They did their work well, and with an independent air that was not unpleasing. His Excellency told us that they would accept no orders from any white servant, but only from Lady Thurston or himself.

The Meteorological observations taken at Suva show a high uniform temperature for the year, the maximum ranging from 86° to 93° Fahr. in the shade, and there is moisture with the heat; but in some months it falls as low as 50°. Still, it is not probable that the white race could be perpetuated there. Production must be carried on by black labour under the superintendence of the white man, who will stay, as in India, for a time only. We saw several Fijians lying about the streets and wharves in a listless manner; they seemed to us to be the very picture of indolence. Our bad opinion of them was increased when our party went into a shop in front of which two or three of them were resting. One of us was anxious to get a specimen of the bread-fruit from a tree that was some hundred yards away, and the shopwoman asked them in the native tongue to go and climb the tree for it, promising good payment for their trouble. They looked up, shook their heads negatively, and sank to rest again. This confirmed in us all the conviction of their exceeding laziness; but a highly competent authority afterwards assured me that, though the natives certainly were not industrious in the same degree that men of colder climes and less fertile lands are, yet we had got quite a wrong impression from what we had seen. The Fijians, he said, who were idling about, were some of them wharf hands whose work was necessarily intermittent, and who were simply waiting for the next ship. Others had come down to the capital to have a holiday after having finished a labour contract on a plantation. The reason why they would not go for the bread-fruit was simply that all the trees there were private property, and they felt as an honest white man would feel if some dark-skinned rogue offered him money to go and rob an orchard. This shows how slow a passing stranger should be to draw conclusions from his first impressions. But, as my informant stated, there can be no doubt that the natives are idle compared with races of men to whom nature is more niggardly; the sunny clime and rich soil, ensuring an easy life, are fatal gifts. The Scotchman, with his raw climate and often sterile fields, is the better man. The Fijian will work when pressed to it; but his object gained, he enjoys rest upon a little fish and native fruits. No race of men have ever worked except under compulsion of some kind. There is the same laziness among other races in tropical climes, such as the Jamaican blacks, and even in Europe in the sunny land of the Neapolitans. An easy life disinclines them to work or effort of any kind; as, indeed, why should they struggle, if they can live at rest?

Even this little, half-savage community furnishes matter for observation to any one who is interested in the various aspects of social questions that different races of men present. For example, the Fijian knows nothing of the equality of men, which the more advanced races are trying to realize. The idea that one man is as good as another has never occurred to him. He has his born chiefs to whom he is ever ready to "Tamar," with appropriate exclamation. But then he takes care that they shall be real chiefs, by paying particular attention to their breeding. Carlyle was eloquent in his description of the true chief, and also in his lament upon the difficulty of finding him. The real King, Duke, leader, was something widely different from the merely titular person. "The chief of men is he who stands in the van of men, fronting the peril which frightens back all others." The original meaning of "aristocracy" was, we know, simply the best men of the country. But how to find them? This no philosopher has told us. The dusky Fijian humbly offers his solution of the difficulty, somewhat—since there is nothing new in the world, whether among black men or white—somewhat after the manner of Plato in old Greece.

The visitor to these Islands, with their mild climate and easy methods of sustaining life, is reminded of the old question about which some thinkers have speculated, as to the superiority of civilised over savage life. Professor Huxley a few years ago, on behalf of the European poor, declared in favour of the savage. He has a quiet life, enough to eat; clothes are no difficulty. Certainly it is painful to contrast the forlorn life of many of the poor in old lands and the hopeless condition of some, with the comparative ease of the savage's lot, and his apparent freedom from care. Yet experience shows that struggle is the condition of progress. The easy-going races stagnate and fall to decay. It will be the glory of our time if the result of our social conflicts shall be to give men a high plane of living and comfort, without destroying that energy and individual effort that is essential, not merely to secure advancement, but to prevent decline.

Since writing upon Fiji, an article has been published in the *Contemporary Review* by Mr. Hogan, M.P., in which the system by which the natives are required to pay their assessed tax in produce is severely condemned. The information gained by a short visit and that one gets from reading, does not enable me to speak positively upon a question that, to understand properly, demands an intimate knowledge of the habits and feelings of the natives. Long experience is necessary to acquire this knowledge, and no man has had experience which can be compared with that of Sir John Thurston. His judgment upon the matter must therefore have weight. A reason that lies upon the surface certainly suggests itself in favour of his policy, namely, that it saves the native from the trader or middleman. The Government take his produce direct, and credit him with the full value of it. The trader would naturally give as little as possible for it, and the necessities of careless natives would induce all the well-known entanglements of the money-lender. Also it may be doubted whether the Fijian would have industry and foresight enough to regularly cultivate his land, unless he was compelled by authority to do so. It is understood that the Colonial Office is giving careful attention to the subject.

HONOLULU.

In due time we arrived at Honolulu, the capital of the Sandwich Island group, which is in the island of Oahu. It is a flourishing and interesting town, with churches, good streets, over which run tramways, high-class hotels, a club-house, pretty suburban residences, electric light, the telephone, and a busy harbour full of shipping. The Americans dominate the place commercially and politically. The islands are only 1,800 miles from California, and their main trading relations are with the United States, with whom they have made, by treaty, reciprocal commercial arrangements. The republic takes their produce in exchange for its manufactures. The population is made up of Kanakas—a fine race, but rapidly dwindling—Europeans, Chinese, and Japanese. Their government was a limited monarchy, with a sovereign at the head, an Upper House of landowners, and a representative chamber that was constituted by popular election. Until lately a native Queen filled the throne, but she was accused of planning to upset the constitution and rule by native power alone, and when we arrived we found the little community in the middle of a revolution. The Queen had been deposed and was living in a private house, while an American gentleman was President of the new republic, and some fellow-countrymen composed the executive. United States troops had been landed, and the Queen protested that she yielded to them only. Lieutenant Harman, U.S.A., says that the United States practically established a protectorate over the islands. The *Times-Herald*,

Chicago, has sent round the question for the answer of a number of their leading men, "Should the U.S. annex Canada, Newfoundland, Cuba, and Hawaii?" Some of our party called upon the deposed sovereign, and were graciously received by her. She was a middle-aged, dark-complexioned woman, who appeared to be kind-hearted, and who spoke excellent English. After the manner of Europeans, she inquired how we liked sea-travelling, whether we suffered from sea-sickness, how long we would remain in her city, and at parting gave photographs. Her house was well-furnished, but without any display of either European luxury or barbaric wealth.

The cursory observation possible during our short stay would not enable one to form any opinion upon the merits of the respective causes of the legitimate sovereign and the successful rebels. But it was interesting to see how exactly all the conditions of victorious *coups d'état*, as we know them in Europe, were reproduced here. All was done in the name of the people; popular election, plebiscite duly held, to ascertain if the nation was favourable to the new Government. But there was the usual question as to whether the election was a genuine one, or only a make-believe. The condition of being allowed to vote, we were told, was that the voter accepted the republic. Certainly the successful party had behind them an armed force, small, but quite sufficient against an inert population, which supplied that base upon which in the last resort all Governments must rest. Whether, if the Hawaiians could have individually expressed their free opinions, they would have deposed their Queen, may be doubtful; but in how many European revolutions have the mere unbiassed wishes of the majority prevailed? How often do they in government at all? In politics, as in war, the victory is to the compact, aggressive corps, skilfully led, not to the sluggish mass, unorganized as they always are. The successful party, too, followed precedent by offering to the Queen a handsome provision if she would renounce all rights to the throne for herself and her daughter, a young lady who was then being educated in Europe; just as the great Napoleon offered the Bourbon heir to France an Italian province if he would renounce his regal rights. He replied in one of the few noble letters that can be ascribed to the Bourbons, refusing the offer, and saying that he would still remain true to the cause of France, though for it he had lost all but honour. The Queen, we were told, replied in a similar strain. Since then we have read of what was said to be an attempted counter-revolution by her partisans. The rising was promptly suppressed, and the usual arrests, trials for treason, sentences, confiscations, have followed. The gentlemen composing the new Government appeared to be clever men, and prompt to act when occasion required. We experienced this ourselves. One difficulty in laying the cable that was projected between Vancouver and Australia, and which it was one object of our mission to secure, was supposed to be the want of British, or neutral, landing-places for the different stages across the ocean. Practical authorities have since declared that the lengths to be spanned are a matter of little consequence, as by aid of modern inventions the cable can be laid in safety for thousands of miles on the ocean bed at a stretch. Before we came some inquiries had been made as to the conditions under which it could be landed, if necessary, for one stage, at Honolulu, and also as to what facilities there were for making a small island, some 300 miles distant, the resting-place, which some preferred as an alternative, since it had never been formally annexed by any power, and so could be taken by England for that purpose. The young republic, however, hearing of or surmising this idea, promptly sent round one of its little ships of war and hoisted its flag over the barren rock. The fact was that the United States Government, with whose wishes they were no doubt acquainted, had resolved to show no favour to the British Pacific cable, preferring to have one from

Honolulu to San Francisco, and so secure the commercial relations between the two places. However, we can lay our cable from Vancouver to Fanning Island, which is our own, without difficulty, though it is 3,232 knots, and it is to be hoped that we shall do so without delay.

The natives are a handsome, lazy race. The soil is so fertile, and the climate so genial, that there is no need for hard work in order to live. Yet at times they will work, when pushed to it. The patient, much toiling Chinese, of whom there are a considerable number here, plods along contentedly from one year's end to another. The Japanese immigrants also are industrious, and the labour of these two races upon the rich land makes the wealth of the country great.

There was noticeable here what one particularly observes in small communities — the pride in titles, names, distinctions of rank and office. Indeed, this feeling is natural to us all, however democratic our ideas may be in the abstract. When trade and artisan societies go out upon a fête day, you will see badges and decorations worn with evident satisfaction by men who would yet recite, with enthusiasm, Burns' scornful reference to the "riband, star, and a' that." Here we found the public men designated by high-sounding titles, each Minister's card bearing upon it the title of the office he held; as for example, so and so, "Minister for Foreign Affairs." To illustrate how strong this sentiment is, even with learned men, I may be excused if I close this long chapter with an incident that happened many years ago in my own province of Victoria. A Supreme Court had been established there from the first, the judges of which used to be addressed by the title of "Your Honour," it being considered, I suppose, that it would be too much to import the old "Your Lordship" from the mother land. In 1853, County Courts were established, and there the practitioners, who were chiefly from England and Ireland, retained, in addressing the Bench, the style of "Your Honour," to which they had been accustomed in those courts at home. But the judges of the Supreme Court resented this sharing of their titular dignity by an inferior jurisdiction, and the authority of the Governor-in-Council was invoked to check the encroachment.

The following notice was accordingly published in the *Victoria Government Gazette* :—

Colonial Secretary's Office,
Melbourne, *4th October*, 1853.
NOTICE.

In order to remove an erroneous impression which has prevailed as to the proper title of judges of the inferior courts, the Lieutenant-Governor directs it to be notified that, until Her Majesty's pleasure be known, the title of a judge of a County Court or the Chairman of General Sessions shall be that of "Your Worship" or "His Worship." Where the name of office is required, the addition to the ordinary address should be "Judge of the ——— County Court," or "Chairman of General Sessions," as the case may be. The titles of "Your Honour" and "His Honour," having been as yet conceded by Her Majesty to the judges of the Supreme Court alone, cannot properly be assumed by or accorded to any other officer.

By His Excellency's command,
JOHN FORSTER.

But how to proceed—how to give effect to these sound views? The County Court judges did not style themselves "Your Honour," and after all was it in their power to prevent the public doing so? In this dilemma the Acting Chief Justice wrote the following official letter to my father, who was one of the first appointed judges :—

Supreme Court,
8th July, 1853.

SIR,—I have the honour to request that you will have the goodness to inform me if it be with your sanction that you allow yourself to be addressed, in the court in which you preside, by the title of "Your Honour."

I remain, Sir,
Your obedient Servant,
R——— B———,
Acting Chief Justice.

To the Chairman of General Sessions
    for the County of Bourke.

My father, who had only arrived from Ireland a short time before, replied that when presiding in his court he was variously addressed by witnesses and others—sometimes simply as " Sir," or even " Mister," often " Your Worship," frequently " Your Honour," occasionally " Your Lordship," and, though rarely, " Your Reverence"; but that he was unable to say that he actually sanctioned any one of these titles. In the end the public, with a natural obstinacy, continued to " honour" the County Court judges more than ever.

CHAPTER III.

CANADA.

WE arrived in Canada early in July, and as we travelled through the whole extent of that vast Dominion, from Vancouver, on the Pacific, to Quebec, on the St. Lawrence, we had many opportunities of observing Canadian social life, and some of studying its political condition. And Canada is vast. To get from one end to the other you go 3,000 miles by rail. You can do this now comfortably in five days and a half: one hundred years ago it took a goods dray three weeks to go from London to Edinburgh. Its mountain system, stretching from north to south, also measures that wide span. Its rivers, some of which are the grandest in the world, number fourteen. Some of the smaller ones would be worshipped as river-gods by us in Australia. It has nine great lakes, two or three of which are rather to be called inland seas of fresh water, besides lesser ones innumerable. Its vast forests still defy the inroads of the splitter and the sawmill. Its total area is not much less than that of the United States or Europe, falling short of the size of the latter division of the earth only by something over 300,000 square miles, which is not much when you are dealing with areas of millions. Though this great country has only a handful of people, speaking relatively to its size, yet its population numbers over five millions; and the representatives of Canada and Australia at the Conference spoke for more than ten millions of the Queen's subjects. In 1820 the two countries had only about half a million of people between them! But since then England has poured forth her sons by the million to find new homes. In 1815 the total number of emigrants who left England was 2,000; in 1852 it had reached 368,000—over 1,000 a day.

The warm cordiality with which we were greeted at all points of our journey, and by all classes of people, somewhat disqualifies one for the duty of critic. Yet, on consideration, I can only speak well of the people. At Toronto, near the close of our mission, we were presented with an address by the Imperial Federation League of Canada. It fell to my lot to reply for the Australian delegates, and I am reported, in the official record of our proceedings presented to the Canadian Parliament, to have spoken to this effect :—

> If anything were needed to give us an idea of the grandeur of our empire, it is to realize, as we go through your dominion—in itself a kingdom—that it is a small part of the great nation to which we belong. Nothing since our leaving home has struck us more forcibly than the men who inhabit the Dominion of Canada. We have seen wonders in nature and the wealth which your country contains. Your scenery is beyond that of most parts of the world. These things are grand, but let me say, that they do not make a nation. It is not the fertility of the soil, the richness of mines, nor great waterways that make a people. It is the men who make a nation. We know that wealth and fertility of land have marked nations which fell into decay; but here we have seen in your people all the elements of progress and growth. We have seen that you are thoroughly Anglo-Saxon in character, and filled with that determination of purpose which has made the mother land, and which has been exemplified in the deeds commemorated by that noble statue we saw at Queenston Heights yesterday—the monument to General Brock.

Often such speeches are only to be taken figuratively; but I can reiterate here what I said then. The people appeared to be of a solid, industrious, self-respecting type; self-reliant, and not apt to be carried away by delusions and vain cries. Perhaps the long winter, compelling as it does individual foresight, energetic industry during the time of the year available for outdoor work, and home life, partly explains it. Snow, it is said, is essential to civilisation. The style of living among the better classes was moderate and without display; the salaries of officials were small. The Temperance party was strong among them. In the cities one does not see that undue proportion of public-houses that is so noticeable in other lands, and at some of the most important entertainments that we were invited to, wine was not displayed in any profusion; mineral water was taken instead of champagne. A picnic was given to us in one of the parks at Ottawa, at which a stately lunch was laid out, but without wine, beer, or spirits. We were told that the conditions of the grant of the park prohibited the use of alcohol within its bounds. A noteworthy aspect of the popular character was shown at an evening reception that was held in the grounds of the Parliament House at Ottawa. It was a brilliant affair; the gardens, which were all ablaze with the electric light through tree and shrub, being crowded till late in the warm summer evening, with the youth, beauty, fashion, and rank of the city. The grounds are unfenced, and abut upon the public way; a rope was drawn across to keep out the populace, who thronged around to see the sight. They scrupulously respected the boundary. Not even a street boy attempted to pass inside. There appeared to be no representatives of the roughs of large cities, the hoodlums of San Francisco, or the larrikins of the colonies. But it must not be forgotten that the Canadians are, as I have said, some five millions of people in a territory nearly as large as Europe. There may be quite new developments when they even reach the numbers of the population of the United States: not to speculate upon the time when Canada is crowded like the old world. Then, at least, if not before, the systems of the new world, social and political, will be tested from Hudson's Straits to Panama, from British Columbia to Florida.

The people appeared to be attached to the Dominion tie and the Federal Government in the more distant provinces quite as much as in the central ones. Some even seemed to me to take a greater pride in the Government at Ottawa than in their own local government; for, while they complained of over-government, their feeling appeared to be rather directed against the local than the central authority. Democracies are tiring of their numerous Legislatures and officials, with the attendant expense and elections, and, feeling now liberty to be secure, turn rather towards some central single authority which would do the work necessary for the State and leave them alone. In the United States several of the local Legislatures have been prohibited by the people from meeting oftener than once every two years. Some of the provinces here have dispensed with their Upper Houses, it is said partly for economy's sake, and are accordingly in this position, that whoever gets a majority in the one chamber, can carry directly anything he pleases within the limits of legislation allowed by the constitution, to the provincial Legislatures. There is no independent executive to check, as there is in the United States. This would seem to be a power that carries with it the danger of abuse, setting at nought, as it does, the old maxims as to the value of two houses— constitutional opposition—and that delay which has been said to be the essence of the British constitution. I suggested this view to a prominent business man in one of the single chamber provinces; but he stoutly combated it, and maintained that the old idea of the English constitution was quite out of date, and unsuited to their condition. "Personally," he said, "I am no politician, and would not touch politics; but once you give a vote to everybody, then it is idle to talk of checks. Delay only irritates the majority, and relieves them of the sense of direct responsibility for what is done. You cannot permanently stop them; by modifying and delaying, you only share responsibility with them. No, let them do what they think best, and learn from experience. The more you stop them, the more bitter they get to go on." Something like this was said more than a hundred years ago by Burke. But this view overlooks the fact that the mere feeling of absolutism is bad for any man or assembly of men, and also the consideration that not every community may be strong enough to afford the experiment. You may learn wisdom, indeed, but only when it is too late.

A curious feature in their politics is that while in their provinces they are mostly Liberal, the Dominion Government and Parliament has been for twenty years Conservative, with only one short break, which was owing to exceptional causes. Indeed, the stability of their administration is a marvel when we compare it with the record of Ministries in the mother country, not to mention the shifting governments of the colonies. One party to be in power for twenty years,—one Minister we met with had been in office for fourteen years continuously. How is it done? And they boast of their conservatism. They do not hide it or pass it off under some other name, such as "Liberal-Conservative," "Tory Democrat," "Young Englanders." I heard a Minister in the House of Commons, Ottawa, speak of the "great Conservative party, to which I am proud to belong," amid loud cheers. Some say that this arises from a tacit agreement among the people that they shall have progressive local politics, but safe, steady, general government. Others give another explanation, and say it is owing partly to the marked individuality of the late Sir John Macdonald, and to the large share that he possessed of that peculiar gift which goes so much to constitute statesmanship, and which is known as the power of managing men. Some say that it depends upon the exercise of a vast patronage, and the influence of great corporations, which revive the memory of the methods of Walpole in parliamentary government. It is also explained by the fact that the Conservatives are protectionists, and supported by the personal zeal of the protected interests, while the Opposition depend upon a public opinion that is lethargic and by no means united for free-trade. Further, it seems that the warm zeal the Government party has always displayed for union with the Empire increases their popularity. All these causes may have co-operated in producing the result, but all would not be of themselves sufficient did we not take into account the staid character of the people, and also their prosperous condition. No bank in Canada has, for the last twenty years, failed to pay its depositors in full. This prosperity will continue if Canada can increase its population so as to utilize its great public undertakings.

But no party, whether Government or Opposition, appeared to lean towards a severance from the British Crown, or a union with the American republic, their proximity to the "Yankees" not seeming to increase their admiration for them. Except the voice of one powerful writer—Mr. Goldwin Smith, and there are angry critics of his views,—I could discover no organ of public thought that favoured union with the republic as their destiny, while demonstrations of loyalty to the Queen, and pride in belonging to the Empire beset us everywhere. "God save the Queen" was sung with enthusiasm at all sorts of gatherings—social, official, business—and more freely and persistently than is the habit in the mother land.

"The Maple Leaf for Ever" may be considered Canada's national song, and often did we listen to its pleasing notes. Its closing verse runs thus:

> On merry England's far-famed land,
>   May kind heaven sweetly smile;
> God bless old Scotland evermore,
>   And Ireland's Emerald Isle.
> Then sing the song both loud and long,
>   Till rocks and forests quiver,
> God save our Queen and heaven bless
>   The maple leaf for ever.
>   CHORUS—The Maple Leaf, etc.

Our conference at Ottawa was closed, after our business labours were ended, by the delegates rising up and singing spontaneously, standing round the table, the national anthem of the Empire.

At this conference, too, an earnest desire was expressed to find in the future, as the trade of England's dependencies and the restrictive policy of foreign nations alike increased, some means of promoting, if not freedom of trade within the whole Empire, at any rate greater facilities for interchange between the mother land and her colonies than would be granted to foreign nations, and thus to cement the natural desire for union with the feeling of mutual interest. In this movement the impulses of the statesman wishing to consolidate the Empire unquestionably predominate over the calculations of the shopkeeper.

The minutes contain the following entry:

> The following was then moved by the Hon. Mr. Foster, seconded by Sir Henry Wrixon: "Whereas the stability and progress of the British Empire can be best assured by drawing continually closer the bonds that unite the colonies with the mother country, and by the continuous growth of a practical sympathy and co-operation in all that pertains to the common welfare, and whereas this co-operation and unity can in no way be more effectually promoted than by the cultivation and extension of the mutual and profitable interchange of their products, therefore resolved that this conference records its belief in the advisability of a Customs arrangement between Great Britain and her colonies by which trade within the Empire may be placed on a more favourable footing than that which is carried on with foreign countries. Further resolved that until the mother country can see her way to enter into a Customs arrangement with her colonies, it is desirable that, when empowered so to do, the colonies of Great Britain, or such of them as may be disposed to accede to this view, take steps to place each other's products, in whole or in part, on a more favourable Customs basis than is accorded to the like products of foreign countries. And further resolved that for the purposes of this resolution the South African Customs Union be considered as part of the territory capable of being brought within the scope of the contemplated trade arrangements."

The objection to the first resolution obviously arises from the vast foreign trade of England outside its dependencies, and the supposed attachment of the English people to the doctrine of absolute free-trade, as some expound it. They are not all agreed in that view, though. At the conference of the National Union of Conservative Associations of England, held at Newcastle in December, 1894, when 1,100 bodies were represented, they passed unanimously a resolution warmly endorsing our proposals, which Colonel Howard Vincent, the Chairman of the Union, forwarded to me, with a note in which he expressed his own well-known views upon the subject. He afterwards brought the question forward in the House of Commons. The Imperial Parliament subsequently passed an Act giving effect to the second resolution upon lines that I had the honour of suggesting at the conference. Lord Ripon, in his two despatches upon the proceedings of the conference, discusses this question, and presents weighty arguments in favour of the view that so far has been taken by the Imperial Government. I refer the reader who may be interested in this question, which is at once Imperial and Colonial, to the Appendix, where he will find these important State papers. Certainly Canada has every reason to be satisfied with her union with the old land. It has perfect freedom, joined to the advantages of being part of a great Empire. It is even allowed, with the formal sanction of England, to make commercial treaties upon its own account with foreign nations, and it has more than once exercised that power. On the other hand, England is proud of her dependencies, and anxious for the tie between them to last and get stronger. Times are changed since a powerful Minister (Mr. Disraeli), writing to a colleague privately, declared that "these wretched colonies are a mill-stone round our necks," and another said that the only objection to getting rid of them was that England, once freed from them, would get too powerful for the rest of the world.

Parliament was sitting while we were at Ottawa, and we had several opportunities of attending it. The old arraignment of the Assembly of the French Revolution in the last century : "Nec color imperii, nec frons erat ulla senatus"—certainly does not apply to the Dominion Legislature. The Senate and the House of Commons presented, the one the appearance of a grave, the other of a reputable, popular assembly. If they have defects they are beneath the surface, and not such as strike the looker-on. The Senate, like all nominated chambers, has little direct power. Some leading politicians told me that such good men did not now come forward as did formerly, and that there was a decline in the character of their Houses. One night an incident happened that seemed to us strange and out of place. A division was being taken in the House of Commons; the members sitting in the chamber, while the Clerk of the House takes the votes by calling upon each member by name. While this was going on we were startled to hear one member loudly call upon another, whose vocal talent was well known, to give them a song. The request was readily complied with, and the tuneful legislator led off some popular air, his brethren joining in the chorus with a unanimity that had not marked the previous debate. Thus were the labours of legislation lightened. But do we not read in ancient verse how the immortal gods themselves closed angry discussions with the alternate strains of responsive song?

It would be out of place for me to discuss the merits of the Ministers of the Dominion, with whom we were conferring. But one thing may be said, that we were struck by the advantage, to themselves personally at least, of their long tenure of office. Perfect official experience, such as the permanent heads in England possess, giving them almost historical knowledge of each subject, enabled them to avoid crudeness in its treatment, and imparted that grasp which familiarity with the inside of questions confers. The long exercise of power, too, alone makes a man stronger. We Australians longed for federation more than ever while at the council board, for, though we worked admirably together, yet while we spoke with six voices Canada spoke with one. Ministers keep up some state here, and during the parliamentary session entertain the supporters and their wives systematically, much in the same manner and with the same object as it is done in

London. This practice, the influence of which is more felt than avowed, has not extended to the colonies.

Turning now to the social aspects of the country, we observe that the bed-rock conditions of all democracies are in our time the same. Surface differences caused by climate, race, and especially by the more or less prosperous condition of the people, may make one country less advanced than another. But wherever power passes into the hands of any people they naturally use it so as to ameliorate their lot. Hence general education, labour legislation broadening into Socialistic lines, taxation imposed at the expense of the classes in the interest of the masses, and a common straining upward from the conditions of mere labour, mark all democratic communities, wherever situated. These also prevail in Canada, but not all in the same degree as they do in poorer countries, or countries with a more impetuous class of people. They still depend more on private enterprise than on the State, and with reason, for private enterprise has done wonders for them. Yet at Winnipeg, 1,500 miles out upon the plains, amid a virgin soil and vigorous settlers, we heard that just before we came, there had been a deputation of the unemployed to the city authorities. This, however, was said to be quite unusual, and owing to local causes of an exceptional nature. In Ottawa I observed posted about the streets the election address of a candidate who declared himself for an eight-hours day of labour in all Government and municipal works, to be fixed by law. In some of the large cities there are branches of the Knights of Labour organisation, and also of the Socialist bodies, who use the same watchwords as in other lands as to the wrong of capital and the injustice of wealth. One leaflet which I got in Toronto stated the case against the present constitution of society much in the same way as we may read it in the older land of Europe or the newer one of Australia, and with the colouring to be expected in a political manifesto. It is addressed to the " Workers of Canada," and headed

"The Wealth Producers, Wealth Wasters, and Wealth Robbers of Canada." Repeating the view of Karl Marx as to the surplus value of labour, which I found the Socialists everywhere to accept as undoubted truth, it declares that the "workers are ground down and made the slaves of the capitalist class," and that "the capitalist is the robber of labour, and the land and water grabber is the robber of the community or state, and the politicians who aid and abet are accomplices of the thieves." Its remedy is that "wealth should belong to those who create it, and the natural objects without which man cannot live should be the property of the community or state." The clergy are denounced, and "the politicians must be put aside." The State of Ontario, however, may claim to be the most progressive in the Dominion, and therefore the most susceptible to the new political ideas. Shortly before we came there had been an election, at which thirteen "patrons of labour," or semi-Socialists, had been elected to the local Legislature out of some forty candidates who had stood in that interest. But I could not find that these views had in any part of Canada the same support from the working class that they have in every part of Europe.

The daily press in Canada, if we except this province of Ontario, did not appear to hold that commanding position that it does in England and the colonies, where it often makes and unmakes Governments. We noticed no paper that overshadowed and controlled Ministries as did the London *Times* in old days, during the Reform struggles of 1832; thus leading the truthful Duke of Wellington, when asked by the recently arrived Russian Ambassador to let him know who was the most powerful man in England, to reply, "Why, Mr. Barnes, of the *Times*." There are many able gentlemen connected with the press in the Dominion; but none occupied this position, not even in Ontario.

But the most curious subject of observation to an inquirer into the social aspect of the state was the province of Quebec, where there is still to be seen a form of society mediæval in tone and free from "the divine gift of discontent." It forms an exception to the general course of communities that enjoy self-government. The original settlement was designed by Louis the Fourteenth, to be governed upon Christian and paternal principles, self-contained as it was, and far apart from the distracting influences of European society. The wild freedom of the forests around it, tempting the more adventurous spirits, interfered at first somewhat with the success of this design; but in the end it must be pronounced to have succeeded, and, despite conquest by Protestant England, the province now remains to this day, perhaps the most abiding monument of the power of the grand monarch. In 1791, when England gave to Canada a new constitution, Burke, in that famous discussion in Parliament in which he declared his friendship for Fox to be at an end, implored the House "not to ship off for Canada a cargo of the rights of man." Certainly, as far as Quebec is concerned such a consignment was never accepted.

The Roman Catholic Church may be said to be established there, but it has the advantage of not possessing that absolute power over others which all men and Churches are so apt to abuse. Protestantism is tolerated. But everywhere you find the place overshadowed by vast Catholic churches, spacious convents, seminaries for the education of the priesthood. In a small village where I stayed one night there was a large church. About six o'clock in the morning of a weekday, upon going into it, I found prayers being said to quite a considerable number of people, though they seemed lost in the big building. Among them were some priests who appeared to be strangers, probably tourists. Outside were beggars, asking alms, which I saw in no other province of Canada. The Laval University, in Quebec, represents rather the independent party in the Church. It has two colleges—

one for the education of priests, the other for that of laymen. I went over the latter institution, and found the reception rooms adorned by numerous portraits of popes, cardinals, and bishops. The bull of Pope Pius, authorizing the establishment of the college, is enshrined for inspection in a place of honour. There was also a painting of the Queen in a prominent position; but that of Lord Elgin, who was Governor-General when the college was established, was an insignificant thing, put away in a corner behind the more conspicuous ecclesiastics. What struck the eye most readily in the library were the rows of theological books, mostly the lives and works of the saints, that one would have expected rather in the adjoining college for priests. The attendant who showed me over the building could only speak the French language. One of the most beautiful spots upon the famed Saguenay River is an imposing hill that rises abruptly from the water several hundred feet high. It belongs to the public, being Crown property. From its crest a large statue of the Virgin and Child looks down beneficently upon the tourists that sail beneath it.

Certainly I never met in any community so much willing deference paid to the authority of religion as here. It commands the attention of an observer, and an attention that must surely be not unmixed with respect, in this materialistic age. They have their Lourdes, too, at the shrine of St. Anne Baupre, some fifteen miles from Quebec, whither resort the sick for cure. I met several educated people, who assured me that they knew personally, cripples and diseased people who had been cured. One young man, who was employed in the public offices, told me that a friend of his who was lame from childhood was completely restored while praying before the saint, that he threw away his crutches in the church, and my informant added that he afterwards saw him run in a foot-race at Quebec. During the season for pilgrims the church and the surrounding village are thronged, upon the appointed days, with sufferers of all ranks and ages seeking relief. Mothers with children stricken too early by cruel fate; young men in robust youth shattered by some accident, and from strength prostrated to helplessness; the blind seeking again the light of the sun; the aged praying earnestly to be relieved from their troubles, near though they be to the refuge of the grave. In the large church at the shrine stands a statue of St. Anne, and beneath it is placed a sacred relic in the shape of one of her bones, which all devoutly kissed. Over the entrance door is a large pile of crutches, sticks, and supports of every description for the lame, which had belonged to those who were made whole. It was explained to us that healing was not promised to all, only to those who had sufficient faith, and by no means to a first or a second pilgrimage. An intelligent priest whom I met, courteously discussed the subject of the cures with me, and said that there could be no doubt that faith, trust, and the effect of the unwonted fervour of the occasion, had much to do with the cure of affections that had a nervous origin. Do any of us, indeed, realize the power, in a physical sense, of a deep, sincere faith? While the people thronged and prayed around, a reverend gentleman exhorted them to piety and newness of life. He spoke in French and then in English—the first fluently, the second imperfectly. Near where I sat I was aware of the stalwart figure of a peasant kneeling long and apparently praying earnestly. Some young friend or relative stood near him. The figure remained fixed for so long that at last I glanced round. He was stone blind, seeking with his sightless eyeballs earthly, or at least heavenly, light. I thought of blind Milton's noble and heroic lines—

> Hail, holy light! offspring of heav'n first-born!
> Bright effluence of bright essence increate!
> . . . . Thou
> Revisit'st not these eyes that roll in vain
> To find thy piercing ray, and find no dawn;
> So thick a drop serene hath quench'd their orbs,
> Or dim suffusion veil'd. . . .

> Thus with the year
> Seasons return; but not to me returns
> Day, or the sweet approach of even or morn,
> Or sight of vernal bloom, or summer's rose,
> Or flocks, or herds, or human face divine.
>
> So much the rather thou, celestial light,
> Shine inward, and the mind, through all her powers,
> Irradiate.

John Milton would have scorned the superstition—as he would have held it—of the poor peasant; but perhaps each of them saw alike the light divine.

Near the church were other buildings connected with the saint, in one of which was the flight of stairs that the religious climb up upon their knees, repeating certain prayers at each step. They were crowded when we saw them with pilgrims struggling up. Religious relics, curios, and pictures were sold all about; and the hotels and inns were crowded. Many of the pilgrims appeared to come from the country parts, and to belong to the middle or poorer classes, and they included several men, as well as women and children. Reverence and the impress of the religious feeling were marked among them all. The *Quebec Chronicle* published long reports of the religious celebrations at the shrine, and of the several cures that were reported to have been effected, as part of the current news of the day. During our stay a large party of people—belonging, I suppose, to the wealthier classes—sailed for Europe, accompanied by their priests, to visit Lourdes itself. The Archbishop preached an eloquent sermon upon their departure, descriptive of their hopes and duties.

I have delayed to describe this Canadian Lourdes because it illustrates the character of the people of Quebec. They are a generation behind their age, having kept to themselves, and resisted the encroachments of modern progress; while, far away from their own mother country, France, they are untouched by its infidel spirit. One is impressed by the virtues that they have preserved in their non-progressive state.

Faith that consoles and sustains in life is, surely, still a great gift for men. They are industrious, moral in habits, and love family life. The new woman is unknown among them. They regard marriage as the privilege and protection of the sex that nature has made the weaker of the two, and maternity as an honour, not a burthen. There is no need here, as in old France, to offer rewards for large families. Large families—sometimes very large—are the rule, and the feeling with regard to them was that expressed to me by an old woman, who said that a number of children all brightened up in youth, like coins rubbing together in a bag, and afterwards assisted one another in life. The gaol in Quebec was almost empty. Vice did not flourish about the streets. The police reports in the daily press were scanty; but one morning they briefly stated that some girl had been charged "with loitering near the post office," and sent to gaol for three months—a Draconian contrast to the immunity enjoyed about the Haymarket.

Whether we view it as a defect or as a virtue, it is a fact that the peasantry in this province do not envy others for being better off than they are, and they do struggle on with the difficulties of this life with a patience that springs from a belief in another. A high official in Quebec told me that there was no such thing as Socialism in their province, and as far as I could learn or see there was not. The Roman Catholic Church undoubtedly condemns it; though the concern it always expresses for the poor, and its denunciations of the selfishness of the rich, has led some people to question that fact. In a later chapter I will explain more fully what I observed of the relations of the Christian Churches generally to the new movement. Certainly in Quebec, where the Roman Catholic Church has more real power than in any other place I have visited, not even excepting Ireland, it represses any such tendencies, and preaches contentment under the troubles of this life and to live in the hope of a better.

On the other hand, as Macaulay expresses it: "The Roman Catholics of Lower Canada remain inert, while the whole continent around them is in a ferment with Protestant activity and enterprise."

This, then, is the old order which is giving place to the new. It could not continue as it has done, were it not linked with the good government and secular liberty secured by the Dominion constitution and the ultimate supremacy of the British Empire. Each of the rival principles of government and of social life appear to the best advantage when held in check and put upon its good behaviour by its contrary. In Quebec you see that of the Church and old conservatism in a favourable aspect, just as the Kingdom of Naples showed it at its worst at the end of the last century and as late as the middle of this. The new order, too, may learn something even from the old. It may learn that there are principles which are active in human nature and which powerfully influence human conduct, which do not centre all in the enjoyments of this life; that to ignore these in any scheme of human government is to ignore a large part of man; and that there may be a contentment, even under privations, which no amount of the goods of this life will alone secure, as the discontent and unhappiness of many of the rich among us abundantly proves.

CHAPTER IV.

ENGLAND.

My return to England was after an absence, with one short interval, of thirty years. Coming back after such a time, changes attract the attention more than if you had grown up among them; just as a stranger notices the alterations in a family more readily than do they of the household. What first and most impressed me was the alteration in the attitude of many, if not the majority, of working men towards the State and towards politics, merely as politics. I by no means include the whole of the working classes. An ardent labour leader told me that their direct followers numbered only about one-fourth of the workers of England. But without doubt, not only among these, but among many who disclaim Socialism, the tone of thought and feeling that now prevails is not only changed, but is in marked contrast to that of thirty years ago. Then, great was Radicalism; and John Bright was its prophet. All men were struggling for votes, and for the ballot to make them free. Cobden and his school were still held in esteem. Mill declared that the problem of our times was the establishment of democracy upon intelligent lines. Some of the finest platform speeches ever delivered were made by Bright, as he swayed excited thousands by denouncing the wrong Englishmen suffered in being denied votes in their own land; while they, if they went abroad to Canada, the United States, to the colonies, were at once welcomed to the full rights of the citizen. The power of voting was then prized, a thing valuable in itself, and destined, in conjunction with general education, to place the working man upon a vantage-ground from which he could mould his own career. For Bright was a resolute Individualist. He was the very anti-type of a Socialist. He had even opposed the Ten Hours Bill. All he asked from the State was that it would leave him alone; though latterly he agreed to municipalities undertaking some kinds of work that used to be left to private hands. It was true that the claims of labour to better treatment and plans for ameliorating the lot of the poor, had been advanced from time to time from the beginning of the century. In 1825 a Committee of the House of Commons reported that the greatest part of the manufacturing labour of England was under the dominion of associations that sought to subvert "the natural relation between the employers and the employed." In the history of Trade Unionism by Mr. and Mrs. Sidney Webb, the reformer Francis Place is quoted as representing the condition of England in 1833 in terms that might be used not inaptly to describe the feelings and objects of the advanced party now; the new element being that they seek to secure their aims, not by their own action, but by the power of the political authority. He says: "The year (1833) ended, leaving the (National) Union (of the Working Classes) in a state of much depression. The nonsensical doctrines preached by Robert Owen and others respecting communities and goods in common; abundance of everything man ought to desire, and all for four hours' labour out of twenty-four; the right of every man to his share of the earth in common, and his right to whatever his hands had been employed upon; the power of masters under the present system to give just what wages they pleased; the right of the labourer to such wages as would maintain him and his in comfort for eight or ten hours' labour; the right of every man who was unemployed to employment, and to such an amount of wages as have been indicated—and other matters of a similar kind which were continually inculcated by the working-men's political unions, by many small knots of persons, printed in small pamphlets and handbills, which were sold twelve for a penny and distributed .... among the working people. These pamphlets were written almost wholly by men of talent and of some standing in the world, professional men, gentlemen, manufacturers, tradesmen, and men called literary. The consequence was that a very large proportion of the working people in England and Scotland became persuaded that they had only to combine, as it was concluded they might easily do, to compel, not only a considerable advance of wages all round, but employment for every one, man and woman, who needed it, at short hours. This motion induced them to form themselves into Trades Unions in a manner and to an extent never before known."

But the idea of appealing to the Government for help in the difficulties of life, and the belief in plans for upturning the social state as being the true remedy, were equally discredited among Englishmen. Independence and self-help were their motto. The Socialists of those days asked for no Government aid; Robert Owen and his friends worked on for themselves on their own lines. The Christian Socialists of thirty years ago, while bitterly condemning the Manchester school, yet disclaimed State aid and tenaciously clung to self-help. It was only the old Tories that were for Government interference. Statesmen and political economists were alike emphatic in condemning what is advocated now by those who claim to be progressive. Bentham, the father of the advanced political thought of our day, and who supported the Household Suffrage and Vote by Ballot in the early part of the century, yet stoutly maintained that private enterprise was the mainspring of the social system. A brilliant Whig of the first Reform days declared that what men would "come out and fight for, was equal rights to unequal possessions."

Cobden said that he would rather live in a country where the feeling in favour of individual freedom was jealously cherished, than possess all the principles of the French Constituent Assembly. Mill pronounced that a people who looked to its Government to direct them in their joint concerns would have their faculties only half developed. Fawcett, in my time an "advanced" Liberal, said that poverty "was mainly due to improvidence," and adds, " in trade congresses and other such assemblies ominous sounds are beginning to be heard that the State should find work for the unemployed. What does this mean, but that upon the prudent and thrifty should be thrown an ever-increasing burden created by improvidence?"

As late as 1878, Mr. Gladstone, writing in "Kin Beyond Sea," of the English and American nations, declared that "they set a high value on liberty for its own sake. They desire to give full scope to the principle of self-reliance in the people, and they deem self-help to be immeasurably superior to help in any other form."

In 1873, so competent an authority as Mr. Chamberlain formulated the demands of the then Labour party to be these three:—The amendment of the law of conspiracy, the alteration of certain clauses in the Crime Law Amendment Act, and the abolition of imprisonment for breach of contract.

Nor were these views confined to the governing or the learned classes. They were held with equal firmness by the working classes. Until quite a recent period, the Trade Unions were pronounced supporters of the principles of self-reliance and individualism. Proposals for State interference and Government control, they resented. Even in 1888 the International Trade Unions' Congress declined to pass a resolution in favour of the Eight Hours Law. It is thus tersely put in Webb's History of Trades Unionism: "*Laissez faire*, then, was the political and social creed of the Trade Union leaders of this time. Up to 1885 they undoubtedly represented the views current among the rank and file."

Now all this is changed, and changed in less than ten years; for in 1893 the Trade Unions' Congress at Belfast pledged itself to complete State Socialism. They repeated the pledge at Norwich in 1894. At Cardiff, in 1895, they re-affirmed all that advanced Socialists expect to get in a generation. A revolution in the tone of men's thoughts and in their attitude to questions, both of a personal and of a public character, was thus accomplished, or evidenced, suddenly. Not that the Trade Unions' Congress represents the whole of the working classes, nor yet that we should conclude that even those who voted had all intelligently accepted the scheme of the Fabian Society; but the turning from self-help to Government help, the merging of political aspirations in social ones, the growth of politics into a social science, all this marks large classes of the wage-earners whether professed Socialists or not, as I have said.

In change alone there is nothing to wonder at, as ceaseless change marks the life of Western civilisation, as change must mark growth of all kinds. How different are our ideas from those of a hundred years ago! How different will they be again a hundred years hence! What strikes one as curious is, not alone that the transformation appears to be so rapid, but that it consists in harking back to old ideas of Government, that in the previous part of the century had been universally condemned as unfit for free men. Now the feeling is all for Government help, and with help, Government dictation in the details of industry and of social life. It assists one to realize the change, if we imagine the reception a popular speaker would now get if he addressed to a mass meeting some of the figures of speech by which orators of old used to rouse Englishmen— if he gloried in the fact that though the wind and rain might beat through the broken roof of their cottage, yet the King himself could not enter except by warrant of law; if he told them that they might be in rags, but never in chains, or assured them that freedom was bread to the labourer! The feeling now of the advanced party is that it would be a very good thing for the public authority to have free access to every one's cottage, so long as it was kept repaired by the State; and as for the chains and the rags, if they must choose, the inclination would be to be well clothed and comfortable, though in Socialistic bonds. As for the old authorities upon political economy and social questions, from Adam Smith to Herbert Spencer, they are scorned upon all sides by the new school. We are told that we suffer because "our forefathers had too much Bentham and not enough common sense." Adam Smith "found wealth and popularity in his musings." John Bright is the "Apostle of Grad-Grindery"; Herbert Spencer is "Poor Herbert Spencer." Macaulay is one of the "middle class crowd." Mill is only saved by its being maintained that he made a good ending as a Socialist; though it does not appear from his published works. Yet these were all men of mental power. It sets one speculating what sort of thinkers the next school of censors will be, thirty years hence, when they, perhaps, will scorn the present critics. For the time "the dismal science" has no friends. It is taken for granted by the progressives that there is nothing in it. Politicians advise the people no longer to "gnaw at that dry bone." Political economy never has been welcomed under popular Government.

I might illustrate the change by referring to a book that is to be found in most public libraries. Robert Southey may be taken as the typical old Tory, laughed at by Byron and contemptuously reviewed by Macaulay. Yet, if we read the critique of the great Whig upon "Southey's Colloquies on Society," the poet now appears to be the advanced man, and the scoffing reviewer the fossil reactionary. Southey declares that a liberal expenditure on national works is one of the surest means of promoting the national prosperity. Macaulay argues that any large expenditure by the Government is certain to be attended by waste and corruption, which our experience in the colonies, as to the waste at least, fully bears out; and adds, "We firmly believe that five hundred thousand pounds, subscribed by individuals for railroads or canals, would produce more advantage to the public than five millions voted by Parliament for the same purpose. There are certain old saws about the master's eye and about everybody's business, in which we place very great faith." He further goes on to jestingly describe Southey's idea of Government :— "He conceives that the business of the magistrate is, not merely to see that the persons and property of the people are secure from attack, but that he ought to be a jack-of-all-trades, architect, engineer, schoolmaster, merchant, theologian, a Lady Bountiful in every parish, a Paul Pry in every house, spying, eaves-dropping, relieving, admonishing, spending our money for us, and choosing our opinions for us. His principle is, if we understand it rightly, that no man can do anything so well for himself as his rulers, be they who they may, can do it for him, and that a Government approaches nearer and nearer to perfection, in proportion as it interferes more and more with the habits and notions of individuals. He seems to be fully convinced that it is in the power of Government to relieve all the distresses under which the lower orders labour. Nay, he considers doubt on this subject as impious. We cannot refrain from quoting his argument on this subject. It is a perfect jewel of logic."

To Southey's theory, that the duties of a Government to its people are paternal (now the accepted formula), Macaulay answers that so they would be, if Governments were as much wiser than their subjects as parents generally are than their children, and if they loved them with as great a love.

Finally, he thus sums up the advanced creed of that day :—" It is not by the intermeddling of Mr. Southey's idol, the omniscient and omnipotent State, but by the prudence and energy of the people, that England has hitherto been carried forward in civilisation; and it is to the same prudence and the same energy that we now look with comfort and good hope. Our rulers will best promote the improvement of the nation by strictly confining themselves to their own legitimate duties, by leaving capital to find its most lucrative course, commodities their fair price, industry and intelligence their natural reward, idleness and folly their natural punishment, by maintaining peace, by defending property, by diminishing the price of law, and by observing strict economy in every department of the State. Let the Government do this: the People will assuredly do the rest." Such was the creed of the Liberal; now it is credited to the reactionary.

So great a change, and one that promises to lead to new experiments of a vast kind, sets one thinking upon the line of progress that has led up to it. I will leave it to more learned men to explain why the peoples of the Western world have, for many centuries, been agitated by social movements that have presented themselves from time to time with ever-growing force, till now, when the demand is to reconstruct society altogether; while other vast populations of the world quietly stagnate in submission and with apparent content, under a *régime* full of ills and oppression. Why have we alone restlessness, with its outcome, progress? The higher type of man always seeks to go higher still, and possibly with us it may spring from the sublime doctrines of Christianity, which proclaim the equality of man before God, the wrongs of the poor, and the perils of riches. Certainly when the dark cloud of the Middle Ages began to lift, it was the religious element that first stirred. The Reformation marked the initial uprising, involving as it did an emancipation of the human mind greater, and having wider consequences, than its champions ever contemplated. England followed with a revolution in which the head of the sacred King was cut off. Then the ferment passed

to the Continent, and powerful writers, with Voltaire and Rousseau at their head, and developing the intellectual advance led by England, accomplished as great results as probably the pen can ever lay claim to, in preparing men's minds for the tremendous outburst that ensued, and the continued ferment that has marked political and social life ever since. The independence of America, the solemn announcement that all men were born equal, the French Revolution, with its fierce assault on all the old principles, human and divine, struck chords that are still loudly vibrating in men's hearts. The Revolution proclaimed not only liberty, but equality, and more than that, *fraternité*, thus pointing to the ideas of to-day. Special causes delayed the advance in England till 1832, and even then the aristocratic party that took it up had no idea of the work that they were in fact accomplishing. They were under the belief that they had completed the work of organic change. They distinctly repudiated universal suffrage, as inconsistent with all stability of Government, and argued that its effect would be to disfranchise all who had an income over a certain amount. The after utterances of some of the hot political chieftains of that time make curious reading now. A few years only had passed when Lord John Russell told the people that the settlement might be regarded as final, and that they had better rest and be thankful. Macaulay may be taken as one of the men who represented the intellect of the great Whig Party. Only ten years after the passing of the Reform Bill, he, in addressing the House of Commons, thus spoke of universal suffrage and the institution of property:—
" My firm conviction is that, in our country, universal suffrage is incompatible, not with this or that form of Government, but with all forms of Government, and with everything for the sake of which forms of Government exist; that it is incompatible with property, and that it is consequently incompatible with civilisation. It is not necessary for me in this place to go through the arguments which prove beyond dispute that on the

security of property civilisation depends; that, where property is insecure, no climate, however delicious, no soil, however fertile, no conveniences for trade and navigation, no natural endowments of body or of mind, can prevent a nation from sinking into barbarism; that where, on the other hand, men are protected in the enjoyment of what has been created by their industry and laid up by their self-denial, society will advance in arts and in wealth, notwithstanding the sterility of the earth and the inclemency of the air, notwithstanding heavy taxes and destructive wars."

It is evident that the eminent men of that time never understood that the movement in which they had taken part was one which, pushed on by natural impulses, must spread its advance, like the in-coming tide, over Western civilisation, until it had run its full course and exhausted the force of the impelling causes. They evidently never understood that it was only one milestone on the road to universal suffrage; and that some who claimed to be the advanced leaders of the masses in the day to come after them, would demand not alone the abolition of private property, but the curtailment of personal liberty, so as to prevent future accumulation. Just as little did it occur to the great men of the United States to contemplate as possible such an outcome to the institutions that they had established. From Washington, the aristocrat, to Jefferson, the democrat, their utterances are uniform upon this point. Daniel Webster, in addressing a popular convention that assembled to revise the constitution of his State, assumes as beyond question the present constitution of society, and declared that neither life nor liberty could be secure unless property was safe. "It would be monstrous to give even the name of Government to any association in which the rights of property should not be competently secured." So thick is the veil that screens the future from even the keenest intellects!

The political advance, however, moved on in England, and necessarily at an accelerated pace. The Conservatives passed household suffrage, murmuring that it was a leap in the dark, and now the ballot, and payment of members, voted by the Commons and adopted by the Government, will substantially give social mastery to the people.

Thus the movement that got its last great impulse from the French Revolution has now, in one hundred years, almost completed its political function. All men are declared to be politically equal—the voice of the labourer to be as important in the polling booth as that of the millionaire; political freshness and vigour is with the poor; education enlightens all; an active press and able political champions are ever ventilating wrongs and ills of life.

Meanwhile an industrial revolution has also been going forward. The accumulation of wealth has assumed proportions that were quite unknown to our forefathers, the workers are separated from the master with whom, in old times, they used to toil conjointly, herded together in vast industrial armies, and commanded by paid servants of the employer, which is probably a joint-stock company. Machinery has increased the power of production beyond calculation, but the *employés'* share of the produce appears to be inadequate. The struggle of life gets keener as all the lower strata of society push upward. Property, too, is divorced from public duties such as it had in the Feudal times. Democracy ousts it from them now; even in England it will do so in due time.

In what position, then, do we find ourselves now? Are we prepared to rest and be thankful? By no means. We are more discontented than ever. Our feelings that were dull are becoming keen, our yearnings take a new direction, and seeing how easily political equality has been accomplished by giving votes and passing statutes, we turn more restlessly than ever to the social sphere, where so much remains to be done, to see what can be achieved there by the same appliances.

There the inequality that results partly from past misgovernment, and partly from the constitution of man, exists; and the question arises whether the equality by law and the inequality in fact can continue to work together. It is the more serious in our time, as with us there are no slaves. The ancient democracies gave free men equal rights, but below them were the slaves to do the menial work. Liberty, it has been said, maintained itself only by the aid of servitude. These ancient democracies were incomplete things. The American statesman, Calhoun, the rival of Webster and Clay, maintained that, in the Southern States, the slavery of the blacks was the surest guarantee for the freedom of the whites. But with us the noble purpose is to embrace all. The meanest toiler is not merely to be free, but to have his share in government, equally with the best. I do not know that Society has yet fully realized all that this new phase of the rights of men — of all men — means. It is easy to see that such a political equality as that, and such a social inequality as we see around us, will not long continue to exist together. Either will modify the other. Political institutions, if they are to be stable, must rest upon and reflect the social conditions of the State that they represent.

The new school hold that the real use and value of political power is to enable the people to get hold of and control "the social machine." They discard the old idea of political privileges being a good in themselves, as teaching "the elector to venerate himself," and to employ his thoughts upon high matters. They have got all these privileges and find that they do not of themselves stay the ills of life. "We have had household suffrage for thirty years, and national education for twenty-five years, and we find life harder than ever," writes a Socialist. "A vote is a thing of a transcendent nature," was the word of a great Whig. "What good is a vote to a man? It does not feed him," was the remark made to me by one Labour leader; while another assured me that he and his friends took little interest in any politics except in so far as they should be used for industrial purposes. At election times the questions put to candidates by this party do not relate to the wants of the nation at large or the interests of the Empire, but to the needs of the worker, and the answers to these determine his vote. At the Birkenhead election, which took place while I was in England, the following series was drawn up and submitted to each candidate :—

(1) Are you in favour of having clauses inserted in Government and municipal contracts, making a standard rate of wages compulsory on the contractor?

(2) Are you in favour of making a contractor-in-chief responsible for the sanitary condition of the workshops and hours of labour, worked under a sub-contractor?

(3) Are you in favour of public contracts having conditions inserted, to ensure that the work shall be done on the contractor's own premises, and in favour of having clothing and uniforms for public servants, manufactured by Government or by the municipalities requiring them?

(4) Are you in favour of having an eight hours day prescribed by an Order in Council as a maximum working day in all Government departments, and restricting overtime to cases of special emergency?

In England we have so long enjoyed personal liberty that the enthusiasm for it has died out. Men take it as a matter of course. And why should they fear the control of the Government, since—the Government? They *are* the Government. To this party the value of politics as a matter of advancing principles and improving men by its exercise, seems to be small; but the prospect of its use in securing social amelioration to be unlimited. Can we wonder that they prefer the material to the ideal? Is it not the natural course of events for men to use power to secure their own objects? Have not the select and the educated classes always done so? And how was it that the wise men of fifty years ago expected the poor to be content with the gift of political privileges without making practical use of them?

A high authority has laid it down that the spirit of democracy is opposed to Socialism; for that though both make for equality, the one is for equality in freedom, while the other is for equality in compulsion and servitude; and the United States is referred to as a democratic country that has shown no tendency towards Socialism. The tendency there, indeed, is not so marked. Fuller political experience does not favour the idea of complete Socialism, though the "populists" there are quite ready even now to go a great part of the way, and of the working classes in both countries, many who disclaim Socialism turn longingly to paternalism, which is government by themselves, for their own benefit. Personal independence they regard with suspicion, as a protest against their authority. They reject local option for districts as regards the eight hours day. Political theories, questions of principle, rights of men, slip into the background.

Hence the change that strikes a stranger on coming back to England. The centre of gravity in the State has been shifted. The people are king. Mere politics bear no fruit. Control and repression that they resented when it came from a power above them, many welcome when it is by a power that comes from themselves, and when the object is to secure what is dearer to them even than freedom—namely, equality and social relief. Powers which they would have limited before, they would make expansive now that they are coming into their own hands. Certainly, if the Socialist party could carry their designs to the full extent, the battle of freedom would have to be fought over again. But it is satisfactory to bear in mind that their immediate object is one we all sympathise with, to improve the lot of the poor; while the means they propose, as they advance, will be judged by the common sense of an Anglo-Saxon people, whether in the old world or the new, and, what is not less important, will be tested step by step by that best of teachers, experience.

CHAPTER V.

SOCIALISM IN ENGLAND.

POLITICAL equality then being established, and the people having power, all attention is now turned to the evils and wrongs of the social state. These are as old as man himself, and partly arise from his nature; we may doubt whether it is the design of Providence that human life should ever be delivered wholly from them. But this doubt should not prevent the most strenuous exertions to mitigate them, and having got thus far in our present stage of human progress, the new reformers step forward with plans for reconstructing society in such a manner as to secure competence to all, while allowing superfluity to none; all to have a good time, and none too good a time. Such plans have often been proposed in the world's history, from the age of Plato downwards. The evil is old, the remedy is old; what is new is the power resting in all the people, told by the head, to carry it out; or at least to try the experiment. Even they cannot make it succeed if it is contrary to the natural conditions of human life.

The Socialist party is stronger in England than in the United States, partly owing to the greater proportion of poor in the former country, and the wider chasm between the different classes of the people. There is also in England a small class of intellectual people with leisure, who have had no practical experience of politics, and whom a humane longing to mitigate the ills they see around them leads to take the Socialist road. In the United States, politicians and reformers are distrusted, the leisured class is apart from public life, and the great middle class is busy and unimpressionable. As might be expected, the movement is more powerful in London than in other parts of England. In other centres, Birmingham especially, the old Trade Unionists appear to still hold their ground, and they favour Mr. Chamberlain's plans for helping the poor and the worker, which are opposed to Socialism in preserving individuality and seeking to increase and distribute wealth, not to abolish it.

When I told a political friend in England that I was going to see as much of the Socialists as I could, and in particular that I desired to ascertain what their precise objects were, he replied that I should be disappointed, as they would not tell me what they really intended to do. My experience, however, was just the opposite to this. I found, both in their published statements and also in conversation, the most explicit declarations of what their present objects were, and also what their ultimate aim was. I speak now of the direct Socialist party. Though much has been written upon the subject, yet, as I meet numbers of educated people who have only a confused idea as to what is held in theory and proposed in practice by that party, I will briefly state the result of my inquiry. Even Socialists own that the complete realisation of their creed is distant, but its influence largely affects the legislation of the day. It thus becomes a matter of present importance to know what they propose to lead us to in the end.

They define their creed to be "The science of reconstructing society on an entirely new basis by substituting the principle of association for that of competition in every branch of human industry." They hold that the present constitution of society is hopelessly faulty—in leaving industry to be a matter of individual effort, and competition between man and man, and allowing as a necessary result from this competition the institution of private property, and the subjection of labour to wealth; wealth thus being enabled to grasp an undue share of production.

Their remedy is for the State to own the land and all the instruments of production and distribution, such as railroads, ships, mills; to employ every one, and distribute the results of the common industry equally among all. Thus there would be no more poverty and no more wealth; no slums and no mansions. Their ideal, when sketched out by fancy, is fairly represented in the popular Socialistic novels that have circulated throughout the world. In the "Manifesto of English Socialists," which was published by the Joint Committee of the Social Democratic Federation, the Fabian Society and the Hammersmith Socialist Society, they state their position thus :—

> It is, therefore, opportune to remind the public once more of what Socialism means to those who are working for the transformation of our present unsocialist state into a collectivist republic, and who are entirely free from the illusion that the amelioration or "moralisation" of the conditions of capitalist private property can do away with the necessity for abolishing it. Even those readjustments of industry and administration, which are Socialist in form, will not be permanently useful unless the whole State is merged into an organized commonwealth. Municipalisation, for instance, can only be accepted as Socialism on the condition of its forming a part of national, and at last of international, Socialism, in which the workers of all nations, while adopting within the borders of their own countries those methods which are rendered necessary by their historic development, can federate upon a common basis of the collective ownership of the great means and instruments of the creation and distribution of wealth, and thus break down national animosities by the solidarity of human interest throughout the civilised world. On this point all Socialists agree. Our aim, one and all, is to obtain for the whole community complete ownership and control of the means of transport, the means of manufacture, the mines, and the land. Thus, we look to put an end for ever to the wage-system, to sweep away all distinctions of class, and eventually to establish national and international communism on a sound basis.

As to how they propose to get the land and the other factors of wealth: briefly, they propose to take them. Taxation is a ready means, and the authority of even orthodox writers is invoked to prove that it may be properly used to accomplish other useful ends than merely supplying the financial needs of the State.

Many of the European Socialists have hitherto not adopted the idea of the equal reward of all under the new system, but have maintained that while the ownership of the means of production should be communal, the result should be apportioned among the workers in proportion to the value of their services. They would allow a man to keep what he earned, but not to bequeath it. The impossibility of practically carrying out this idea when you abolish the competitive system has become apparent, and in the introduction to the American edition of the "Fabian Essays" what appears now to be regarded as the true principle, is stated to be an equal provision for all. The alternative plan, it is laid down, would leave the individual, as now, to be well-to-do or to want, according to his strength or weakness, and keep alive, although in much less glaring contrast, the economic distinctions of this day. "Nationalists, on the other hand, would absolutely abolish these distinctions, and the possibility of their again arising, by making an equal provision for the maintenance of all, an incident and an indefeasible condition of citizenship, without any regard whatever to the relative specific services of different citizens. The rendering of such services, on the other hand, instead of being left to the option of the citizen, with the alternative of starvation, would be required under an uniform law as a civic duty, precisely like other forms of taxation or military service, levied on the citizens for the furtherance of a commonweal in which each is to share equally. The law of service must be uniform, but the services rendered will vary greatly—with many entire exemptions—according to the abilities of the people. The inequality of contributions will in no way prejudice the invariable law of equal distribution of the resultant sum. It is confidently believed that all Socialists will ultimately be led by the logic of events to recognise, as many now do, that the attitude of the Nationalists on this point is the only truly Socialistic one." So able a writer as Mr. Sidney Webb says:—"The Socialists would nationalize both rent and interest by the State becoming the sole landowner and capitalist. . . . Such an arrangement would, however, leave untouched the third monopoly, the largest of them all, the monopoly of business ability. . . . The more recent Socialists strike, therefore, at this monopoly also, by allotting to every worker an equal wage, whatever the nature of his work. This equality has an abstract justification, as the special ability or energy with which some persons are born, is an unearned increment due to the struggle for existence upon their ancestors, and consequently having been produced by Society, is as much due to Society as the 'unearned increment' of rent." To this certainly it would come, whatever be the reasoning, were the system established.

While this is their ultimate object, they admit that it cannot be realized for generations, and meanwhile they urge forward all the social reforms that lead to it, and particularly the assumption by the Government, or by municipal bodies, of as much industrial work as possible. The more that is done by the State, and the more private enterprise is curtailed, the further they get upon their road. The more industry is brought under political control, the more property is taxed in any way or for any purpose, till it becomes useless to the holder; the more of public works the State can be got to undertake, the further advance is made towards the terminus they would arrive at. Anything that tends to break down the present social conditions is acceptable as paving the way for the new ones. An American Socialist told me that he supported the cause, though he believed that the ultimate prospect it held out was quite impracticable, simply because it was the best means for subverting the existing system. It is a feature in the situation that many who disclaim Socialism are at one with the Socialists in several practical proposals of the day, as the doings of the London County Council show. Politicians do not know what to make of the apparition, and claim to be Socialists, half in jest. A vast amount of legislation has already proceeded upon lines, which, if sufficiently prolonged, become Socialistic; and projects for municipalizing gas and water-works and tramways, and for the purchase of the railways by the Government, are favoured by many who would indignantly disclaim being classed as followers of Karl Marx. The more that is done in this direction the more the Socialist rejoices, as it brings him nearer the time when the State will be the general employer, and the individualism alike of the strong man and the weak will be merged in one equal common employment. All will agree that there are some public purposes that are best effected by the joint action of the community. All good men endeavour to act towards their fellows with that sympathy of feeling which honourably marks much Socialism, but is not peculiar to it. Thus many descriptions of reformers are toiling away together with the Socialists in altering the industrial conditions of the commonwealth.

There stands the social structure, the product of twenty centuries of growth and toil, with the workers, many-tongued, surrounding it. The direct Socialist is for pulling it down altogether, gradually perhaps, and digging out the foundations. The semi-Socialist and political Socialist is quite agreeable to take off the top storey, but not to demolish the whole building or destroy the substratum. There is also the Conservative architect, who wants to alter, enlarge the walls and make repairs, so as to increase accommodation, but all with the object of preserving. So long as the top storey only is coming off, the first two classes can merrily work together; the second, protesting that the idea of destroying the whole building is absurd; and, as far as alterations go, all three can combine; though the true Socialist will object to anything that would make the old framework stronger, as his object is to undermine it. Thus he entirely objects to the "three acres and a cow" policy. What the half Socialist and the political Socialist will do when the first storey is off, depends upon what the public then think of it. They are not enthusiasts like the pure Socialists.

I found several associations at work in spreading the principles of the new school, for new as a live power it is in England, dating from some ten or fifteen years back, though the principles are old. First there is the Fabian Society, which carries the brains of the party in the literary sense, and which forges arguments, forcible or presentable, which are used by plainer men upon every platform in the world. As one goes from country to country and meets a succession of adherents, you find these presented to you again and again, like coin from an imperial mint that runs everywhere among the subjects. At the Sydney Federation Conference in 1890, one of the public men there, an ex-Premier, and a man whose singleness of purpose none could doubt, told me that he had been converted to Socialism by the Fabian Essays, and urged me to study them. There can be no doubt that their influence, and that of the other publications of this Society, has been great, partly on account of the cleverness with which they are written, but also because the evils they attack are obvious to all; the inconveniences of the present system come home to millions practically, while the reasons in favour of tolerating that system rest upon intellectual conclusions from the teachings of man's history. Also their views are founded upon a generous belief in the perfectibility of man, and they avert their eyes from his defects, while adverse criticisms call to mind those defects, which have hitherto constituted the difficulty in all human institutions.

The Fabian Society is a teaching body, a sort of university for the Socialist cause. The members number about seven hundred. In their report for 1894, they declare that their Society consists of Socialists, that their object is the emancipation of land and industrial capital from individual and class ownership, and vesting them in the community for the general benefit, also the transfer to the community of the administration of such industrial capital "as can be conveniently managed socially." These measures are to be carried out without compensation, "though not without such relief to expropriated individuals as may seem fit to the community," and rent and interest thus added to the reward of labour. It seeks to permeate by its lessons other political organisations, rather than to swell its own ranks of membership. It nominates no candidates at elections, but often gets its members accepted by others. It does not try to get other bodies into its fold, but sends its members out among them as missionaries of the cause. Its direct work consists of the publication of tracts, leaflets, questions for candidates, and Acts of Parliament, to the working of which it desires to attract popular attention, such as "The Parish Councils Act;" and also in promoting public discussions, and the delivery of lectures. The General Secretary states that in four years they published 35,000 copies of the "Fabian Essays," 214,000 tracts, 700,000 leaflets, besides their monthly issue of the "Fabian News," which is sent free to all members. They have correspondence classes for students throughout the country, and boxes of selected books and papers are sent on loan to all the associations that are in sympathy with them.

The Social Democratic Federation is the oldest of English Socialist bodies, as it dates from 1879, and it is directly political in its action. It advocates the advanced Socialistic programme, including the abolition of private property and the standing army; "the people to decide on peace and war;" the production and distribution of wealth to be regulated by the community; meanwhile cumulative taxation upon all incomes exceeding £300 a year, and "every person attaining the age of fifty to be kept by the community, work being optional after that age."

That branch of Socialism that primarily attacks the private ownership of land is represented by the English Land Restoration League, the Land Nationalisation Society, the Scottish Land Restoration Union, and some smaller associations. Henry George's "Progress and Poverty" is their text-book; and some years ago that gentleman advocated his principles at an open-air meeting arranged by the Land Restoration League, and held in the heart of the City of London, on the open space in front of the Royal Exchange. He took as his text the verse inscribed over the entrance to that building—"The earth is the Lord's and the fulness thereof." This League describes its work as consisting of "lectures without number in the London clubs, meetings in town halls, open-air meetings in the parks and open spaces, conferences on the land question, newspaper correspondence, a voluminous output of leaflets and pamphlets, and an occasional 'Henry George' campaign." In 1891 they organized the "Red Vans" for travelling through the English villages and carrying their propaganda there. They are covered waggons, coloured red, in which the lecturer travels, drawing up at convenient places and times, and haranguing the peasantry.

The Land Nationalisation Society was started in 1881. Its object is to secure the compulsory taking of land by the State, not merely the taxing of the rent as the Original Single Taxers proposed. It employs the usual machinery for spreading its views, including a "Land and Labour Cart" for the villages. One of its members gave a special donation of £500 to assist in organizing a series of meetings. It initiated the first Land Nationalisation Congress, which was held in London in 1894, and at which forty organisations were represented. The Scottish Union was constituted by five other land societies uniting with it. Its object is the imposition of the Single Tax upon land.

In Ireland these views are not as prevalent as in other parts of the United Kingdom, for there the

Gladstonian legislation has improved the position of the tenant effectually at the expense of the landlords, most of whom are impoverished. The tenants are not favourable to their interest in the land being taxed away for the common good. There are some cases of municipal socialisation of land, but the general scheme of Socialism does not find much favour in Ireland, partly because, as has been said, the people have the land, partly because Home Rule occupies the aspirations of many, and partly because the Church of Rome discountenances it. Mr. Michael Davitt, when he visited Australia in 1895, told a large audience that he addressed in Melbourne, that "He did not believe in Socialism. It had failed in Paradise with only two beings to observe its laws, and how was it likely to succeed in the present day, with hundreds of millions of beings of divers opinions and capacities?"

The condition of the labourers in several English counties, as shown by the reports of the lecturers and agents of these societies, is so abject that revolution would be welcome if it would improve it. Both owners and workers of land are now more than ever impoverished by the free import of agricultural produce from the fresh fields and favourable climes of the world. They cannot compete with this.

The English Land Restoration League has upon its General Committee three members of Parliament, thirteen members of the London County Council, six graduates of Universities, and five clergymen. Its principles are explained by a few words that are printed on its card of membership: "Don't buy the landlords out; don't kick them out, but tax them out."

"The Independent Labour Party" is one of the most active of the Socialist bodies, though its influence in practical politics appears to be small. But the important question with regard to such movements is, not so much their immediate political strength, as whether they are likely in time to impress the people. Their Secretary, Mr. Tom Mann, says: "What we aim at is such a reconstruction of society from its base as shall make the existence of poverty in our State an absolute impossibility. 'Not the relief of poverty, but the abolition and prevention of poverty, is the end to be held in view.' The special means whereby it is proposed to get rid of poverty is by the effective organisation of industry, *i.e.*, the actual public organisation of the trade of the country. The community, by means of its committees and duly elected officers, knowing as they would what the year's requirements were, and knowing the effective working capacity of the country, would so apportion the total to be done that none should be overworked and none left without work." Its members are chiefly young men, whom the Secretary considers are more amenable to reason than old men. It distrusts both Liberals and Conservatives, and supports those who give direct support to the Collectivist or Socialist programme. A leading member of this body expressed to me their utter disbelief in the ordinary party politician. They felt no interest in politics, except as a means of advancing Socialism. One party was as bad as the other. Among the objects specified in their official programme are: the eight hours law, remunerative work for the unemployed, provision for all sick and aged, taxation to extinction of unearned incomes, and "the substitution of arbitration for war and the consequent disarmament of the nations." It has branches throughout England and Wales. At the election for Leicester in 1894, its candidate, though defeated, polled 4,402 votes.

"The New Labour Army" mainly directs its attention to the work of the Parish Councils called into existence by the Act of 1894. The real meaning and the far-reaching scope of this measure did not appear to attract much attention in England. When it has time to work out its natural effect, the result will be that the local government of the country will be transferred from the squire, the parson and the farmer to the peasant and whoever he may then follow. This seems to an observer from outside to be a more important change than many others which attract fierce opposition when proposed. This Labour Party seek to introduce advanced views into this new sphere. They distrust Parliamentary action, and declare that the people "follow Parliamentary leaders merely to be deceived by them." Their object is to permeate the Parish Councils with the principles of the progressive party that have ruled the London County Council, and to take practical steps to improve the lot of the poor (in which it must be said that they get support from all parties), directing them, however, all the time towards the Collectivist end that they have in view. The London County Council and the Parish Councils strike a stranger as the most promising field for the exertions of the Socialist party in England, considering all that is involved in their wide and practical scope of action, and that party seems to fully realize the fact. There was truth and meaning in the statement of Mr. John Burns, when he said that he would rather be a doorkeeper in the temple of the London County Council than a dweller in the tents of Parliament.

The London County Council was constituted only a few years ago, to govern, in municipal affairs, the whole of the metropolis outside the City, and according to the gentleman just quoted, "it was called into existence mainly by political exigency." It has already made a marked impress upon social matters. It contains several titled and wealthy members, but up to the time when I was in England (1894), its practical working was guided by the Labour and Socialist element. The one had distinction, the other power. Mr. Ben Tillett is one of those elected by the Council to the important position of Alderman. The electorate is practically based on universal suffrage. If roused and united the wage-earners can govern. There is as yet no payment of members. The work done by the various committees is enormous, as the minutes show, and varies from the direction of great public works down to the purchase of a cab for one of their officers, or a billiard table for the use of firemen at their station. It is in these committees that the real business of the Council is done. One gratifying feature is the number of reports that are adopted for providing gardens and open spaces for the poorer districts. Another which gives one, fresh from the United States, more pause, is the manner in which large money values are dispensed in works ordered to be done without tender or other test, in full (and at present justifiable) reliance upon the perfect disinterestedness of all concerned. But this seems to lead to waste, and prominent members of the Council maintain that the Finance Committee should exercise a closer supervision than it does.

The election of 1892 was openly fought on the issue of Municipal Socialism, as the newspaper and magazine articles of the time testify, and resulted in a sweeping victory for the Socialists. It must be remembered, however, that so far they are only dealing with the top storey of the building, and that numbers of general reformers agree in most of the work as yet in sight. All agree that much excellent business has been so far accomplished. All rejoice at improved dwellings for the poor, better wages, more public reserves and recreation grounds, sweeter sanitary surroundings; these are things in which men of all parties cordially co-operated, and which it delights even the passing stranger to see taken in hand. The advanced party, in addition to these objects, steadily push the Collectivist policy. The employees, as might be expected, appear to sympathise with it. A complaint was made by the National Free Labour Association that some of the Council's foremen on their works inquired of all applicants for employment whether they were members of trade unions, and refused employment to those who were not. The Works Committee inquired into this, and reported that the charge was, except with regard to one foreman, who had since left their service, unfounded. They state that they have instructed all their foremen not to ask, before engaging a man, whether he belongs to a union. But the very instruction is significant. It was reported that some of the Council's workmen availed themselves of the easier hours of work to take private jobs in the intervals. In November, 1894, a resolution was passed forbidding this, and directing a standing order to be drawn up prohibiting it, but no further steps were taken, and the matter was dropped.

In a paper read before the British Association at Oxford, in August, 1894, Mr. Sidney Webb explains and defends the "economic heresies" of the Council. He states them to be threefold, namely, establishing a trade union rate for skilled and a minimum wage for their unskilled employees; giving their contracts, where they did give any, only to employers who also respected this accepted wage and "moral minimum"; and further endeavouring to dispense with contractors wherever it was possible, and doing the work by their own officers and workmen. The minutes of the Council show many instances of the application of their policy. When several tenders are sent in for some work, the Council will reject the lower ones, if not satisfied that the contractors pay trade union rates of wages. Repeated reports are made by committees, and agreed to, that works, often of a large kind, be done by the Works Committee without the intervention of a contractor. Some question seemed to exist as to the practice of not accepting the lowest tender, for one member gave notice of a motion, while I was there, that the lowest tender should be taken "as a general rule, and in default of strong reasons to the contrary." The progressives assert that this policy has produced excellent results —that by paying good wages they get good men, and that, by dispensing with the contractor they get better work and also cheaper work. Their course would be easy, supported as it is enthusiastically by many for political, as well as for social reasons, were it not that the rates continue to go up; and though the collectivist does not care for this, the ratepayer does. This money difficulty comes in the way, at some time or other, of most reforms, and makes the men who have to pay critical, who were before indifferent or even favourable. Sir John Lubbock, who is not a mere caviller, says that in the last year of the Metropolitan Board of Works, which the Council superseded, the expenditure was at the rate of 10·1d. in the pound, while the Council's estimate for 1895 was 18·1d., which, however, was brought down by the increased Exchequer contribution to 14d.; while at the same time the rateable value had risen from thirty-one millions and a half to thirty-four millions. He states that the undertakings of the Works Committee, dispensing with the contractor, were marked by "excessive cost," and refers to a report of the Parks Committee, which, after giving details, said: "It will be seen that the seven works which the Works Committee undertook, and with the estimates for which they reported to the Council that they were satisfied as to their sufficiency, have actually cost no less than 36·14 per cent. above the estimate." A return was prepared by the Parks Committee of all works carried out by the contractors. These were eighty-two in number. The officers of the Council estimated the cost at £52,000; they were completed for £49,000 by the contractors, or six per cent. less than the estimate, while that done by the Works Committee cost thirty-six per cent. more. Sir John Lubbock also mentions that another committee complained of the cost of a wall erected by the Works Committee as being excessive. "They referred the matter to the architect, who reported that he could not account for the excess, but that the bricklayers appeared to have only laid on the average twenty-three bricks an hour. The Chairman of the Committee denied the statement, and assured the Council that the number of bricks laid per hour was at least forty-six."

An outside observer has no means of judging of the correctness of details such as these. But the Socialist party certainly met with a marked check at the elections that took place not long after Sir John Lubbock spoke in 1895. They had only a slight advantage in the number of members returned, instead of having as before a sweeping majority, while the actual majority of votes was cast for the moderate party. Later in the year the press gave the report of the Works Committee, which showed a loss of £3,000 on £180,000 worth of work without the contractor. The causes which, it was stated, were assigned for this result were—the architect, who was too exacting, the manager too sanguine and easy-going, and some of the men, who were alleged to be indolent and careless.

One hears different views expressed as to the ultimate working of the system of city government thus established in London. One Labour leader declares that the citizens will become more attached to it than they are to their Parliament; that it will be the centre of the boldest progressive views, and will even become to the Commons at Westminster what the Jacobin clubs were to the States-General at Paris. Some say that if things do take this turn, it will mean what they term the "Tammanification of London." Others anticipate that it will continue to be simply a powerful but legitimate engine of useful municipal work, guided by the common sense and moderation of Englishmen. If its members continue to be men of the same stamp as at present, this will doubtless be so. The difficulty will present itself if it becomes an arena for city politics. With paid members, large financial operations to be dealt with at discretion rather than by fixed rule, and an army of employees powerful in the electorate—and one man with a personal interest is more potent at an election than twenty of the apathetic public—then the problem of the government of great cities by universal suffrage will present itself in earnest to London. A popular authority cannot itself manage a business concern on business principles the employees of which are its electors. The examples of the good work done by Birmingham, Glasgow, and other English cities are not in point, as they have so far avoided the political element. That problem has certainly not been solved in the United States. There it is admitted, as it also is in the colonies, that while all should have equal votes for the general political government, some test of direct contribution should be required from the voter in municipal affairs. All will hope and trust that it may be successfully dealt with in the mother land. If it is, she will have given the world a grand object lesson, and a new one.

There are a number of church associations in England, some of which nibble at Socialism, and some profess to swallow it, while the Labour churches swallow it in earnest, ejecting any theological elements that may be in the way. I will explain what I observed of these afterwards.

CHAPTER VI.

MEETINGS.

I DESIRE to give some account of different meetings that I attended, Trade Union, popular Socialist, scientific Socialist, general political. There is nothing new in such meetings or in a report of them; the leading newspapers do not give much of their space to that purpose, and I gathered that it was not the policy of those papers, either in England or in the United States, to afford prominence to such discussions as one hears at them. The number of these gatherings would alone justify this: yet, in no better way than from them, can an inquirer learn what ideas are taking hold of the popular mind. The very extravagances that one sometimes hears, and seeing how far they are successful in impressing the audience, and how far they fail, are instructive to the observer. And possibly some things may present themselves to a stranger in a new light.

As much that I am going to say will necessarily be critical, I desire to premise that I take for granted the value and blessing of fearless, open discussion. It is a noble privilege for a man to be able to speak out boldly the word that is in his mouth, whether it be wise or whether it be foolish. And this freedom necessarily means that much that is unwise is spoken. Further, it must be borne in mind that a public meeting is not the place for thought. It would be unreasonable to expect it. Indeed, the very qualifications that go to make the successful platform speaker, are just those that impair the power of the thinker—warmth, colouring, the knack of seeing only one side and seeing that forcibly, the art of putting forward the most telling points, which yet may be by no means the true ones. The orator—and especially the platform orator—must see only one side of the shield. Yet, in fact, truth is generally not wholly with either extreme; but the man who would attempt in a public discussion to discriminate, is usually marked as a trimmer. I do not speak of popular meetings only. The last quarter in which one need look for dry truth is any public discussion. For when you get to the public discussion, the time for thinking is past and that for action has come, and the victory is to those who strike out direct and push forward with daring against the foe. You might as well expect the soldier in battle to keep making his ammunition, as ask the public speaker to keep weighing the truth of his propositions. What both are wanted to do is to fire off. With the meeting, too, when the impulse to the desired side is once given by the vigorous push, men are swayed over to it by the general feeling that prevails, which acts with a sort of mesmeric force, and mere mental operations have little to do with the result. Most political meetings, too, have their weak side, concealed from public view, their factions, and personal rivalries, that render each leader apt to play the winning card, whatever it is, lest the game should slip from his hands. They thus, though often imposing when seen from afar, appear, when we come close to them, to resemble one of John Bunyan's characters who "was a tall man and somewhat more comely at a distance than at hand." But their value as a means of learning the trend of popular movement is great.

The most important meeting that I attended in England was the Trade Unions' Congress at Norwich, held in September, 1894. It was the twenty-seventh annual meeting, the first Congress having been convened in 1868. The original project was essentially English in its design. It was for a representation, corporate in its character, of all Trade Unions at an annual meeting, where questions that practically affected the common interests of the workers would be discussed. The letter proposing the first Congress is given in Webb's "History of Trades Unionism"; it states its purpose thus:

"The Congress will assume the character of the annual meetings of the Social Science Association, in the transactions of which Society, the artisan class is almost excluded; and papers previously carefully prepared by such Societies as elect to do so, will be laid before the Congress on the various subjects which at the present time affect the Trade Societies, each paper to be followed by discussion on the points advanced, with a view of the merits and demerits of each question being thoroughly ventilated through the medium of the public press. It is further decided that the subjects treated upon shall include the following:

1. Trade Unions an absolute necessity.
2. Trade Unions and political economy.
3. The effect of Trade Unions on foreign competition.
4. Regulation of the hours of labour.
5. Limitation of apprentices.
6. Technical education.
7. Courts of arbitration and conciliation.
8. Co-operation.
9. The present inequality of the law in regard to conspiracy, intimidation, picketing, coercion, etc.
10. Factory Acts Extension Bill, 1867; the necessity of compulsory inspection, and its application to all places where women and children are employed.
11. The present Royal Commission on Trade Unions —how far worthy of the confidence of the Trade Union interests.
12. Legalisation of Trade Societies.
13. The necessity of an Annual Congress of Trade Representatives from the various centres of industry."

Such was the creed of the working man's wants in 1868.

Since then they have met each year in some city of the United Kingdom, which is chosen by vote at the Congress of the preceding year.

Delegates from England, Ireland, Scotland, and Wales attend. For this year, the ancient city of Norwich, notable for having Nelson's birthplace in the neighbourhood, was selected.

They follow orderly methods in their discussions, and have a sort of Cabinet, or Front Bench, in the shape of a Parliamentary Committee, and a General Secretary, elected by the Congress. The Committee is supposed to look after the interests of labour generally, and, being composed of the most experienced and trusted members, "to lead the House." For some time past, however, a divergence had sprung up between the Front Bench and the Congress; the former having been composed mainly of men of the old Trade Union School, who depended on self-reliance, and were opposed to the new Socialist ideas; while those ideas were suddenly taking hold of the rank and file of members. At Norwich this difference appeared to have been obliterated, for the leaders vied with one another in advocating the full Collectivist programme.

Though the total number of workmen represented this year was only 1,100,000, yet there can be no question that they reflect ideas that permeate thousands of others, and which may be properly termed progressive, in the sense that they are coming to the front to be considered by the community, and dealt with in one fashion or another, as public opinion may determine. There were 378 delegates, with about a dozen women among them, who were accredited by 179 societies, and I was informed that one hundred members were either Members of Parliament, of School Boards, of Trade Union Councils, or were Justices of the Peace. Some Members of Parliament took an active part in the discussions; and some, who were not delegates, attended as spectators. The galleries were filled with people belonging to all classes. Many of the delegates were plain operatives, and appeared in garb and aspect as such; many others assumed the dress and bearing of the better-off classes, and appeared to have emerged from the position of workmen into that of local leaders, or secretaries of clubs. Some of the most extreme views were advanced by the best dressed. The meetings, which lasted about a week, were held in St. Andrew's Hall, and were opened according to custom by the President's address. The Parliamentary Committee presented a business-like report, stating the results of the past year's progress in industrial reforms. The printed Orders of the Day fill a pamphlet of twenty-six pages, and deal with every description of subject, from the most national to the most minute, that could interest the wage-earner. The discussions were fairly carried on, the tone adopted toward employers and capitalists being, however, marked by that colouring that we have become accustomed to upon such occasions. Some resolutions were passed that one would have expected at any meeting of labour representatives, but there were others that did not appear to be the result of any deliberate opinion of the meeting; they were of so grave a character, yet adopted so suddenly, and after little discussion. "No. 36, Surplus Labour," was as follows:— "That this Congress is of opinion that it should be made a penal offence for any employer to bring, or cause to be brought, to any locality extra labour where the already existing supply is sufficient for the needs of the district." This was seconded by a delegate who was a Member of Parliament. A leading Labour member, who was sitting next me, said, when the motion was read, "This is absurd." Nevertheless, it was carried, *nemine contradicente*, but with one vote against it. A motion was made, "That in the opinion of this Congress at least six working days in each year should be set apart as National Holidays, and that the Parliamentary Committee be instructed to introduce a Bill at the earliest possible date." The mover maintained that they worked far too many days; but he met with no support, and his motion was quietly dropped. A resolution to "prohibit the landing of all pauper aliens who have no visible means of subsistence" was carried, as was also one condemning the use by the Government of things made by prison labour. The principle of payment of Members of Parliament was adopted with enthusiasm, as was also that of fixing by law the daily hours of work at eight. A motion, that all persons employed in the Government workshops should be paid Trade Union rates of wages, "with a minimum of sixpence per hour for all labourers," was carried, with the omission of the latter words. Another proposal that was advocated was that female workers should be paid the same as men. This appeared to be popular; but one of the women delegates put a somewhat new complexion upon the subject when she rose to speak. "What does this mean?" she said. "Simply that only men will be employed. It will work the women out. Some of the men are honest enough to admit that this is their object." It was not persisted in.

A large number of practical questions appear among the one hundred and twenty-six subjects upon the notice paper, several of them referring to the proper inspection of factories and machinery, and the sanitation of workshops. The amendment of the Poor Laws, the further dealing with the law relating to the Liability of Employers, the Truck Act, Bake-houses, Co-operation and Trade Unionism, the Liability of Trustees, the Report of the Labour Commission, the law relating to Colliery Engine-keepers, Technical Education, the necessity for providing Life-saving Appliances round the coast, amendment of the law relating to Merchandise Marks—these, and subjects like these, formed the more feasible part of the work of the Congress.

But the most interesting motion, which one expected to hear discussed with some keenness, as it involved the question between the new Trade Unionism and the old, was that affirming the Collectivist or Socialist principle of carrying on national life and industry. I had been told by a Socialist authority in London not to miss the keen discussion that might be expected at Norwich upon this subject. But the manner of its treatment was disappointing. What discussion there was, was short and heated—all on one side—and the dissentients, such as they were, seemed cowed. The motion was, "That in the opinion of this Congress it is essential to the maintenance of British industries to nationalize the land, mines, minerals, and royalty rents, and that the Parliamentary Committee be instructed to promote legislation with the above objects." On this the simple amendment was moved by Mr. Keir Hardie, M.P., to omit after "land" the words, "mines, minerals, and royalty rents," and insert, "and all the means of production and exchange," thus affirming the complete Socialist programme. One delegate objected that this meant a complete revolution in the national life, and that before it was accepted proof should be given as to how it would work, and whether it would work at all. Were they to throw over altogether the spirit of enterprise, self-reliance, thrift, personal foresight? He agreed to the State taking the land and mines, because they stood upon a special footing, and were different in their nature from the other instruments of production. This solitary champion of the old school—though, indeed, it was the dominant one only ten years ago—fared badly in the fight. His position was forthwith attacked, and with some acrimony, by several of the leading members of the Congress, who appeared not only to feel strongly in favour of the Socialist programme, but also to feel that confidence, that is imparted by being on the winning side. They had a good opening for their onset in the fact that their opponent was willing for the State to take the land, though not to take anything else. If the one was right, why not the other? If the one needful, why not the other? If there were oppressions connected with the private ownership of land, were there not just as great wrongs owing to the domination of capital? Why be half-hearted, and halt on the broad road to justice and reform? Had the dissentient objected to all State ownership, his position would have been stronger. Each leader appeared to be eager to show that he was in no way behind the most advanced men of the new Socialist school. The motion, as amended, was supported by two delegates who were Members of Parliament, and carried by an overwhelming majority of 219 to 61. At the Liverpool Congress, four years before, it was rejected by an equally decisive majority.

I remarked to a Labour leader who was sitting near me, that there had not been that interchange of views and conflict of debate upon the question, that I had expected. He said that further talking was not required, as the whole subject had been fully considered when State Socialism was affirmed by the Congress at Belfast the preceding year.*

It was only to be expected that during the discussions of nearly a week some erratic effusions would break out. It was during the brief debate upon Socialism that a prominent Labour leader, in opposition to its solitary champion, denounced "thrift" in terms that excited some comment afterwards. His words were: "Thrift is the invention of the capitalist rogues to deprive thrifty fools of their right standard of living and comfort." He added, "Commercial enterprise was the last resort of scoundrels." This seems strange language, especially as addressed to wage-earners, who, in the present order of society at least, will certainly sink into pauperism in old age if they despise thrift.

* We learn by the papers that at the Cardiff meeting of 1895 the Congress declared against the Collectivists by large majorities, and were only prevented from repealing the resolution above referred to by a technicality. Yet we are also told that they adopted a proposal for nationalizing all *land*, *minerals*, and railways. The Socialists may feel consoled under their defeat. As they would say, their opponents are building better than they know. The action of both Congresses show what confusion of ideas there is on the subject, and how hastily conclusions are voted and rescinded, without the scope of either decision being fully realized.

The statements are obviously contrary to fact, and further, they put out of sight the reasons why, from the earliest dawn of civilisation, moralists of all nations have lauded the qualities that make for thrift. It is not alone that men may secure for themselves an independent living—though surely it is something not to have to live on others—but on account of the moral powers that thrift develops—industry, self-denial, preferring future good to present indulgence. If these qualities are wanting in any people, more healthy and vigorous nations will soon outstrip them in the race, no matter what form of social state be adopted. If these qualities were to be discarded by the Western World generally, the decay of our civilisation would not be far off, despite all the new schemes of public economy that could be devised. The speaker was himself a man of temperate habits, and a great worker, which makes his teaching the more harmful.

Another leading speaker denounced the desire of getting cheap things vigorously. "The great curse of this place is that every one wants to get things cheap—cheap clothes, cheap furniture, cheap tools" —this he said in a scornful, sneering tone. They must, on the contrary, get such a command of the instruments of production as would enable every man and every woman to keep up a high standard of comfort, and not to depend upon a few shillings, more or less, of wages. It was also very emphatically, almost angrily said, that women must be treated in all spheres of work with absolute equality to men. It was declared that "competition with all its fearful evils must disappear, and collectivism with brotherly feeling take its place. The democracy must own all the industrial forces of the nation." A delegate noticed one result of invention and progress in mechanical appliances that appears to be unavoidable, but is not the less unsatisfactory. He said, "The division of labour is ruining us. It prevents a man from being a good workman in anything."

A feature in the proceedings was the contest for the position of Secretary to the Parliamentary Committee, to which a salary of £200 a year is attached. Mr. Fenwick, M.P., had held the position for years, and was again a candidate. He was universally respected, but he was opposed to the State regulation of the hours of labour, and had warmly supported in Parliament the amendment moved to the Eight Hours Bill to leave, according to the old ideas of liberty, an option to each district to adopt that limit or not. As the majority came round more and more to approve State control, his position became more awkward; but he had, nevertheless, with commendable toleration, been re-elected several times. The limit was reached at this Congress. He reminded them that he was responsible for his votes to his constituents only, and claimed independent action; but upon the ballot being taken he was found to have been rejected, and a strong supporter of the Eight Hours Law, without qualification, elected in his place. This would seem to establish the position either that the Secretary should not be a Member of Parliament, or that if one, he should be able to anticipate that the decisions of the Congress are agreeable to his constituents as well as personally to his own judgment.

Excellent order was maintained throughout the proceedings, and the proposals for improving the condition of the workers that appeared on the notice paper, were discussed in a practical manner. One pleasing feature was the attention shown to the women delegates. Precedence was always given to a woman when she rose—which was seldom, and chiefly upon matters affecting the sex; and upon one occasion when the women wished to speak upon a topic that had been passed, the Standing Orders were suspended to allow women only to address the Congress. Thus consideration for the weaker sex honourably distinguishes men, even though they may deny the conditions out of which it arises. Mr. Colman, the Member of Parliament for the district, hospitably entertained several of the delegates and their wives at his estate near Norwich; four-in-hands and carriages of various kinds being drawn up outside the Hall, awaiting the end of the day's work. But some looked askance upon these Greek favours, and one member declared in Congress, amidst applause, that many of them regarded it as a degradation to be thus entertained.

In one of the rooms of the Hall there is a fine life-size portrait of Nelson, whose native place is near, and who first went to school at the Norwich high-school. It is said that the Trustees of the National Gallery are trying to get this picture for the public. What a change in the ideas of men less than a century has brought about! What would the hero have thought had he attended this Congress and heard declared the condemnation of capitalists, the abolition of property, the evil of thrift, the danger of cheap goods, the equality in all things of women with men, and all by persons, some of whom held good public positions, assembled in open meeting and debating with the full sanction of the law and of public opinion? And what would the delegates have said to the absolutism that then prevailed in the Navy, even under so just a commander as Nelson? Nicolas, in his "Despatches of Nelson," gives under the date of October, 1804, an instance of the despotic powers that commanders of the King's ships exercised in those days over the King's subjects. Lieutenant Shaw informs the Admiral "that misconduct had taken place among his men on board the brig *Spider*," and as he could not discover the guilty party, he had flogged them all, "calling them over by the watch-bill and giving them a dozen each." Nelson gravely rebukes this action as "foreign to the rules of good discipline and the accustomed practice of His Majesty's Navy," and adds, "I trust that your watchful conduct will prevent any such confusion or disposition to riot from happening again." But the Congress would have used stronger language than the hero!

There was a women's meeting held during the week,

under the auspices of the Congress, with the object of promoting the formation of a Trade Union among the female workers of Norwich. An immense crowd, chiefly of men, assembled, and were addressed by Lady Charles Dilke, Mr. Tom Mann, Mr. Ben Tillett, and others. Lady Dilke spoke with that clear and accurate pronunciation which the educated English seem to keep to themselves, as it has not extended in its native perfection to their brethren in America or in the colonies. While partly the result of training, it also appears to be connected with a dignity and reserve of manner that prevents the speaker from being in a hurry, and makes him feel that what he has got to say is worth being said completely, as to each word, and listened to. Lady Dilke mentioned some sad cases of distress, and urged all to "take up their cross—for it was a cross—and fight for a better system of life." Some of the other speakers dwelt upon the social evil, and held the capitalist *régime* answerable for it too.

Taken as a whole, the chief result of the Congress appeared to be to mark, in its ranks at least, the victory of the Socialists; but this rather because the political trend set in that way, and political leaders led on, than from any distinct conviction in its favour in the minds of the delegates, or any clear feeling beyond the natural feeling in favour of anything that promises to lessen the hardships of the toiler's life.

The workmen of the United States held their great Congress at Denver some months later, and there the Collectivist "plank"—it was familiarly known in America as "the tenth plank"—was rejected. But neither do I regard this as proving a mental conclusion on the part of the operatives there against Socialism. Some, no doubt, do disbelieve in it, but others voted against it because they considered it premature. They are a business-like people, and more than one Labour leader told me that they were going to vote against the tenth plank at Denver because it was impracticable at present, though they fully believed that it was bound to come in time.

The outside public and the newspapers did not seem to be much impressed by the deliberations of the Congress. As an institution it appeared to have lost the charm of novelty and youth, and to have somewhat outlived the usefulness of its original purpose. The complete Socialist objects to the lingering influence of the old Trade Unionism in it, and to so much of its action as still savours of individualism. The old Trade Unionists are dissatisfied with the new policy, and some proposed to recede from the Congress now that absolute Socialism had been adopted.

Some Members of Parliament told me that much weight was not to be attached to their decisions, as many voted for proposals knowing that they would and could go no further. Others maintained that the views of English workmen generally were different from those expressed by the minority there represented. One gentleman considered that the mere meeting of the Congress would lead to the return of two Conservatives for Norwich at the next election. But I will briefly give the judgment pronounced by some prominent authorities in different spheres of public influence, upon the Congress, and upon its declaration in favour of Socialism.

Mr. Chamberlain said that this declaration "was impracticable and absurd," and was duly challenged to take part in a public discussion upon Socialism by Mr. Hyndman. This he declined, but in doing so stated "that he had never attacked Socialism," as he was accused of doing, "because there are some kinds of Socialism of which he highly approves. What he has called impracticable and absurd is the Collectivist resolution of the recent Trades Union Congress."

Addressing a meeting at Leeds shortly after the Congress sat, Mr. Chamberlain further said :

"Neither do I think that the bulk of the working classes have any real faith in the new theories put forward by the Trades Unionism of to-day, borrowed, and I think incompletely understood, from foreign sources. I have found that the working people are quite ready to appreciate the fact that this Collectivism—which has been, I admit, most frankly and clearly stated—is a policy which is neither more nor less than a confiscation of every kind of property—of the savings of the poor quite as much as of the capital of the rich. I do not think that the good sense of the people of this country will ever lead them to adopt a community of goods. I think that they see that these new doctrines tend to interfere with their rights and their liberties, even more sharply and injuriously than they would with those in a better position, and I think they also see that a policy of this kind, tending as it does to bring every one to a dead level, would be fatal to their liberty, energy, independence, thrift, and to all the qualities which have made us proud, and justly proud, of the British working man."

Mr. Balfour, the leader of the Opposition in Parliament, speaking at a meeting early in 1895, contented himself with saying that there was no fear of Socialism if care was taken to do justice to all, that no good could come out of wrong to any class, and that much might be properly done by legislation.

Mr. John Burns, at Battersea, gave the highest praise to the Congress and to most of what it had done; but he differed from the resolutions concerning the exclusion of aliens and proscribing prison labour, and touched lightly upon the Collectivist resolution, simply saying that it was nothing new.

Mr. Michael Davitt, who fully accepts several Socialist proposals, declared at a public meeting in Melbourne that probably many of the delegates when they voted for that resolution did not clearly realize what it meant.

Mr. Bryce, speaking in Lancashire some time after the Conference, thus stated his views upon the main question :

"What was the present position of Socialism in this country ? It had still comparatively few believers, and that was doubtless the reason why, though most of the leading spirits in the independent Labour party were Socialists themselves, the party did not call itself by that name. Sometimes the dreams of yesterday became realities to-morrow. The difficulties of what was called the Collectivist scheme of reconstituting society were enormous. They were not merely economic difficulties, nor difficulties attending the transition from the present order to the new one desired. They were difficulties also of the ethical kind, and lay deep in the constitution of human nature itself. . . . The proper policy for a party of progress, and the policy which the Liberal party had practically followed in the past, was to examine each particular proposal on its merits. Some of the plans which had a touch of Collectivism were, he believed, perfectly sound, and ought to be pushed forward. . . . The millennium or nothing, and the millennium all at once or nothing, seemed to be the Collectivist motto. But social and economic reconstruction was far slower than political; it was only destruction that was easy. What the Collectivist party desired was nothing less than to persuade mankind to change the road on which they had been travelling for centuries. Let them, by all means, press their propaganda. England was a free country; let all have fair audience."

One marked incident of the Socialist discussion at Norwich was the manner in which it illustrated, as I have stated, the weakness of the position of those who would save the State by confiscating property in land, while they would hold sacred all other kinds of property. I will next refer to a meeting that was held in Philadelphia, because there, also, it so happened that this same point was forcibly illustrated. It met under the auspices of the Single Tax League of Philadelphia, in a large and handsome hall in the principal street of that city. The audience, though not very large, was distinctly "respectable," all being well-dressed, and apparently well-to-do. Several ladies were present.

Two or three ready speakers explained and lauded the principles of their cause. No man was entitled to own land, though he was entitled to hold any other kind of property, and the State should therefore resume possession of its value, as it is when unimproved, by quietly taxing it away. In support of their argument, they laid down, with that calm confidence that Americans often display in dealing with fundamental questions, two propositions as being incontrovertible: one, that no man could have a right to anything that he had not created; and, two, that he had an absolute right to what he had created. This seemed to me a very imperfect analysis of the question. When a man catches a fish, he does not create it, but he has expended labour on it, and is the first in possession. When Abraham argued his right to the well with Abimelech, he did not pretend that he had made the stream of water that he wished to enjoy; it was only a natural gift, improved and made available first by his labour. "I have digged this well." These theoretical reflections were soon, however, interrupted by a practical episode. A rather sour, ill-favoured looking man rose up from the audience, and requested to be allowed to address the meeting. This was agreed to and he came upon the platform. They told me that he was a well-known workman of the city, who lost no possible opportunity of addressing meetings. He had a vigorous style of declamation, and evidently thought that the stronger expressions he used the better. He said that he addressed them as an absolute Socialist, who would confiscate all property, and then went on to denounce the Single Taxers as contemptible halters between two opinions. They said it was right to take a man's land; if so, why not his tramways? (the tramways were then unpopular with the working classes of Philadelphia, and I always found that general principles were coloured by the local grievance in each place). The law secured the one just as much as the other. Free land might be a sop. That was just why he opposed it, as it might allay discontent and delay the time of general reckoning, when they would crush all the propertied classes. Single Taxers allowed a man to keep his interest upon capital because the law allowed it;—the law equally allowed the robbery of rent. And what was the use of giving him a block of land unless they gave him capital too? He could not cultivate it with his ten fingers. The Single Taxers were merely playing into the hands of the Democrats. The national banner, the stars and stripes, was every thread of it a fraud, all for the capitalist. The people must fight. He wound up by denouncing religion and marriage. A Single Taxer replied, contending that Socialism would make all the people slaves, just like the blacks before the war, well fed, fairly cared for, but free men no longer.

Though the meeting did not go with the Socialist, and some of the ladies appeared to shudder at his language, yet he carried off a more successful impression of the argument than did the advocates of the Henry George scheme. Partly this was owing to the success that attends the more pronounced opinion in any popular gathering. The man who goes half-way only, should keep in the closet and not tempt the platform. But it was also owing to the fact that he really had the best of the argument, as also had the Socialists at Norwich against the delegate who would take the land but nothing else.

The man who says that the State is not justified in doing a wrong, even for the supposed benefit of the people, and that having sanctioned private property for centuries, and induced people to put the fruits of their labour into it, cannot now honestly seize it—occupies a logical and just position. The man who says that the safety of the people is the supreme law, and that it now calls for the appropriation by the State of all the means of production and exchange, comes also to a logical, though unjust conclusion. But the man who says all property is sacred except land, and the State must confiscate all the land, but nothing else, occupies a position that is both illogical and unjust. Land is a fit subject, owing to its limited nature, for special regulation and for taxation, suited to the circumstances of each State; if need be, limiting the amount that may be held by any one person, giving free play to all the agencies of distribution, and taking, to be sure, all that the public may want for public purposes upon payment of reasonable compensation. But a man's right to land rests upon the same immediate foundation as his right to a ship, namely, the authority of the law and custom of his country for centuries, which has led him, relying upon the public faith, to give what his labour produced, for it.

A meeting was held in a fashionable part of London, under the presidency of Mr. Keir Hardie, M.P., and the patronage of the Independent Labour Party. The notices announced the expected appearance of several prominent leaders of that party upon the platform. Boswell mentions the blank astonishment with which he contemplated the mere idea of any one presuming to designate his patron as "*Sam* Johnson." A similar feeling of reverence does not now obtain in public circles, for I found that the fashion prevailed of giving contractions of the Christian names of the prominent men who were to speak. Thus it was "Tom" this, or "Ben" that, "Fred" or "Frank," that figured in the bills. People like to call their favourites by some short name or nickname. It comes naturally, as indicating the popularity of the object, in some cases; in others also the familiarity that is claimed by his admirers. In the United States, where this popular fancy has full play, few successful public men have been known to the people by their own proper names. There it has generally been some short designation descriptive of the calling of the man, or of some personal peculiarity. It is "the Rail-splitter," "the Flat-boatman," "the War Horse," "the Stonewall," "Tippicanoe," "Little Mac." The familiar prefix "old" has been in frequent use— "Old Hickory," "Old Hutch," "Old Bullion," "Old

Pig-iron," "Old Rough and Ready." Even the rogues of New York had their "Boss Tweed."

Mr. Keir Hardie, whose name appears to defy contraction, took the chair. His appearance and manner convey more the impression of complete sincerity than the power of sober judgment. The large hall was crowded by a poor but respectable-looking throng—many of them women—whole families sitting together, and the daughters at intervals going among the people selling the tracts of the Socialist and Labour party. The leaders, including some Members of Parliament and several candidates for that position, occupied the front of the platform, supported by several Socialist reformers, among whom was a well-known Russian patriot who had to flee his own country. At the side was a brass band and a choir of girls, who performed between the speeches some of the Independent Labour Party chants, which, with the music to match, were sold in the room. Among these were the "Marseillaise" and Burns's "A Man's a Man for a' That," and some songs by other authors that expressed the bitterest feelings against the classes who possess property, and the clergy.

It would be hard to expect speakers upon such an occasion to break new ground, and none of them did so. An impressive speech was made by a young working woman, but its effect was wholly owing to the intense and almost hysterical feeling that she displayed. She fully adopted the warning addressed of old to the orator: "If you want me to weep, weep yourself." She was denouncing the wrong done to the worker when he was turned out of work and bread by the invention of new machinery. It was impossible not to sympathise with her. The speech that most engaged my observation was one that was made by a gentleman who was stylishly dressed, and whose manner presented something of the theatrical aspect. As a platform speech it was the most successful of the evening, the chairman's being tame in comparison. His argument was simple. "Why are you poor? It is because others are rich. Why do you live in garrets? It is because of the palaces that you see in this neighbourhood around you. We," he exclaimed, "make war on these palaces; and we equally make war on your garrets. We would abolish both, and have all well housed and well provided for." The effect of such declarations to a meeting of people many of whom are badly off is irresistible. They carry all before them. The speaker also made several jokes and points, at which all laughed, and he had a certain oddness in his manner that inspired merriment; he led the whole meeting triumphantly. People like to be entertained, and something of the funny prompts a fellow feeling that the austere tone of the highly self-respecting man fails to inspire. A strain of the common, or even the queer, strikes the public fancy and attaches the speaker to the audience. They will tell you that they like to hear a "live man." Some of his strongest expressions were vociferously applauded, especially by the women, who appeared to accept the most extreme utterances more readily than the men. A number of girls carried plates round the hall, making a collection for the expenses of the evening. As at Norwich, marked consideration was shown to women. At one part of the proceedings a young girl appeared on the platform and commenced giving a recitation. It was poorly done, and annoyed the people by delaying the speeches that they were anxious to hear. Some near me commenced muttering disapproval, but they were promptly silenced, and general attention was given till the girl had completed her task. When the meeting was over you saw mothers calling their children and families collecting together to go home.

The novelty in gatherings such as these lies in the new conditions under which the ills of social life are now ventilated—when people are no longer resigned to them as a necessary fate, but, under respectable auspices, question all things, and work out, when they have the power, any change that they may think right.

And it is easy to condemn any institution, if you look only to the evils that result from it. I was not able to be present at, but I heard of, a smaller meeting of those who hold advanced views upon the relation of the sexes. There the institution of Christian marriage was assailed with equal facility. Is it not a fact that thousands who marry are unhappy—why should this unhappiness be made lifelong? How many marriages are made for love only—and is it a marriage at all without love? Why should the wife be tied to the drunken husband? Why crush the unfaithful wife, but give immunity to the unfaithful husband? Here, again, the objections are obvious, but the reasons that justify the old belief want searching after.

In this connection another assemblage that I was at may be referred to, where the institution of private property was attacked also with vigour, though not with the same apparent success. It was in an English county, where a "red-van" lecturer was addressing from his cart a number of the villagers and country people, who appeared to have sauntered up to listen, rather than to have come up to attend the meeting. His questions and arguments, like those of the popular man in London, were certainly not easy to answer off-hand. " Why should one man own half a county when you have not grazing room for a cow? Why should you live in hovels by the thousand in order that a handful of the gentry may live in mansions?" Why, indeed? Yet he did not make the same impression that the speaker did in the city. The people seemed to listen in a stolid manner. The effect of generations of suppressed life and energy cannot be thrown off by a few years of freedom. Or possibly it may be the external manner only that is sluggish, and there may be feeling within. A note which is stated to have been sent to one of the "red-van" lecturers by an old Wiltshire labourer would seem to show that there is this feeling. It runs thus:

"Our parson preach yesterday of We Labourers Being Dissatisfied and Discontented With our Wages murmering of it he said

We Labouring men ought to Be satisfied with what we got. Be satisfied. We Wish You to Publish it Plese."

I heard these same fundamental questions put at a meeting in the United States, but with a local colouring that was imparted by the circumstances of the audience. It was a gathering of a Social Labour Club at their Labour Lyceum, which was chiefly attended by shoemakers, whose industry was at the time much depressed, work being uncertain and wages low. They all sat about smoking while a young operative spoke. He first addressed himself to the general view of the question between the poor and the rich, and advanced the usual arguments, or rather asked the old questions. The wealth of the United States was enormous, more than sufficient for all. Why, then, were they poor? Because the rich robbed them. He also said, what was asserted at Norwich, that cheap things were a mistake. What they wanted was dear things and good wages. He denounced, in violent terms, both the great political parties, and all politicians from the President downwards. All this was listened to, and applauded more or less, but the freest applause came when he went on to show how it was that they in their industry had bad times and often low wages. It was wholly owing to the exactions of a ring of property owners. Their raw material, the hides, was grown on the distant prairies, and the first robber was the ranch owner. Then came the railway companies, the fellmonger, the factory owner, the shopkeeper, all these had to be appeased, and so, little was left for them. Had the people all these instruments of production and exchange in their own possession—the lands, the railways, the factories, the shops—all would be rich, and two hours' work a day would be sufficient to produce what the community wanted. They should confiscate all property, just as they did the slaves.

But perhaps the saddest audience that the rights and wrongs of property were ever discussed before, was that which thronged the galleries of the hall in Chicago where the Labour Conference met in 1893. One of the delegates gave me the particulars. It was a hard winter; there was great distress; numbers whom the boom time had attracted to the city were now left without work, without food, and without lodging. During the night many slept on the steps and about the porches of the building, and crowded into the galleries when the meetings were held, for warmth and shelter, to hear the delegates, and to ponder upon the rights of the wealthy. A tragical sight it must have been to see these social wrecks eagerly listening to denunciations of property as being the cause of their misery, and hearing the promise, under the new system, of ease and plenty for all. Hard after such comforting words to have to go out and face the cold reality of the world as it is to-day! He told me that it was no easy matter to oppose any Socialistic proposals with such surroundings. When he and some others did so they were vehemently hissed by the hungry galleries. No wonder! But this spectacle at Chicago is not a bad illustration of how the whole social system stands now upon its trial, even before the poor. It must justify itself, and justify itself even to them.

In London I attended a widely different kind of meeting. It assembled to hear a lecture from a member of the Fabian Society. The room was capable of holding about one hundred people, and was well filled with a miscellaneous audience—some well dressed, some apparently poor, some that seemed to be students or to belong to the literary calling; women as well as men. The chair was taken by a clergyman. Nothing could exceed the attention paid to the speaker. He was as far removed as possible from the type of the platform declaimer. His manner was cold, hesitating, critical; his matter logical (granting his premises), skilfully marshalled, and erudite. He attacked the old school of political economy, and among other things laid down that the poor not only *could* not save, but that they *should* not, till they had reached a good standard of living. What this was, was left unfixed. He appeared to admit the ancient maxim that the waste of the rich is one of nature's ways for equalizing things again, as he said that luxury was useful in scattering wealth. In explaining the principles of the Socialist community, he declared that in it they would not produce more than was wanted from time to time for the day that was passing over them; nor would they save. He did not discuss the effect that such a policy would have on invention, new discoveries of machinery, energy, and the progressive spirit. "Rent" and the evils connected with it were explained in a learned manner. He wound up by warning his hearers that they must not tie themselves too much to facts; they must often act without them; they must have faith. The flaw that marred the effect of his argument was the manner in which he imputed bad faith to the adherents of the orthodox school. In disputing their propositions he repeatedly remarked, "The trick here is in assuming" so-and-so. The unfairness of this was the more marked as he stated it without the least degree of heat—merely as an obvious conclusion from the facts.

When he had finished, a number of intelligent questions were put, which clearly showed that the questioners had thought over the subject carefully. Some who spoke were obviously those upon whom prosperity did not shine. That old problem of political economy, the true meaning of "value," was acutely mooted. The meeting may certainly be termed an intellectual one, but the impression it left was how small a part of the road towards great changes mere intellect goes. It may start the ball, but once it begins to roll, rough practical hands come to the fore to push the mere thinkers aside and trundle it along in their own way. Movements grow more owing to the strength of the feeling in their favour, than to the exactness of the reasoning that supports them, and it is experience that shapes them. At the shoemakers' gathering in America, and at the Labour Party meeting in London, one saw the practical side to the metaphysical cogitations of the lecture-room.

Another meeting that I attended in London was at a Labour church. I call it a meeting, though strictly speaking it was the Sunday service of the Socialist brotherhood. The absolute Socialist breaks with the religion of the day. He does not go to church, nor let his children go. He regards the churches merely as part of the capitalistic system. Where he can, he establishes a church of his own, and there are a few such in England. There are only a few, however; for numbers care to go to no church, new or old, and many who are ready to break with most things do not wish for an ostensible change to a fresh form of faith. The service or meeting was held in a large church that had originally been built by some Christian body, but was now taken over by the Socialists. It had an organ and the usual fittings of pews, pulpit, and reading-desk. There was a small attendance of people, apparently belonging to the middle class, a few of them being women. A gentleman of some position in the Socialist world acted as minister or leader to the gathering. He read a portion of the Bible, and then gave a prayer which made reference, but not in any undue manner, to the evils that they were seeking to remedy. One or two of the ordinary church hymns were sung, and this concluded the religious portion of the day's business. Some one from the congregation then came to the reading-desk, and spoke at length of the ills of social life and how they ought to be remedied. Society was not a healthy body, but a diseased one—the stomach swollen, yet refusing to feed the emaciated, worn-out hands. The extravagance of luxury was shameful. One lady had given £7,000 for a pair of ear-rings, and a gentleman gave £1,000 for a breastpin, and yet there were starving poor. Some other members then spoke, and one denounced property owners in more bitter terms than I had heard at any other meeting in London. He declared that he looked forward to taking personal vengeance upon them. The hearers loudly applauded from time to time. But the minister, in closing the discussion, dissented wholly from the vengeance view of the subject. The system, he said, was to blame, not the people who lived and worked under it. The law allowed and encouraged people to hold property. It was unjust to cherish hatred against them. How many of themselves, he fearlessly asked his hearers, would not enjoy property just like others, if they could? His remarks were not ill taken, but they did not excite the same warmth of feeling that those of the vengeful man did.

This gathering was a failure however looked at—whether regarded as a religious exercise or as a political display. The two functions that it endeavoured to fulfil were not merely different, but inconsistent. Fighting against the evil conditions of this life is one thing, and cultivating the spirit that teaches us to rise superior to them in the hope of a better, is another thing. The essence of Socialism is not to waste time in vain yearnings after another life, but to make this present one as comfortable as possible. The leader appeared to be a thoughtful and humane man, but the short ministrations by which he commenced the proceedings had an air, unintentional though it was, of mockery about them. It was so unreal. All felt that they came there for a different purpose than to pray and to sing soul-consoling hymns. The attitude of Socialism to religion bears so directly upon the question of how far the new creed is likely to ultimately prevail, that it will demand further consideration later on.

I went to a service of a similar kind at Washington, at what was called the People's Church, where a reverend gentleman preached who I was told not to miss hearing. There was a moderate attendance of what we call the middle class of the people. Pamphlets and leaflets that condemned all monopolies and all aggrandisement of capital were sold in the hall. They were moderate in their tone, and admitted that no one's property could be honestly taken without compensation. A sort of litany, descriptive of noble sentiments and of kind human sympathies between men, was read, and hymns were sung, some of which were religious, though not of the orthodox type, and some philanthropic. The minister, who was the only speaker, delivered a purely secular discourse, which was at times warmly applauded by the audience. One of the main topics was the bad condition of the ordinary politics of the day. A true man could feel nothing but contempt for both parties. The only interest that they felt in either was what they could get out of them for mutualism. Votes of the electors were often bought for a few dollars. He cited some newspaper which gave particulars of this in one State. The elector said, "These men are only going in to make what they can of it—why should not I also make what I can?" He also attacked the press. The strong vote that the people had just given at the elections, which had come off a few days before, in favour of the Republicans, was not based on any thought, but it was a blind rushing about from side to side of the ship staggering in the storm. The chief reference that he made to the distinctive views of his own school was when he declared that the great Trusts and Corporations had learnt the evils of competition, and were teaching the people the same lesson, and preparing their property to be held by the people's representatives. He concluded by saying that the era of competition and selfishness was doomed, and that of mutuality coming in. All his thrusts against the politicians appeared to be highly acceptable to his hearers, yet he and they were anxious to hand over their affairs, private as well as public, to those very men. What struck one as marking a difference between this People's Church and the one in London, was that here there was less religion and also less bitterness. The service was more secular, and there was a broader and more tolerant tone adopted towards the well-to-do. They were dealt with as creatures of a system, not as criminals.

These may be taken as representative of the different kinds of meetings that take place for the discussion of Labour and Socialistic questions. I will only add one other, and that is one of a political character, such as used to excite enthusiasm when I was in England before. It was announced to be held in Hyde Park on a Sunday, and was styled in the handbills "a grand national demonstration" to urge upon the Government to take immediate steps to abolish "that mischievous and useless hereditary chamber," the House of Lords. Twenty-six different points in the suburbs around London were notified for the different crowds to assemble. Strict injunctions as to the times of departure from different points and the lines of route were given, and complete obedience to the marshals and to the police was commanded. Eleven platforms were erected, with parties of speakers announced for each. Of Women's Liberal Associations seven were to be represented, and one platform was given over wholly to women. The resolution of the day was to be proposed at all the platforms at the one time to the sound of the bugle. All this recalled to mind the days of the old Hyde Park gatherings, when fifty or sixty thousand people assembled, broke down the railings when they found the gates closed, smashed windows, and threatened the mansions around, so that Mr. Disraeli gravely informed the House of Commons that he was not quite sure whether he had a house to go home to or not.

Nothing, however, could be tamer than this display. The old fire was extinct, or was burning in other directions. The day was beautiful, and the crowd considerable. Various trade and other societies came up, headed by their bands, and bearing their banners. These latter bore some mottoes that are getting rather old-fashioned with the more advanced party—"Labour conquers all," "Industry the source of wealth," the praise of "the workers," "The dignity of labour." These do not fit in with the doctrines that I had heard —of two or three hours' work a day being sufficient, and of producing from time to time only enough to keep the community going. Speeches were made from the eleven platforms upon the iniquities of the House of Lords and the oppressions that it perpetrated upon the people; but they excited little enthusiasm. The crowd stood about or lay on the grass in an indifferent way. What enthusiasm there was came from the Irish element, which was well represented, and was indignant because the Lords had recently rejected the Home Rule Bill. People crowded about the women's platform. A few appeared disposed to be jocular, but they were quickly silenced by that chivalrous feeling of consideration for the other sex that marks both Englishmen and Americans. Yet it was a sorry sight, these women straining their voices to cry aloud denunciations of the guilty peers. What imparted a hollowness to the whole display was the fact—which the people generally are quite aware of—that the Lords dare not resist anything that the public really want. They have formally surrendered ever since 1832. They could reject Home Rule only because England was against it. Unlike the Senate in the United States—which does stop any legislation that it disapproves of, quite irrespective of the wishes of any majority in the lower house—the Lords claim only to delay till a decided majority of the Commons declare themselves. Long-headed Radicals desire nothing better than to leave the House of Peers just as it is. But the indifference of the crowd was also owing, as it seemed to me, to that decay in the popular interest about merely political questions to which I have previously alluded.

Meetings such as these that I have described remind one of the change in the political condition of England that little more than half a century has produced. Then the feelings and grievances of the poor found their outlet in mob demonstrations, sometimes with violence, and at all times with the rough and crude announcement of demands that were then regarded as quite outside the region of practical discussion. Sir

Robert Peel assured the House of Commons that England need have no fear of mobs, as "in England the mob can do nothing," there being a power and moral feeling in the country that "could at all times put down any mob." When the petition for the People's Charter was presented to the House of Commons, that body refused, by a majority of nearly six to one, to hear the promoters at the bar in support of it. Now the points of the Charter are for the most part embodied in the constitution, or accepted by the leading political party in the State, and instead of tumultuous gatherings of the mob you have formal meetings of the electors, presided over by Members of Parliament, at which in polished harangues the upsetting of all things is proposed. Doctrines that would subvert the social state in a more fundamental manner than the Chartists ever thought of, are announced amid the most respectable surroundings. Electoral changes have gone faster than educational influences. These meetings are not tribunals well adapted for passing judgment upon what have been termed the unseen foundations of society. These being out of the general sight, the causes and manner of laying them, be they on right lines or wrong, can only be adequately investigated when you know all the many-sided facts and reasons and think carefully over them. This cannot be expected amid the excitement of a popular assembly, so when the cause is called on, judgment goes for the time by default against existing institutions, for want of appearance. Only one side is or can be heard. Any man can then readily ask a question that no man can readily answer. All easily see the force of the adverse arguments; for the evils of the present system are felt by all, as some evils must be under any system. But the judgment given is only an interlocutory one. The appeal is to the whole people, many of whom do not go to these meetings, but all of whom are set thinking even by the very fallacies and extravagances that are at times proclaimed at them.

It is just here that the value of open discussion

comes in. It gives vent to ideas and discontents that as a fact are prevailing among the people. It does not create them — they exist already — but it brings them to the light. In so far as these are just, it ensures that they will be attended to—that right will be done, and this is a great public gain. Where the impossible is demanded, public opinion will in time stand in the way. Though, amid the excitement of the platform, the extremist seems to carry all before him, yet when people awake next morning to the facts of the workaday world, and meet the other people, they find their ideas modified. More, too, is said at these meetings than is meant; and much that is meant by honest enthusiasts they themselves admit to be impracticable now, and to be realizable only in a distant future. Numbers, to be sure, are now sovereign in the social state, but yet have not an absolute sovereignty. There are some other powers to be reckoned with. Truth is one, and like Milton's angel it may be wounded, but not killed. The common sense of the whole people is another; and the more discussion there is, the more these two ultimately come to the front. We must think this, even if we only take the modest estimate of the popular wisdom formulated by Abraham Lincoln, when he said, "You may fool some of the people all the time, and all the people some of the time, but not all the people all the time."

I mixed with many poor people and many rough people at different gatherings, but always saw kindness of feeling and consideration for others displayed. I have mentioned some instances regarding women. Certainly tender-heartedness often finds its home among the lowly. I may mention an instance from my own experience. When a member of the Victorian Parliament, I once, when driving through a lonely part of the country district that I represented, was stopped upon the track by a gaunt, hard-featured looking bushman, who had hurried across from a neighbouring paddock, where he had been burning the scrub. Begrimed with smoke and dirt, his rugged features would not have led you to suspect that a heart as fond as a woman's beat within his breast. I had just known him—no more, for he was not of the loquacious type of man or elector, and he so seldom troubled me that I wondered what he wanted me for now, supposing that he had some of the usual personal troubles of the elector. And he had a personal trouble; but I will let the conversation tell what it was:

He: I wanted just to see ye for a minute.

I: Oh, very well. What is it about?

He: It's about this yer burying-place beyond here, near the township.

I: Well, is anything wrong there?

He: They say the Guv'ment are going to close it.

I: Yes, I heard something about that. They will give another ground wherever you all like.

He: That's not it, quite. It's closing it up altogether.

I: Well, I suppose it is getting too full—it's so small, though there are only a few of you about here.

He looked round without speaking, so I repeated that the Government would make all arrangements for a new place. Then he began fidgeting with the harness of our buggy. He looked away from me down the bush track and slowly continued:

"Ye see, it's this way. My little boy is buried there. He's dead these two years. An' the mother an' I would feel lonesome lying anywhere else."

He broke off shortly, leaving, however, his objection to the absolute closing of the cemetery perfectly clear.

CHAPTER VII.

SOCIALISTS I HAVE MET.

In carrying out the purpose of my mission, I lost no opportunity of meeting and conversing with representatives, men of every description of Socialist views, from the intellectual and discriminating speculator down to the toiler, whose wishes were mainly moulded by the wants that pressed him and the hopes that the new system held out to him. Public speaking has been said to be a knack which can be acquired by practice, and which does not show you what is in a man, or whether there is anything in him; whereas in conversation you can get at what he really thinks, if he does think. Certainly in the platform you have one means of knowledge, in publications another, and in personal converse a third, and the last is instructive as showing what people's thoughts are running upon, irrespective of the value to be attached to the opinions themselves. You can thus often get, by a short cut, to what is wanted. I told all whom I met that I was commissioned by the Government of Victoria to make inquiries, and that I hoped to publish the result. But I have avoided recording anything that I gathered was intended for private converse only; of this there was little. Most of those whom I met were confident in their views, or at least in the feeling of their wants, and anxious to have all widely known. One of the ablest thinkers and advocates of the Socialist cause in England favoured me by giving me more than one interview, at which he explained his opinions very clearly. Socialism, he said, was a principle of the new organisation of society: not a system or Utopia. They aimed at substituting State control of industry for that of the individual, and their purpose was therefore correctly described as being the nationalization of all the means of production. But there were many points which were still quite unsettled, as, for example, the respective spheres of the central government and of local or municipal government in the work. Also, though they assumed democracy, the form of it which would prevail, and the extent of popular voting to be allowed, was uncertain. For immediate practical proposals the report of the Socialist minority of the Royal Commission on Labour was the best guide. Everything would be done gradually; no forced change. The Duke of Norfolk, and even his son, might have their land, but after that it goes to the State. His object was to secure equality of opportunity, as far as possible, to all. At present the workmen were reduced to the position of mere machines under masters; and this state of affairs was only preparing for the time when the collective State would step into the shoes of the private master. Changes were going on all about that were almost unnoticed, but were preparing for this final change. It would take, however, generations to complete that change. Taxation would be one great lever to bring it about. Tax away all property quietly, perhaps slowly, but surely. Both Mill and Bentham advocated using death duties, and altering the law of inheritance so as to pare down large fortunes. But he would not favour any immediate dividing up of large properties; though he would tax away for other purposes than revenue getting. High authority among economists approved of this. There would be a gradual levelling-up of wages to a certain level, and a disinclination to allow anything very high, and thus things would be getting more on an equality. In the social state there must be strict discipline: the ranks of workmen would not be allowed to elect their own heads; they would only have their vote for the general election of representatives. The idle would be subjected to some form of penal discipline. The mere struggle for wealth was despicable, and would not be countenanced; but he did not see how they could prevent a man or a woman getting exceptional payment for exceptional service. If a Paget or a Patti were refused a high fee, they might decline to operate or to sing. I asked what, under such a system, would be the use of a large income, even if permitted. He said that they must, he considered, allow a man to keep for his life what he earned, though not to bequeath it. As he left the form of political government uncertain, I inquired whether he contemplated the possibility of having the industrial state and men's personal rights, with the private concerns of home and family, in the hands of such men as the free government of the United States produced, to rule New York, Chicago, San Francisco, and other great cities? He spoke disparagingly of America, said it was no example, and that there would be no fear of such things with Englishmen. They would have all appointments during good behaviour, a strict Civil Service examination, and all salaries would be so equalized that there would not be great temptation to favouritism. But now there was the worst possible favouritism under the system of individual training. In no public government system could there be worse. Authorship would be provided for by having professors who would be maintained by the public, and devote their leisure time to literature. He would allow honours and distinctions for all good service done to the State, and stimulate ambition in every way. And men would strive to serve the public for these. Look at the way many of the colonials worked for their petty colonial titles. I put the old question as to how the menial work of the State would be apportioned, but do not think that further light was thrown upon this difficulty during our conversation. It is dealt with, as far as it can be, in the "Fabian

Essays." He admitted that the Socialists do centre their hopes in this world, and discard the sanctions of another; but this he considered all the working classes do now: the Socialists were by no means peculiar in that respect. He saw thousands hungry and ill-clad about him—his object was to help them; about other prospects of man he could not say. Also, undoubtedly a great change was coming over the sex relations, and in the new state they would have to be reconsidered. But all this, and much that he had discussed, belonged to the future.

The weak points in this interesting expression of views appeared to me to be—allowing the earning and holding of private gains, which is contrary to the view of most Socialists and subversive of the scheme of the new system; the taking for granted the absence of political abuses in the future; and the position indicated (rather than directly expressed) for religion and women in the coming state.

I saw another gentleman in England who was also a thoughtful exponent of the cause. He, too, said that generations must pass before their complete scheme could be secured. But they would go on taxing away gradually the value of land and of all other wealth, at least where inherited, to the vanishing point. But if the State wanted to take any one's land immediately for some public purpose, compensation should be given. There would be more freedom for the working classes under the Socialist system than at present, though those who were now the upper classes must lose much of what they enjoyed. No doubt something of the spirit of enterprise would be lost to mankind, but was not much bold spirit lost when the marauding Barons were suppressed? It was shown by experience that the shorter the hours for any class of artisans, the better style of men they were, and so, when under new conditions, all worked only three or four hours a day, the labouring class would improve still more. I asked, might not here be an illustration of John Stuart Mill's plaintive criticism that the worst of reformers was that they never knew where to stop? Rightly shocked at fourteen or sixteen hours' toil a day, they reduce it to eight, and then four; then, if production warrants, to two. But what becomes of the habit of industry and labour that conquers all and keeps human nature sweet? He said that the leisure time would be occupied fully in self-improvement in all its varying developments. The eight-hours day was merely a stage in the advance. He agreed with the gentleman who spoke at Norwich that thrift was wrong, if it prevented a man's children from being well provided for and fully educated. The limitation of population was not necessarily one of their planks, nor essential to their system, but as a fact, the better off people became the more it was limited, and this would be more fully realized than ever in the Socialist state. I questioned whether if all were provided for by the public, and none could rise above the common level, the motives that now lead to late marriages and small families would still operate. He considered they would, and said that directly they improved the condition of any class of operatives, their proportion of children became distinctly smaller than that of the worse-off classes below them. Women must have absolute equality with men in political rights. He did not enlarge upon the position that women would hold in the new State, beyond saying that many Socialists believed in greater freedom of the marriage tie, but that it was not now one of the planks in their platform. It was a subject that for his part he did not pronounce upon either way. They made it a matter of duty to contest as many municipal elections as possible, and to stir up the people throughout the country to work upon proper lines the new Parish Councils Act. It was upon this line that the actual advance of Socialistic principles must be looked for. He referred to what had been done by the London County Council.

I will take next an interview that I had with a

prominent American gentleman, who is also one of the thinkers upon this subject, and whose interest in all that affects the lot of the working classes is well known, even beyond the borders of his own country. He said that Socialism, as such—*eo nomine*, as lawyers would say—was not, among the masses in the United States, a growing creed, but that the desire for State ownership of many things was. For example, that the State should purchase all the railways was eagerly desired by the shareholders, in order that they might get rid of a bad property, and by the workpeople, in order to become their own employer. But some of the industrial combinations of the artisans did not thrive well. The Knights of Labour had one million adherents a few years ago; now they have only 200,000. The Socialist or Labour party showed very poor results at the last election. But both the Republican and the Democratic parties would go as far as possible to secure their votes, for the Populist party was growing. Upon the general question his view was, that we were faced by vast evils, apparently arising out of the present industrial system, or at least not cured by it; and what was the remedy? Society was dumb. The Socialists propose a remedy. He inclined to think that it should not be rejected without a trial. It was impossible to say it was a mistake without giving it a chance. Some radical measures were wanted. At the same time it would possibly be that the first success of their cause would be its destruction, as experience would show the difficulties in the way of working their system which at present they did not realize. The best chapter in Kidd's book on "Social Evolution" was the first, which showed society dumb and helpless before the problem of the day. There must be some solution: why not try this one? "This," he said, "was the mental attitude of many thoughtful men in America." This is, in fact, the old "leap in the dark" view of Mr. Disraeli's party in 1866.

It will be observed that his own opinion was by no

means fixed upon the merits of the new system. It was
evidently coloured by a deep feeling for the sufferings
of the poor and a generous wish to agree to anything
that promised to help them. But he referred me to a
gentleman in his office who had written a book on
Socialism and who did not share the hesitation that
embarrassed his chief. He said that the principles of
Socialism were certainly growing among the working
classes in the United States. You could see it in a
hundred different directions. It was owing to those
principles that the people thoroughly distrusted both
the great political parties—the Republicans and the
Democrats—because neither understood the true nature
of the present industrial situation. Much the same was
declared to me by an English Socialist concerning the
Liberals and Conservatives there. The new system would
gradually and after many generations ameliorate the
human lot, but it would take a long time. In these great
changes in human history the interests or fate of any
one generation were as nothing. Successive generations
died away like the flies in summer; they could only
regard the final result, when the Government would be
the father of the whole people. One of the first practical
steps would be for the State to own all the railways. I
suggested the difficulty that presented itself of giving
either of the political parties, whom the people so little
trusted, the immense patronage and political power
that the control of the army of railway *employés* would
confer, operating as they do throughout the United
States. He said that the government of the service
would have to be specially provided for, by officials
appointed independently of the party in power, or elected
by the people. He sketched out the new social state as
he would have it, but did not, in the conversation,
grapple much with the difficulties that suggest themselves; with regard to some of these he referred me
to a book that he had published; as to others which
seemed to me important, he said that they were mere
matters of detail which would settle themselves as ex-

perience would dictate. I often found this answer given to such objections, and the speaker sometimes added that he was a practical man and did not concern himself with the future. Yet it is surely important to know whether the ideal we are told to work towards is a possible one or not. But his view upon the question as to how, under the new system, services were to be remunerated was clear. All should be paid alike—"the crossing-sweeper," he said, "as much as the physician. He kept the streets clean and prevented disease; the other cured it."

Turning for the moment from the theoretical to the practical aspect of views such as these, I might relate a conversation that I had with some working people. The speakers at the single-tax meeting and the shoemakers' meeting, whom I have referred to in the previous chapter, may be taken as representative of some of their class, but not of all; for I found others who held Socialist views without the absolutely destructive ideas that these men proclaimed. I met a number of artisans who had informally come together to see me, in a workshop in a back street of an American city, on a week-day morning. They all professed the Socialist creed. Work was then very slack, and I understood also that there was a partial strike going on, so there were a number of idle men about the house. They repeated the usual formulas of Socialism, particularly as applied to their own case. If the State owned the factories, all the people would get the produce; there would be no men overworked and none without work, and they would not be turning out lots of stuff more than was wanted. If they themselves, they in that room, had the factory in their own hands, they would run it better for the people than the boss did. The question whether all could be depended upon to work fair they regarded with indignation, and mentioned the case of one lame man, whom they all helped to make up his task, so that he got the full union rate of wage as well as the best of them. General consent appeared to prevail so far, but a difficulty arose when I asked them if they had sufficient confidence in their politicians, to hand over all to them. Several said emphatically that they had no confidence whatever in them. They did not trust them one bit. I asked how then was it that they elected them time after time every two years. It was not as in England, where they had a seven years term, and could not be ousted during that time, no matter what they did. One of them answered me briefly—"It's the boodle, sir, that does it; they may be honest when they go in, but they can't stand the boodle." Stead's book on Chicago, he said, was perfectly true—no exaggeration. Were such men, then, to manage the public industries, or, if not, who was? I asked. They had no solution to this difficulty. One said that he would never agree to the Government having things in their hands. Others said that the Government would be improved under the Socialist state; everything would be better. Another remarked to me that what they really wanted was what Bellamy had sketched out—an easier life than they had now. Why not, then, try what co-operation would do? Let working people own the factories and divide the profits. This would never do. They had tried it; there was a co-operative factory here doing well, and then came one managed by a boss and undersold them directly. Under the new plan all must get the same wage. If one man made three pairs of boots in a day, and another one pair, would each get the same return? To be sure they would; the man who only made one pair might have worked harder than the other. One said women must get just the same as men. Another replied, "Not at all; they can't stand the work. Why, I've seen them come into the factory with their medicine bottle just as regular as their food. It's all nonsense." But under the new system three or four hours a day would be enough work for all. They need only produce enough stuff to supply what was actually wanted by the people about. Towards the end of the interview a gentleman came in who held some official position in their Union. They mentioned to him some of the difficulties that I had suggested; but he disposed of them quickly. Afraid of jobbery in the public service and railways? Get a proper Civil Service system, or better still, disfranchise State *employés* altogether. Co-operation? Perfectly useless so long as you allow outside competition. The great thing is to kill competition. That is the root of the whole matter. No one should be allowed to own any land whatever. As for fear of abuses if the Government own the railways and industries, there was more corruption of the Government now by the railroad corporations, than ever could be under any other system. The whole Government was corrupt; both the political side and also the judicial, from the Supreme Court down, all was in the hands of the capitalist.

One often finds the official in labour associations to hold more absolute views and language than does the plain working man. During the conversation a number of artisans stood about the room listening with more or less attention. One young fellow, in a corner near, kept partly watching the speakers and partly practising in dumb show what seemed to be some new step in a dance or hornpipe. When we were about parting, he broke in, and, addressing the leading spokesman, said: "I tell yez, it's all very well, I hope ye will settle it as ye say, but I don't believe it. We must fight, there's no other way out of it. It's not to be done by this talking, like. For meself, I'm ready to shoulder my musket any time, right off." And he made a suitable movement with his arm. A few seemed to nod assent, but the others only smiled, and the man addressed asked him in a deprecating manner not to make a noise. Most of them seemed conscious that no fighting was needed by men who can control the ballot box.

The thinkers upon this subject are, however, by no means confined to those who sit in offices and write books. Two of the most instructive conversations that I had were with two working men—one in England, the other in the United States. The Englishman was a firm Socialist, while the American had been a Socialist, but now doubted its being practicable, and so must be regarded as a convert or a pervert according to the views of the reader. The first was by occupation a carpenter. He spoke with calmness and a tone of moderation, and expressed indignation at the violent language that some Socialists had used, saying that all the harm was done that way. He emphasized what truly is an argument for collective action of some kind, either by co-operation or the State—namely, the great advance in the use of machinery, and the dwarfing of all individual action or industry. Not only were there now no artisans working by themselves or by twos or threes, but all small employers were being swallowed up, and vast machinery, impelled by steam, and attended by troops of *employés*, produced things in great profusion, his share of which the worker did not get. It had been calculated, he saw, in the United States that machinery had increased the productiveness of labour 3,000 per cent.; but the gain to the working classes was estimated at only twenty per cent. How much, with all our machinery, had we reduced the hours of work in the last forty years? But in the Socialist state the whole people would get the full benefit of the improvement in machinery, which was quite illimitable: steam, electricity, compressed air—soon it would do everything. When he was a youth it was considered good work for a man and a boy to make twelve flooring boards, tongued and grooved, in a day. The boy held the machine on the end of the board, while the man slowly pulled it down. Now one machine will make twelve thousand of these in the same time. True, all had the benefit of cheap boards; they had floors now of wood, instead of bare earth; but what became of the workmen and the boys? But while he believed in the State owning the land and all the great instruments of production, the change could only go on very gradually, from time to time, as the people became fitted for it. He saw well enough that they were not fitted for it at present, and he objected rather, therefore, to the collectivist resolution carried at Norwich; but only because it was premature. He had always told them of the need of going slowly. He admitted that he had little faith in politicians, and it was a difficulty, who was to govern the great industrial society in the future. Yet some Government departments were fairly enough worked now—for example, the post-office, with its numerous *employés*. I had this illustration of the feasibility of Government management given to me several times both in England and in America. His idea of the Socialist state would be that men should be paid or rewarded according to their work; but then all would help the weak ones, just as is done by the trade unions now. The Communist says, to each one according to his needs, but the Socialist, to each according to his deeds. To the question whether this would not lead back to all the evils of competition—private property for the earner's life, at least—and the weak not being as well off as the strong, he could give a no more satisfactory answer than other more pretentious men. Incidentally he said that the idea which a few entertained of helping industry by some form of protection was nonsense. It could only cause more poverty. Look even at the wealthy United States. It was not necessary for him to say how the idle would be dealt with in the new State, how menial work would be apportioned, who would devote themselves to inventions, literature, science, and art; for all that was in the distant future, and must be grappled with when we come up to it. He wished to go on quietly now helping the poor and the toilers. He liked Burns' poetry much, and often thought of his words about man's inhumanity to man, and he wanted to remedy it.

The side of the problem that seemed to press him to his conclusion was the growing power of machinery.

And thinkers of various schools have more than once called attention to the revolution machinery was making in industry. It was calculated that in 1886 the machine power used in the United States was equal to 3,500,000 horse-power; this represents the work of twenty-one million of men, and only four million were employed. And the power and scope of machinery increases daily by strides that our forefathers never thought of, and men are pushed out. This points to united action, large operations, and a better division of the produce as a necessity. The Socialist says that this can only be brought about by taking both men and machines into the service of the State. But great economists hold that an equally good result could be brought about by some system of co-operative production, if men were sufficiently advanced to work it intelligently. For this, foresight and self-denial would be necessary.

My other friend, the artisan in the United States, held an important position in the labour world, and was a firm supporter of the rights of the workers. He had been for some years active in the Socialist ranks, but had come to disbelieve in the solution of the problem of the day which that party offers. He said that he saw clearly that it meant slavery for all, and even if they were fed and clothed, what better would they be than the negroes before the war of emancipation? Only a few of those were actually ill-used; most of them were well fed and cared for; yet the people had spent millions, and spilt their blood all over the continent, merely to make them free men, able to work for themselves as they liked, not as they were ordered by their master. White people would never settle down to a similar helpless state to that of the old blacks. But that was really what it came to. They all knew what sort of governments many cities and States now had in America, and how did they know that they would get better ones under the new system? It would be a nice thing to have a set of men like some of those, deciding what your son or daughter was to go to, and perhaps some rogue of a fellow keeping them out of their rights for some of his relatives. Why, now the men in the State service were only slaves—they dare not say a word, or they might be turned off, and whether or no, lots were turned off when a new set of politicians came in. The Socialists said that all government would be pure and just under them; but he did not see why that should be; and suppose they were mistaken, and it were not so, what a mess they would all be in. And money was not the only difference between men. If it was all equalized, still the clever, active man would in other ways be able to lord it over the rest. Men were as selfish now as they were 500 years ago; and were they all to become different under the new system? The Socialist ideas all came from Germany, which was the home of Socialism. Still, though he did not go with the Socialists to the end, he felt the force of their position when they attacked the present state. They said, "You have been going on the old lines for eighteen centuries, and they have not brought happiness to the people; now let us try new lines." He was all for fighting the capitalist and forcing him to do his duty. The Labour party must fight them; and they had fought them and taught them a lot. Why, every few years showed a change for the better in the ways of the capitalists. In a week or two some of their leading men and some professors were to meet Labour delegates, in Chicago, to discuss industrial questions with them. They would not have thought of that ten years ago. He would not abolish private property, but try and diffuse it by a graduated income tax, death duties, and by promoting profit-sharing in industry. The rich must be taught their duty, and the labour organisations could teach them. There was a political side to society and an industrial side. The people ruled the one, or thought they did, the capitalist at present the other, and he must be taught, and industry improved by securing to the worker a proper share of production.

Profit-sharing was one step in advance; but Bellamy and his military Socialism had no real weight with the people of America.

I asked him how he first came to distrust the views of the party he had been so long acting with. He said that he used to attend all their meetings, private and otherwise, in New York, and that what first set him thinking about the real meaning of the system was the view of marriage and the family that some of them maintained. He mentioned the name of a well-known lady, and said that he had heard her and her friends denounce marriage and the family as "the root of all evil." When he came to look into it, they were right, if the Socialist ideal was right. It, when worked out, meant the loss of all independent life, even between husband and wife, or father and child. They were going to propose their tenth plank at Denver—that is, the Collectivist resolution adopted at Norwich, and we would see what would come of it. He did not think that they would carry it.

Such were the views of this working man, and he certainly expressed them with force and intelligence. At present a good many in America agree generally with his conclusion, though they have not thought it out as he has. But he bases that conclusion upon the hope that a more just distribution of wealth can, and will, be wrought out by other means. If that hope were to prove a delusion, his following would be small.

Here I may mention that in England I met some Birmingham artisans who also expressed their dissent from the Norwich Conference resolution; but they did not appear to have thought about the matter like the Americans. They said in an uncertain sort of manner that they thought it was going too far; it was too much. The old Trade Union plans were better. They seemed to be under the influence of Mr. Chamberlain's opinions, and said more decidedly that his scheme for enabling them to purchase freeholds was just what they wanted. One of them was a workman on the railways.

I asked him if he and his friends favoured the State owning the railways. He said emphatically that they all did; and honestly and ingenuously added, "It would be so much more comfortable for us." Another said that of course the Government service was best; all of them tried to get into it. He had tried to get into the dockyards, but it could only be done by influence. When they got in they were provided for.

The Populist party in America is like the Independent Labour party in England in condemning both the great political divisions in their respective countries, and it adopts several of the Socialist's views, but, unlike its English counterpart, utterly repudiates his ultimate conclusions, or thinks it does. It goes, however, a good way on the road with him; but declares it will part company with him at the dividing of the ways. I had some talk with one of their leading representative men. He said that their party was rapidly growing in voting power, they were growing evenly all over the States, though as yet they could command few electorates. Last election they had polled two million voters; next, they would poll four millions. The future was with them. Now their legislators were generally distrusted and the best record was no record. They would alter all that. As for the Socialists, they had no real weight; they had never worked out their schemes. Bellamy had made no progress among the working men. The tenth plank might be endorsed at Denver; but few of the delegates would really believe in it. They all regarded it as imaginary. His party was quite distinct from the Socialists, as much as it was from the Republicans or the Democrats. But they were strongly in favour of the State owning all the railways, taking them after paying compensation; of a graduated income tax to take away large fortunes; and of limiting the holding of land to those who make use of it. The Single Taxers had no weight here; the farmers would go as a unit against it; but the large grants of land to Railway Corporations and to English capitalists ought to be recalled on payment of compensation. There was corruption everywhere; he did not know how the people stood it so long. Would there not be a fear of more of this if the State owned all the railways, with the million of *employés* new civil servants? He would deprive them all of votes. When the Populists got power the first thing they would settle would be the silver question; then the banking. They would pay all their debts in silver. Land and railways would come afterwards. It was a question whether universal suffrage was a success—whether it could stand against money. This would be proved on the silver question. The danger of America was the slums and the millionaires.

Another prominent Labour leader, whom I met in New York, though he was not identified with the Populist party, spoke in the same strain regarding Socialism, while yet he likewise adopted many of its immediate proposals. He was one of the foremost men in the American Federation of Labour, which proclaims as its object, "The organisation of the working people, by the working people, for the working people," and had given many forcible addresses inculcating their views, which were printed and widely circulated. He said that Socialism was merely a passing phase, that it had no real hold on the people, and that the vote which would be given at the Conference that was about to be held at Denver would, even if in favour of the "tenth plank," not show any real opinion upon the subject. As for Bellamy's book, people regarded it as a dream. I asked how it was, then, that Henry George polled so many votes in New York. He said that thousands voted for him who had no belief in his views; they voted merely against the party of corruption. So far, he seemed to be going upon the old lines; but, he added, that they were universally agreed upon the necessity for the State owning all the railways, and other monopolies, and being the common employer; in shortening the hours of labour to eight to-day and less to-morrow; and in securing by State power, if no other, adequate wages, so long—he expresses it in one of his published papers—" so long as the wage system may last." He holds strong views upon the right of the workman to get a better share of the general wealth, and to be a partner in the produce of the land and of machinery in a manner not yet recognised. The great weapon, he considers, is the Trade Union system, when kept in full vigour and development, and the powerful strikes that it can direct. President Cleveland was quite wrong in interfering in the Chicago strike; he should have left them to fight it out. At a Sunday afternoon gathering of artisans, which I went to in the same city, the opinion generally expressed, was in favour of the whole Socialistic plan, if it could be got; but many said it was at present impracticable. All, however, were for the Government owning the railways, and becoming the people's employer wherever possible.

The Socialist regards views such as these with satisfaction, and he has reason to do so. They may say that they don't agree with him, but they do in fact agree with him for the present. They travel along the same road and the parting of the ways is distant. He says that by the time they get to the parting, they will have gone so far upon his track, that they will find that it is the only possible one upon which to continue their journey.

The most pronounced Socialists with whom I met, were two gentlemen in the United States, both of whom were educated men occupying positions, the one in the literary, the other in the official world. I will briefly record their views. The former said that the Socialist party was growing slowly in America, but the Populist quickly, and that they certainly would be in power by the year 1900, perhaps by the elections in 1896. The Socialists were quite content to go along with them and let them do the work, for they were agreed upon much that was now in sight. As for the present Government and Legislature, they were quite corrupt; but that was owing to the big corporations and the power of money.

There would be no fear of this in the Socialist state. The Courts, too, were all corrupt, from the Supreme Court down, in the sense of being under the domination of capital. The only difficulty would be in the transition to Socialism; once there, the system would be easy to work—when you had a generation educated in it. There would be no fear of production falling off under the new plan of life; the country could always supply itself, and Foreign Trade was only wanted for luxuries. Machinery, now the ruin of the working man would then be his slave. All would be paid alike, and no private property allowed. If Patti wanted a couple of thousand dollars to sing, she would not get it. All positions would be equalized by giving equal honour to all. The bailiff would be as much respected as the judge; the positions in the Government of the day would have no attractions; they would be no better than any that we call humbler. If any were idle and would not work, he would let them starve; but there would be no idlers, for all would take a pride in doing their public duty. Was the sentiment of honour and regard to general approbation to become extinct? As to disagreeable work—call for volunteers. Did not men volunteer their lives away when the colonel of the regiment called upon them? There would be no crime under Socialism. The motives for crime were money and women, and neither would operate then. There would be no private money, and there would be a freedom in the relation of the sexes that does not now exist. Marriage would not then be the fixed thing it is now. Now it was greatly abused. Parents, too, were the most unfit persons to educate their own children. The family makes selfishness. Bring the children up together in common. Nor would there be any need of religion then. Religion was wanted to preach contentment to the miserable; then there would be no miserable and no need of preaching. Years ago we read of such views being ascribed, not without a shudder, to the outcast Nihilists. Now they appear amid respectable surroundings, and proclaim themselves with immunity in the midst of that society they would destroy.

In much the same strain spoke the other exponent of the full Socialist programme. I hope that I do them no injustice in only giving the conclusions that they arrived at. In the long interviews with which they favoured me, they gave reasons and urged arguments which, while they were far from convincing me of the truth of their views, satisfied me of the sincerity of the speakers. But it also seemed to me that in both cases the thinking process was coloured and perverted by prejudices and visionary ideas.

This other gentleman held quite as pronounced a view as the first, upon the low condition of public life in America. The politicians were thoroughly distrusted by the people, and so were the judges. The Supreme Court, while not corrupt, was yet biassed in favour of the great corporations, for whom the individual members of the Bench had been acting all their lives as attorneys. They should all be elected direct by the people, and only for a very short time. I asked if they would get good men then, and referred to the fact that Judge Cooley, a man of unspotted character, and whose profound writings were studied by lawyers all over the world, had been unseated at an election by a nobody, after twenty years' service.

He quite justified this, and said it was right to reject him. The Senate, too, must be altered, and elected in a different way. He always liked to have his hand on the shoulder of the public officer. At present they bought their way into the Senate. He was a pronounced Socialist, though he doubted if Socialism would work out in the manner that many expected; but he went with it, so as at any rate to break up the present system. The Government should own all the instruments of production. Political liberty without economical liberty was useless. Voting did not make a man free; nor did it feed him. He would tax away the value of the land and allow no compensation. It would be done gradually. All would be paid equally, the policeman as much as the general. This would not interfere with production. The man who could make twice the number of pairs of boots that another could, would still exert himself to make them. That was done every day by the Trade Unionists. In the Socialist state there would not be the same motive to increase production, and why should there be? All they wanted was to have enough to go on with. But men would invent and make improvements for the honour of it. Human nature would then manifest itself in a new direction; no more mere selfishness. Even if Socialism did not last itself, it would lead to something better. There would be no fear of a continuance of political corruption in the new state, because then there would be no motive for men to strive for the Government places, as they would have no high pay hanging to them; and they would be so carefully watched, owing to the personal interest of all in their doings, that there would be no chance of their going wrong.

To these two I will add the views of another literary man who was editor of an important organ of the Labour party. His opinion was that the working men were getting distinctly more Socialistic in tone, but that they had no clear ideas on the subject. They adopted no scheme or plan, and did not care to do so, as they were practical men, and all they wanted were some practical things now. Some of them professed to be Socialists, but many of them professed to be the very opposite, to be Anarchists; while some were Individualists. They would take the best points from each creed as far as they could get them. In the distant future, no doubt, they would have pure Socialism, when selfishness was eliminated from human nature, and there would be no more poverty to induce it, as now. What, then, did they desire at present? Oh, only for the Government to take the land, railways, telegraphs, and let the land be worked by the people on co-operative principles.

There is a small sect of Anarchists in the United States, and they, too, adopt one important proposal of the Socialists, though diametrically opposed to them upon the main issue. I met the two principal office-bearers of one of their clubs and heard their views with interest. It was stated subsequently in the colonial papers that I had been interviewing Anarchists, and a Melbourne illustrated journal produced a lively sketch of my precipitate retreat from the Anarchists' den, leaving my hat behind, to avoid a bombshell which a diabolical-looking ruffian had placed ready to greet me. The best dictionaries describe an Anarchist as one who excites revolt or promotes disorder in a State; so the popular ideal of him is not to be wondered at. But the reality, at least as I met it, was widely different. They were educated gentlemen, rather of the refined type, who were engaged in business, and devoted their spare time to promoting the principles of their society. These they declared to be that they condemned all government except what was absolutely necessary to prevent crime. Men should be a law to themselves. Sixty millions of men had no right to coerce one million. For example, they would have no debts collected by law; let people who choose to give credit look to that themselves. Bentham was cited in support of this. Often the advocates of peculiar views fasten upon some passage in the works of a great writer, which they adduce as a high authority, though they treat with contempt nearly everything else he has said. Mill has thus often been quoted as favouring protection in young countries; Washington as condemning foreign commerce. They would do everything according to the law, until they could alter it. The true Anarchist was the perfect gentleman. They totally dissented from the Socialist idea of the Government taking the industry of the country under its charge. It was preposterous to think of it. Just look at their Government. The less Government interfered with individuals the better. It would only bungle and oppress. In what, then, did they agree with the Socialists? In taking the land. They were all agreed to support Henry George's single-tax, and do away with all other taxes. It would be more than sufficient if Government was confined to its own proper sphere. They, of course, objected to the State taking the railways into its own management. Poverty was growing in the United States; but as yet there was no hatred between the poor and the rich as such; though it would come. They thought that Socialism was growing among the working men, because great social evils were growing. The worst possible forms of sweating prevailed in some of their cities. Laws were made against it, but made in vain.

This is the intellectual form of the Anarchist's creed. It is not likely ever to have much weight; for while it would subvert what the experience of ages has shown to be essential for the safety of men in human society, it utterly disclaims the longing to use political power to secure social benefits—practical "fruit"—that is the marked characteristic of our time.

Leaving now America, for the present, I will revert to some interviews that I had with representative Socialists in England. One gentleman whom I met held a high position in the Labour party, and no one hearing him could doubt his sincerity, though his opinions were evidently coloured by his feelings. As a boy, he said that he had heard much of Cobden and Bright, but he had never believed in them. He and his party were at eternal war with the property classes, but they regarded the workers of all nations—French, Germans, Russians—as their brothers. They took no interest in ordinary politics; the Liberals were just as bad as the Conservatives. If they looked to politics at all it was only that through them they might get hold of the social machine. He would confiscate all property, land first and the rest afterwards, and employ the people; but he would do it by law, not by social revolt. It was a better way to do it, as well as an easier. Would that be honest after your laws sanctioned it, and thus pledged the public faith? The people's laws did not sanction it; only the plutocrats' laws. At present about one-fourth of the working men agreed with them; but they were growing fast. The first thing they would do would be to take the land and use it for employing the people, without scanning very closely the profit that it would then return. Would there not be the danger of political interference in the management of that and other industries under the proposed system? He would give the Board of Trade, or some other body, quite distinct from politics, the whole management. Such abuses as were feared, existed in New York and Chicago, because their Governments rested upon an individualist basis; and money was there. A few hours' work a day, three or four, would be quite enough. He had no fear of men idling the rest of the day; they would cultivate literature, music, and such things. There must be absolute equality between men and women, and all would work from a principle of honour. Selfishness would decline. He and his party broke absolutely with the religion of the day—Christianity as it was taught—and took their children away from Church and Sunday school. Where they could, they established Labour Churches and schools. Their paper was the "Labour Prophet." He showed me a letter that he had just received from a clergyman which said that the writer could remain in the Church no longer, owing to its attitude upon social questions, and that he was open to take an engagement as a Socialist lecturer. He had some papers connected with one of the Labour Churches. Their object was stated to be "The realisation of Heaven in this life by the establishment of a state of society founded upon justice and love to the neighbour." Edward Carpenter, the author of "Marriage in Free Society," was a representative Socialist and good man in every way. But as for himself, he did not wish to express any opinion upon the question of greater freedom for married life.

In these conversations I was an inquirer, and did

not urge my own opinions further than might be useful to discover truth by the conflict of thought. But I questioned what he seemed so sanguine of, namely, the possibility of keeping the new State free from political evils any more than the old, inasmuch as their origin was in human nature itself, and you could never calculate upon getting perfection out of any system of voting by imperfect men. The ballot-box could not do everything. It could not ensure public rectitude. Upon this he rather turned upon me, and said that it was no use going further if I did not believe in the people's voice. But while I hold that the system of government resting upon the people's voice is the best and the only form now possible, I am far from believing that their vote is the wisest means for always ascertaining truth. There is a fanaticism about the worship of the ballot-box, as there is about most other faiths. I remember hearing of an instance of this under a popular Government. Two rival places in a district were competing for public money to be spent in the search for coal. Each claimed to have the true geological indications. How to decide? Perplexed politicians proposed a public meeting, where the matter should be discussed and voted upon. This was in fact done, and the rival claims of the two localities—carboniferous indications against those of limestones of the oolitic series, and so forth—were settled by the ballot-box. But will Nature thus give up her secrets? And was not the Labour leader also expecting too much from it?

The next person I met was to me an object of much interest, for I expected him to throw light upon a subject that we colonial politicians have long been exercised about. He was a working man who had practical knowledge, from the worker's side, of the system pursued by the London County Council in carrying out its operations without the intervention of the contractor, under the direction of its Works Committee. When a political body has to do industrial work, the employment of a contractor, if he is selected by some known and fixed rule, at least has the merit of disposing of the question of patronage. Where it acts directly, patronage must rest somewhere, and when the system works out to its natural results, it becomes political patronage. In some of the colonies where the Government is the direct employer, men are taken on upon the recommendation of the Member for the district, and are not taken on without it. If the foreman wants to dismiss, the man claims justice from his Member. I know that we Members regard this patronage as a burden, trying to ourselves, and not useful for the public. We all endeavour to do our duty and show more independence than we sometimes get credit for; but the system is bad. The mixture of politics with industrial work is a mistake. The best workman may never be heard of at election times, and may not have the knack of conciliating influence; while the man who has, may not be a good workman.

I was anxious, therefore, to hear whether the London County Council had as yet encountered any of these difficulties in the working of their new policy. According to my informant, who declared himself an enthusiastic Socialist, they had steered clear of them. They were going, he said, on distinctly Socialist lines, and with great success. Abolishing the contractor and doing the job under their own foreman was working excellently. They paid the highest Trade Union rate of wages, and there was a general striving to get into their service. If a foreman dismissed a workman, he had an appeal to the Sub-Committee of Works, which was composed of eighteen members, four of whom were working men. There were several such appeals. If a man had a grievance, he went to the member for his district, if he was a friend to labour, and he would bring it before the Sub-Committee; or if the man was wrong, the member would tell him so, and then he would be satisfied. I saw, I may remark, in *The Daily News* a statement that a foreman had dismissed a number of men for idleness, and that the Committee had supported him. My informant said that the men all worked with a will now, to show that it was cheaper not to employ a contractor ; but when the new system was well established, he thought that they should be allowed to go easier, for then a man would take more interest in his work, when he could give time to it and finish it properly. This was much better than hurrying through it. Not only did the Council give good wages for their own work, but when they did employ a contractor they made him give good wages too. The Blackwall Tunnel was an instance. There they made the contractor pay in all £26,500 more to the men than he wanted to, and it was a good thing for him also, as otherwise there would have been strikes. He had been through several political agitations himself. At one time a complaint was made that a foreman was employing all his own relatives, and then this was forbidden. Sir John Lubbock's statement, which I have cited in a previous chapter, gives the other aspect of this subject.

Mr. Sidney Webb, in his "Socialism, True and False," adverts to the doubt whether the workers under the social state would be able to ensure the best terms for themselves. He says, "As citizens and electors, the workers, we may presume, will see that the hours of labour are as short, the conditions of work as favourable, and the allowance for maintenance as liberal, as the total productivity of the nation's industry will afford." The experience of democratic countries, where the Government acts as an employer of labour, gives no countenance to this doubt, and the impression left by the remarks and the tone of the London workman was, that the County Council in due time, and when the ranks of its *employés* are increased by its different new undertakings, will learn that a body which is elected by popular suffrage, if it is also a large employer of labour, is governed by its *employés*.

I had heard much about Christian Socialism, and so was glad to be allowed a conversation with a reverend gentleman who held an official position in one of the social unions. He was a Church of England and an Oxford man, and gave the impression of a noble feeling of sympathy with the poor. He said that all the young clergy were Socialists, that the movement was as strong at Oxford now as the High Church outbreak was seventy years ago. Most of the clergy about London were the same. I remarked that it was stated that nearly all the working classes, and many other classes, renounced religion wholly. He replied that many were infidels, but that they had a Christian love of their brethren, and he looked hopefully to the future. The working-girls of London were wretchedly paid and hardly used, but not one of them would go into domestic service; he was trying to get up a Union among them. I was anxious to get his opinions upon the different proposals of the Socialist party, and asked him if he approved of taking people's land from them without compensation. But he only said that he knew nothing about these political ideas; he was a practical man and confined himself to helping the distress he saw around him. He was an instance of how many different kinds of people are included under the general name of "Socialists." For him Socialism simply meant active benevolence towards the poor.

I met a lady who holds a high position in the Socialist world of letters, and, like others, felt the charm of her conversation. But her views are already made known to the world by her clever pen. Also, I had the opportunity of conversing with some other ladies who held advanced views. I ventured to suggest as a worthy object for woman's ambition a reform of the system of domestic service, rendering it less distasteful to the fancy of young people, and restoring something of its old character when domestics were part of the household, and cared for as such. Pepys, I think, records his satisfaction at engaging a young lad to serve him, who could also play on the flute and accompany him in his music. I mentioned this upon one occasion in America, when I had the honour of meeting, at a deputation, an elderly lady, whose whole life had been spent in helping the poor of her own sex. Among those present was a lady who held the position of State Inspector of Factories in the city where we were. The elderly lady agreed that the value of a good system of household work that would attract girls was immense, and she added that to have some one to take a motherly interest in them, and advise them, was a great thing. But the inspector disputed this, and said that they should be advised by no one but their own mothers. "Let them exercise their own judgment." Her view appeared rather to be that of Mrs. Besant, who says, "The great servant problem will be solved by the disappearance of servants, the wide introduction of machinery, and the division among the members of each domestic commonwealth of the various necessary duties. The prospect is really not so very terrible when quietly surveyed." A cleavage of thought was at once disclosed between these two ladies.

Among those whom I met on my travels I might mention one, who was certainly not a Socialist. Mr. Cleveland, the President of the United States, did me the honour of allowing me an interview while I was in Washington. He has often denounced that incipient form of Socialism termed Paternalism, and at the time when I saw him he was the object of the direst invectives by the silver party of Socialists. He expressed interest in the proposed Federation of Australia, and seemed to have some knowledge even of our affairs. He gave one the idea of a man who possessed natural force of character, improved by the exercise and responsibility of power. Of the world's leading potentates who have personal authority, Mr. Cleveland is one and the Emperor of Russia the other. But Mr. Cleveland, the autocrat who rests upon the people's will, occupies the first position, as he represents what it seems not improbable may be the future type of democratic Government, when the influence of Parliaments may have waned.

If one were to judge by the opinions and wishes

expressed by representative people of all classes, you would not conclude that there was among many, any defined belief as to the value or the feasibility of the Socialist creed. Joined to a feeling of discontent with the present conditions of life, which in part is justifiable, and which increasing intelligence renders more acute, is the sense that they possess the power, as they are assured on all sides, to alter these conditions as they please. The immediate proposals made—to tax down property, and to substitute Government for private employment— naturally commend themselves to all. They embrace these gladly, and do not trouble themselves with any scrutiny of the more distant prospects that are held out to them. But they would object, I believe, to the practical working of these ideals, if they were really brought up to them. Even with the thinking Socialists their clearest ideas are all destructive, and the immediate impulse that actuates them is compounded of a sympathy with poverty and a hatred of competition and its complement, private property, which they accuse of being the cause of poverty. They sketch plans of the new social state in which these evils are to cease, and where all are to be equally well off; but they do not seem to be oppressed with anxiety as to how it will really work out. It is enough for one generation to clear the ground for future building. They are right in not prophesying. The path of the political prophet is strewn with failures. The pioneers who fought for freedom in the past, would be astonished at the turn things have now taken, and we may at least be certain that the observer in the future will be surprised by equally unexpected developments.

CHAPTER VIII.

THE UNITED STATES.

THE United States of America must always have a great interest for the inquirer into social questions; the scene of experiment is so vast, the spirit so fearless, and the conditions so novel and so favourable. If the results are not as faultless as sanguine prophets in the past expected them to be, it must be remembered that America has had not only to deal with its own population, but has, in carrying out a noble policy of freedom, to assimilate a much larger foreign population, consisting of the poorest, and some of the worst, of the Old World. Had it barred out strangers since the days of Washington and been limited to its own people—native Americans,—though its progress would have been much slower, there can be no doubt it would have been sounder. It is interesting, indeed, to speculate upon what, had this been so, America would have been like to-day. On the other hand, we must not fall into the fallacy of short computation in considering its great political and social experiments. It is too soon to pronounce upon much that one sees in this vast continent. Even a century is a small time in the life of a nation, and until this land is filled up with a population such as older lands have to grapple with, the real time of test and trial will not have come. But then, while the difficulties of the problems will have increased, the wisdom taught by experience will have increased also, and the amelioration of social life by the operation of natural causes will have been going on.

Every political student knows that America has a stronger central Executive power than England. Much that was happening while I was there impressed this fact upon me. The Federal Constitution makes a great profession as to the power of the people, just as that of England does of the power of the Sovereign; but there is a good deal of make-believe about both. In America all power is ascribed to the people, everything is done in the name of the people—in Courts of Law evil-doers are prosecuted by "The People"; there is no suggestion anywhere of any privilege or any authority outside the mandate of the majority. But all the while the reality is there. The President certainly springs from the people, but once chosen he is a real King, and not only has great powers, but, unlike some European Sovereigns, is perfectly free and safe in exercising them. The Senate is a veritable second legislative voice for the nation, and quite independent of what, in older lands, is called the popular Chamber. The Supreme Court is outside both the President and the Legislature, and will stop them both if they attempt to do what is contrary to the Constitution. This Constitution, it is true, is only a piece of paper, and I met Socialists and Populists who said that they would soon tear it in pieces. But there it is, a fundamental law unto the whole people, until altered by a process that it is almost impossible to achieve, except at a time of great excitement and unanimity, or by a revolution. Thus President, Senate, and House altogether, and backed by the whole people, could not make a law impairing the obligation of contract or providing for taking any man's property without compensation (these being forbidden in that piece of paper), which the Supreme Court would not annul, if appealed to. The Constitution thus powerfully protects minorities; also it embodies the principle of their representation. One-fourth of the people have as many Senators as the remaining three-fourths, and all the Senators are elected, not by the people directly, but by elected bodies—a method, however, from which more was expected than has been realized. Horatio Seymour says: "It is a remarkable fact that ours is the only system of Government which declares that the majority shall not govern in many vital respects; that it has devised a plan by which it can be held in check; and that each individual has defences against the will of the body of the people and the power of the Government which represents them. The distinctive features of American Constitutions are, not that they aim to give power to majorities, but that they aim to protect the rights of minorities."

I had the opportunity of observing some practical illustrations of this. In the middle of 1894 a contest upon the amendment of the Tariff was being fought between the two Houses of the Legislature. The "House" sent its Bill up in the form that it desired, and the Senate promptly amended it, in many respects fundamentally. Outside, the battle was raging between the adherents of the high tariff and those of the low, and the cries of the contending parties reached to the heavens. The "House" denounced the proposals of the Senate; but the answer of the Senate was direct: Take your Bill as we want it or not at all; we don't approve of your proposals, and we do not intend that they shall become law. And this position was quietly accepted by the "House" and the public, as being in the ordinary course of the Constitution, and the Senate practically had its way. During the Chicago riots—of which more hereafter—a proof of the growing power of the Central Executive was given. That city was believed to be in danger of being pillaged, but the Governor—who was elected by the foreign element of voters—was not alive to the danger. Thereupon the President sent down the United States troops, over the head and against the expressed wish of the Governor, and soon quelled the riots. This episode illustrated not only the strength of the Central Executive, but the weakness and maladministration that marks some of the States Governments. President Cleveland also, under the authority of an old Act, floated loan after loan, binding the United States, in order to keep up the gold supply of the Treasury, in defiance of the opposition of Congress and against a strong "Populist" sentiment in favour of silver. The Income Tax Law, which was passed by President and Legislature, and which was immensely popular as being a burthen upon wealth only, has since been declared void by the Supreme Court on the ground that class taxation is forbidden by the Constitution.

On the other hand, a stranger who read books about the Constitution in England, and heard formulas, would believe that the people were quite in the background; while in fact, unlike their brethren in the United States, they can, when roused and united, do whatever they please. A majority in the House of Commons can do anything, unrestrained by fundamental compact, Peers, or Sovereign. Whoever gets this majority is the real King; for the executive power, as well as the legislative, rests with the Lower House. All is centred there; not divided among different trustees, as in America.

Neither the aristocrat nor the democrat is really anxious to fundamentally alter this peculiar condition of the Constitution which gives the phantom of power to two branches of the Constitution and the reality to the third. The aristocrat—surrounded by all the make-believes of power, enjoying undisputed social position, and often respected by his tenantry, to whom many high aristocrats are excellent landlords—does not realize that when a crisis comes the determining power rests with the Commons, while he and his peers have only the dignified make-believe of authority. He feels the prestige and, as he considers, the usefulness of his position in the first Legislative Chamber of his country, where he honestly does his duty, and he looks forward with pride and hope to his son fulfilling the same high functions. A Peer of high character told me that I was quite mistaken in supposing the House of Commons to be more looked to by the people than the House of Lords. It might appear to be so in some meetings about the city, but in the country the toast of the Peers was always received with more enthusiasm than that of the Commons. While in England, I read letters in the papers from supporters of the old Tory party, deprecating any "tinkering with our ancient Constitution." In social life the supremacy of the aristocracy is unquestioned; and this is a very important sphere, especially to those who rule it. Secure in the sense of superiority that this imparts, they are apt to feel that nothing in politics can alter the natural conditions of birth and hereditary station, and so, they can let the Radicals have their own way in many things; indeed, they can almost afford to be Radicals themselves. They have no desire, then, to see any reform of the House of Lords that would impair its hereditary character. On the other hand, the intelligent democrat wishes nothing better than to see it remain just as it is, not powerful enough to stay anything that the Commons really want, but powerful to impair that middle-class Conservatism which is the dread of the revolutionary party, by identifying it with the hopeless cause of hereditary privilege. The indirect influence of both the Crown and the Peers is at present great, and finds its expression in the House of Commons. But when the time comes round for the popular current to rise, and that body is captured by some people's party led by a powerful leader—the Gladstone of the future—there is nothing political left to stand in the way. Certainly the English people are surrounded by ancient institutions and conservative tendencies transmitted from past ages. The Americans are more restless and more disposed to follow after new things because they are new. But they have a strong rider, with a powerful curb; the English, if they did want to bolt, have neither rider nor curb.

Much in the United States is instructive, not alone from the direct lessons that can be learnt, but also from the incidental teaching which its history affords. Many of the social reformers whom I have met in different countries, while they propose tremendous changes in human affairs, justify them by confidently predicting certain results as sure to follow from the practical working of their projects. In this land of experiments one is surrounded by, or reminded of, humiliating proofs of the inability of even the ablest and clearest sighted men to foretell how human institutions will work, or what operation the most skilfully contrived political machinery will, in fact, have. There have seldom been an abler set of statesmen engaged upon any undertaking than were the men who framed the Constitution of the United States. Yet much that they designed has turned out differently from what they expected. Could they reappear upon earth they would not recognise the work of their hands in the Government that they would see to-day. Devices that they elaborated with deep anxiety and care, have worked in a direction exactly contrary to that which they intended; dangers that they dreaded have proved illusory; evils that they never dreamt of have overshadowed their plans; advantages that they calculated upon have proved vain; political action has manifested itself in new directions that they never thought of. The *Federalist*, in which they explained and justified their plans, is a monument to their mental power, but also a standing testimony to the inability of men to mark out beforehand the lines on which human institutions will go. In reading its pages you feel like one viewing a gallery of ancient sculptures. You are admiring the genius of a past age. Men's affairs advance in their own way, as public needs and public impulse push them on. At whatever part of the Constitution we look, we can see some examples of this. The plan of electing the President by the independent voice of an electoral college of chosen men was excellent as a plan, and was proudly regarded by the Fathers of the Republic as a guarantee for an intelligent, independent choice of the first magistrate. It soon degenerated into a form that nullified the principle of the method. Madison, again, is at pains to prove that the President must always be a man of national repute and character; for the whole nation must choose him, and, while one State might make a petty choice, all, he takes for granted, could not. He also notices the possibility of the President abusing his power by turning out of office a fit man in order to give his place to another. But he quickly disposes of the possible risk thus:

"The danger consists merely in this: the President can displace from office a man whose merits require he should be continued in it. What will be the motives which the President can feel for such an abuse of power, and the restraints that can operate to prevent it? In the first place, he will be impeached by this House before the Senate for such an act of administration; for I contend that the wanton removal of meritorious officers would subject him to impeachment and removal from his own high trust."

It never occurred to him that, within about half a century, President, Senate, and House would all agree in regarding public offices as political plunder. In justice to him, we must remember who were the men and the statesmen then governing America. This is how Washington writes of one proposed for an office:

"My friend . . . . I receive with cordial welcome to my House and welcome to my heart, but, with all his good qualities, he is not a man of business. His opponent, with all his politics so hostile to me, *is* a man of business. My private feelings have nothing to do with the case. I am not George Washington, but President of the United States. As George Washington I would do this man any kindness in my power; as President of the United States I can do nothing."

What a change when we come to General Jackson— the "Old Hickory" of the wire-pullers—with his "To the victors belong the spoils." And yet it is not one lifetime from the patriot down to the political boss.

The Constitution carefully limits the interference of the general Government, for the suppression of domestic violence in any State, to where it is asked for by the local Legislature; or, where the Legislature cannot be convened, by the Executive. Now, the imperious necessity of the public safety has compelled the President to put down riots in a State, against the publicly declared wish of the Governor of that State; and the Supreme Court has declared his action lawful. Such are samples of the unexpected developments of a people's life under new conditions, and the changes that only a century's experience has wrought in the lines laid down in the ablest written Constitution ever devised, and which was planned, too, by practical politicians.

The course of American history also illustrates how blind the best informed men are in their attempts to prognosticate the trend of human events, particularly under new conditions of progress; and it need not be said that no conditions are so novel as those of the revolution proposed by the Socialists.

There were few keener observers of political institutions than De Tocqueville, and he studied those of the United States for years. He declared that America's greatest danger was the weakness of the Federal Government, and arrived at two conclusions: one, that there was no fear of a great war there; but, secondly, that if war did come, the Union would be destroyed by it. Some thirty years later, one of the greatest wars that history tells of devastated half the continent, and, at its close, left the Union stronger than it ever had been, or than its founders ever intended it to be.

Lord Sydenham, when Governor-General of Canada, writing for the private information of the English Government, assured them that, in case of war with the United States, the slaves "in the South would soon settle all that part of the Union." Afterwards, when war came, the slaves devotedly served their masters, raised the crops and protected the families while the white men were away with the armies; and this though the war was to free them, and the victory of the South meant their continuance in slavery. Macaulay, speaking in 1845, said truly, that slavery in America was worse than slavery in Brazil; and that, while it was not improbable that in eighty or a hundred years the black population in Brazil would be free, there was no such prospect for the slaves in the United States. Within twenty years the American blacks were all free men.

Examples such as these—and they might easily be multiplied—make us sceptical of the social forecasts that we hear to-day.

The attention of the political traveller is naturally first drawn to the politicians of the country he is in. They get their tone from the public and from the conditions that surround them, and impart it to the institutions that they work and directly control.

I am far from believing all the evil that I heard attributed to the representatives of the people in the United States, and do not doubt that as good a proportion of noble men is to be found in their ranks as in those of similar bodies in older lands. But the undoubted and marked change that is seen in the type of representative is of more pressing interest to us than ever, now, when it is proposed to enlarge the dominion of the State indefinitely. If the State is to manage everything, who are the State? I say "representative," but the character of representative is disappearing. A representative occupies a great position, the distinctive characteristics of which were marked out by Burke in the last century. He is, indeed, elected by one constituency, but, when elected, he is to exercise his judgment for promoting the interests of all, if need be, against the particular claims of the people of the place that he primarily represents. He is chosen for his ability to think wisely for the country at large, and his duty binds him to do this irrespective of local demands or prejudices. It requires one sort of man to adequately discharge this great function, but another and a different sort of man to be a delegate, whose business it is to carry out local instructions and to promote local interests. The delegate is not wanted to think out opinions and propound them for acceptance or rejection. Obviously also, he is not selected owing to his superior judgment, and then left free, subject to his declared principles, to exercise that judgment as occasion requires. He is returned pledged to carry out certain views that the Party Caucus have adopted, and which the people are supposed to have sanctioned. The successful leader, too, is not the man who sees ahead, perhaps out of the general sight, but he who is quick to gather, and able then plausibly to express what is in the public mind at any time. The people want their will given present effect to; they become sensible of mistakes from experience, and they care little for the statesman who should discover and proclaim those mistakes before the rest become aware of them. Early reformers used to maintain that extending the suffrage would not alter the character of representation. Alexander Hamilton here, and Cobden later in England, predicted that the electors would choose much the same class of members as before. Only as lately as 1877, Mr. Gladstone declared that the new voters would "lean freely and confidingly on the judgments of those who have superior opportunities, and have also, or," he adds enigmatically, "are supposed to have, superior fitness of all kinds." But experience shows that with universal suffrage, directed by Jeffersonian principles, representation has a tendency to lose its high fiduciary character, and to become merely a mechanical substitute for what was possible in the small ancient democracies—the assembly of the whole people in the market-place.

The change and its consequences are largely developed here in America. Its first champion and exponent was Thomas Jefferson, who enjoined on the people to limit the exercise of discretion on the part of their representatives, and to insist before all things upon implicit obedience to orders given. This political thinker, indeed, explained that his system would only work amid a scattered agricultural people, and that it would be inapplicable with a large population of artisans massed in cities; and, accordingly, he had objections to artisans and manufacturers intruding into his ideal State, just as Washington was sceptical as to the value of commerce. This was as if an architect should draw a plan for a house to shelter you, but explain at the same time that it would only protect during quiet weather and so long as there were no storms or rain. Jefferson's conditions of Arcadian simplicity passed away; but his principles remained, and, being suited to the taste of the people around him, soon became recognised as their standing law. The United States Tariff of 1828 was thus passed under instructions from the constituencies, contrary, in many instances, to the declared judgment of the representatives, who yet supported it in obedience to the popular behest.

If you add to this the local idea by which the Congress-man is expected to think first for his own district and afterwards for the country, you do much to alter the nature of representative institutions and the character of the men wanted as representatives. The whole thing comes down to a lower level, and you have not statesmen concerned only for the common weal, but agents busied with the selfish struggle of places and classes.

Here, in the States, you see the system of local delegation worked to its natural outcome, and certainly with the result of impairing the position of the representative. Some other conditions of political life also conduce to this end. The incessant elections and the work of committees and primaries, demand the services of a class of men who give themselves wholly to it. Those who have a business or industry of their own cannot combine politics with it. There is no range of choice for the electors; they must choose a resident of the district. There is no length of tenure for the member, as the principle of the rotation of new men for each election prevails. He only sits, as a rule, for a short time, too short to gain experience or acquire authority as a legislator. Reasonable rewards, such as in the ordinary course of human affairs incite to exertion, there are none. An honest man devoting himself to politics can expect neither honour nor profit. He has nothing to look forward to; when he is old, or before he is old, he is cast aside for those who are younger and fresher. As one old politician expresses it, with more vigour than grace, "The great goers are the new men, the old troopers being all spavined and ring-boned from previous hard travel. I've got the bots, the fetlock, hip-joint, gravel, halt and founders." The tendency of these conditions again, obviously, is to produce a class of representatives whom the public disparage as "the politicians," and who, indeed, are not much better than any one else, and who often would not justify the claim to the high position and the freedom from dictation of the old representative.

There is much to explain this decadence from the representative to the delegate. The people are intelligent; the press brings information to every cottage and cleverly discusses it. The public forms a judgment often as good as the ordinary representative could give them. What they want is generally settled before Congress is called upon to act. Further, it is not to be denied that this system has some advantages for the people, if not for the politicians. It ensures that they are really cared for with such wisdom as may be at hand, and with a solicitude for them that few of the statesmen of the old world have displayed in past times. But the representatives are dwarfed. Often they do not appear to be strong enough for their duties. The Legislatures here do not seem able, for instance, to grapple with the Corporations. The tendency of our civilisation appears to be that, while grander designs

are opened up, there are poorer workmen to advance
them; nobler objects, but meaner instruments. In
time all this may lead to the public outgrowing representative institutions altogether and legislating for
themselves by some direct method. The justification
of representative bodies is, that they do represent and
care for the whole people. If they become the arena
for the hostile struggle of agents, each elbowing the
other in the struggle for their own particular clients,
they fail in the purpose for which they were intended,
and some new form of political life will in the natural
order of things be developed upon the decay of the old.

The representative character in the United States
appears in its worst aspect in municipal affairs. The
government of great cities is a difficult problem in all
countries and has long been a trial to patriotic
Americans. Here we come on the delegate who is
engaged with matters of municipal concern, local works,
contracts, employments, street franchises, and industrial
affairs that have money in them, to use the common
phrase. A generation ago Tweed and his gang degraded
the municipal government of New York to a lower level
than that of any city in the world, except, perhaps,
Constantinople. Rogues in the place of honour, honest
men plundered, public justice bought and sold, embezzlement of the public money reduced to a system—the
people looking on for years indignant and helpless. A
foreigner would hesitate to give such a description, were
it not that all honest Americans use even stronger terms.
At last the outbreak came, and by a convulsive effort
the city rogues were cast out and honest government
instituted. It remained so for a while, and then again
became corrupt. When I was in America, New York
was in the throes of another death struggle with its
depraved City Government. The Lexow Committee
was investigating abuses. Certainly they were startling.
The Americans make no secret of their evils. They
rival the Irish, who were said to be fair people, because
they never speak well of one another. The Press all

over the continent announced and denounced, trumpet-tongued, the profanation of government in New York. To take one extract at random, out of hundreds, this from the *Washington Evening Star* may be cited: "The Lexow Inquiry into the iniquity of New York City has adjourned for a while. The revelations which that prince of examiners, John W. Goff, has compelled with his keen probes of persistency and patience, have shocked and appalled decent American society. The police force of the community, which Tammany has proudly styled the 'best governed city in the world,' has been shown to be plunged in the lowest depths of degradation. Its *personnel*, from the highest to the lowest official, stands forth in the light of public scorn, smirched with the foulest filth of corruption. The investigation has proven beyond doubt or question that the good and the bad, the virtuous, upright business classes, and the vicious, that prey upon the morals and stability of the city, have been compelled alike to pay tribute to the gang that holds New York in its clutches. The question naturally arises, how the people on Manhattan Island, knowing so well the pernicious system under which they lived, should have submitted so long and so tamely to its continuance. It is inexplicable to the honest and courageous that business men of standing should have paid, regularly and irregularly, for so-called police protection, instead of rising up and demanding redress. It is a sickening thing to look upon the picture presented by the witnesses before the Lexow Committee."

The evidence that I read justified even such comments as these.

Again the people rose, and this time proposed not only to drive out the robbers, but to prevent their reappearing, by taking the government of the city out of the hands of the citizens themselves and entrusting it to the State of New York. The excitement during the election resembled that in a town assailed by a foreign enemy, whom all brave men were invoked to come forth and fight. Not only were the usual means of political war exhausted, but the clergy of all Churches joined their voice of warning and exhortation. The papers contained reports of the sermons. One reverend gentleman adjured his people by the love they felt for the honoured mother, or the pure-minded sister, to go and vote boldly against a government that rested upon the support of the brothel and the tap-room. Another said that the question before the country was—"The Ten Commandments: for or against?" When casting the ballot, they were to consider that their dear boy too, the light of their life, might live to have his honest mind perverted, if rogues and only rogues were always to be to the fore. The struggle was severe; the voting extensive. There were nineteen and a half million of ballot papers printed, being sixty-five for every voter. It took five weeks' incessant labour to prepare them. Twelve large vans were required to transport them, there being two hundred tons of paper to carry. Policemen, we read, watched them day and night, though we were not told *quis custodiet ipsos custodes.* In the end the honest party won a complete victory, and reforms have been again commenced in New York in earnest. Over three thousand of the old employers have been turned out to make room for better men. Yet I met some honest people who said that it would be a mistake to take away the government from the city and give it to the State. It was contrary to American principles. Let the people stew in the sauce of their own making till they learned themselves to improve it.

Mr. Bryce, in his valuable work upon America, gives a graphic account of the evils of city government as he observed them—the vicious politicians with all their ways of falsehood, malversation, ballot stuffing, "repeating," as also the embezzlements of the more audacious rings. He quotes Mr. Roosevelt, whose name is a household word here, for a description of some of the men who then ruled the people:

"In the lower wards (of New York City) where there is a large vicious population, the condition of politics is often fairly appalling, and the (local) boss is generally a man of grossly immoral public and private character. In these wards many of the social organisations with which the leaders are obliged to keep on good terms are composed of criminals, or of the relatives and associates of criminals. . . . The president of a powerful semi-political association was by profession a burglar; the man who received the goods he stole, was an alderman. Another alderman was elected while his hair was still short from a term in the State prison. A school trustee had been convicted of embezzlement and was the associate of criminals."

He says, in another part of his work, when illustrating the national characteristics of the Americans, that "when William M. Tweed was ruling and robbing New York, and had set on the bench, men who were openly prostituting justice, the citizens found the situation so amusing that they almost forgot to be angry." They seemed to take it more seriously this time. Honest men, vastly in the majority though they were, literally groaned under the rule of the blackguard. A business man told me, with a hopeless, indifferent air, that he regularly paid tribute to the police. It was the only way out of it. Another, who spoke highly of Mr. Bryce's book, said that its only fault was that it made too little of the evils under which they suffered. Some said, even after the victory, that it would be just like the overthrow of Tweed—only for a time.

Certainly, why the people support such men is a perplexing question; and they must support them, or at least tolerate them, for when they like they can throw them off. Not that corruption in Governments is anything new, from Russia to China. The awkward thing about such corruption as this, is that the people are involved in it, and that the people govern. Mr. Roosevelt is also quoted by Mr. Bryce as saying:

"Voters of the labouring class in the cities are very

emotional; they value in a public man what we are accustomed to consider virtues only to be taken into account when estimating private character. Thus, if a man is open-handed and warm-hearted, they consider it as being a fair offset to his being a little bit shaky when it comes to applying the eighth commandment to affairs of State. I have more than once heard the statement, 'He is very liberal to the poor,' advanced as a perfectly satisfactory answer to the charge that a certain public man was corrupt."

Some say that the people tolerate these corrupt Governments because they save them from even a greater evil—the rule of sincere fanatics, who would plunder them on principle to carry out some of the theories that I have heard propounded during my journeys. They prefer a greasy Boss Tweed to an incorruptible Robespierre. They call in, or at least submit to, the men who rob them to supply their needs, rather than have the men who would rob them to carry out their principles: for the one set are satisfied when they are full; the other, not till you are empty.

In this connection it is curious to notice the way in which they have solved the city problem at the capital of the Union. Washington used to be one of the badly ruled cities of the continent; indeed, one of the worst; and it offended the sense of fitness of the leading men of the Republic to have always thrust before their observation, under the very walls of the Capitol, all the visible signs of vulgar misgovernment and corruption. So they determined to reform it, and this they did by abolishing self-government in Washington and in a considerable tract of the surrounding country. The people of that city for twenty years past have been deprived of all power of voting in the prescribed area, whether for President, Congress, or city. No election meetings for these are held; no votes canvassed for; no ballot-boxes shaken; no tons of voting papers printed. A generation that grew up there would have to go to some other city to know what political electioneering meant. The President appoints three Commissioners, one of whom is always an officer of the U.S. Army, who have vested in them all the powers necessary for the complete municipal government of the city. They levy rates, enact bye-laws, grant and control franchises, and govern with perfect success, all being done with business ability and without a breath of suspicion of jobbery or favouritism. In the peculiar circumstances under which they work, they are able to combine the benefits of both the autocratic and the democratic principle, being surrounded and controlled by an enlightened public opinion, which heartily supports them while they act in the line of public duty that is so easy and obvious to honest men. The municipal arrangements of the city appear to be excellent. Some of the residents who remembered the conditions of the old *régime* spoke to me of the relief they felt in being delivered from it; but a few of the Populist party resented the change as involving a slur upon democratic institutions, though they did not dispute that there were good practical results. It certainly does seem odd, when you come to the land of the ballot-box, to find it proscribed in the capital city itself. But the Government thus established is essentially democratic in spirit, while freed from the defects that mar the rule of the market-place. It may be that the future of democracy has in store a solution of the problem of general government upon some similar lines.

Other facts that one reads of or learns here, convey the impression that the regard of the people for their Legislatures, and their pride in them, is waning. The most popular proposals that can be advanced in conventions for revising State constitutions are those which limit the powers of the legislative body, especially in regard to money matters. The Referendum, by which final legislation is taken out of the hands of the Legislature, is the popular plank in all platforms of the people's parties. Mr. Bryce says: "It was formerly usual for the Legislature to meet annually, but the experience of bad legislation and over legislation has led to fewer as well as shorter sittings; and sessions are now biennial in all States but five." A business man who had given some attention to politics from outside, told me that it was the belief of all commercial men, that the only way to get intelligent uniform dealing with the Tariff question was to take it away from Congress altogether, and let it be dealt with by a permanent non-political body.

One inquiring into Socialism has his attention arrested by what he sees here of the city politicians, not in New York alone, where the foreign element is considerable, but in other cities, where the citizens are fairly well conditioned and intelligent. For dealing with large questions of policy and State concern the representative system often produces noble men; but it does not afford managers of a reliable type for industrial work. These latter, if they are to resist the temptations of their position, would require to have even grander moral qualities than the statesman. When we are told that in the future the Government is to do so many things for us, what one sees and hears here makes us ask with anxiety, is it to be a Government such as this? What surprised me with many of the Socialist and Populist champions whom I met, was the union of unmeasured condemnation of the present trustees of the public, joined to equally unbounded confidence in those of the future.

Direct Socialism has not the same hold on the United States that it has on the Continent of Europe, or even on England. Bellamy's sketch, which is taken seriously abroad, is smiled at here. All new projects are allowed a fair field. The presumption at first is rather in their favour because they are new, and so many come to nothing, that public opinion has a sceptical tone. Notwithstanding the enormous fortunes of some, and which appear, indeed, to be increasing in number, there is still a great distribution of wealth among the people, and there is plenty of free land yet in the newer States. The education of the school, and of self-government for generations, also, has its effect. Unquestionably, too, the distrust of politicians, and the dissatisfaction with the results of Government action in its present sphere, indisposes many to the paternalism of the State. When they do adopt a proposal in that direction, they are sure to do so upon the ground of immediate practical wants, and to repudiate any advanced theories on the subject. Their manifestoes and pamphlets often, while claiming the same thing as similar publications in England, do so in a more temperate and common-sense manner. To illustrate this, I will give two extracts from pamphlets, both advocating the nationalization of the land, one written by an American, the other being "Fabian Tract, No. 42."

The English writer puts it this way :

"Yet into whose pockets does the whole of this value go ? Not into the pockets of the men and women who create it, but into the pockets of those who, often simply because they are the sons of their fathers, are the owners of the ground rents and values. Robbery is the only accurate word which a Christian Socialist can use to describe this state of things. . . .

"Now, what we Christian Socialists urge is, that a Parliament of the people, if they will but take the pains to send honest and obedient delegates to carry out their will, ought gradually, but as quickly as possible, to reverse that process, to take off all taxation from the articles of the people's consumption, and by degrees to tax the land values, till at last, taxing them twenty shillings in the pound, you take the whole of the land values for the benefit of those who create them."

But the American says :

"We who demand justice should be willing to do justice. Landholders did not steal the property of the people ; they bought it with the consent of the people and the positive sanction of their laws. When thousands have invested hard-earned wealth in land in good faith, under the sanction of our laws, it is hardly fair for us to turn about and take the property, or, what amounts to the same thing, its benefits, from them. Let us rather choose methods that we would not denounce if we ourselves were heavy owners of land. The change from the system of private ownership to a system of public ownership is for the benefit of the whole community, and the whole community should bear the just cost of the change."

A representative of the Socialist Labour party in Philadelphia, who was candidate for the position of "Congressman-at-large" in July, 1894, gives, in his letter of acceptance, as able, logical, and temperate a defence of the Socialist theory as I have read anywhere, political manifesto though it be. Himself a thorough-going Socialist, he has no mercy upon the mere Single Taxers, who concede a principle but won't give full effect to it; and he declares that the "mystification and illogical reasoning so rampant in the book of the author of the Single Tax," mark also the declamations of his followers. This gentleman was a German, and the most active Socialists in America are Germans; other foreigners swell the ranks, and there are, so far, only a few native-born Americans.

What may render the progress of the Socialist creed slower in America than in other lands, is that there they have had considerable experience of voluntary Socialistic and Communistic undertakings; and though, as I have before remarked, the failure of these does not prove that State Socialism would fall to pieces in the same way, it indicates that it would do so, unless in so far as it was sustained by force. As far back as 1824 Robert Owen commenced the experiment in America with his "New Harmony" settlement. Mr. Washington Gladden states that at least eleven similar communities followed in different parts of the United States, springing from this parent stem. In 1842 a fresh start was made owing to the writings of

Fourier, and partly due to the influence of Horace Greeley. True to its character for fearless trial of new projects, America soon had no less than thirty-four Socialist settlements in full working order. Noyes's well-known history of *American Socialisms* is based upon a close observation of the working of these communities. They all failed. He enumerates the varying causes of failure as being the spirit of self-love, the members not being "superior beings," dishonesty in the managers, everyday squabbles, too many engaging in talking and law-making, some men and women making it their sole occupation to "parade and talk." Mr. Gladden adds: "The nucleus of these associations, Mr. Greeley said, was almost always a little group of unselfish and enthusiastic men, but about them soon gathered a motley crew of 'the conceited, the crotchety, the selfish, the headstrong, the pugnacious, the unappreciated, the played-out, the idle, and the good-for-nothing generally, who, discovering themselves utterly out of place in the world as it is, rashly concluded that they are exactly fitted for the world as it ought to be.'"

There are a number of small Socialistic communities in America which rest upon a religious basis, and when celibacy or carefully restricted marriage is the rule, these are more successful, as they develop the spirit of self-sacrifice and resignation that religion teaches. This is the secret of their success, such as it is. But they are all under the rule of a few able men. There is no such thing as self-government, and, beyond question, the plan of life as exemplified by them produces a dead level of individual stagnation. The community known as "Shakers" may be referred to as an example. The sexes are kept separate, not being allowed even to shake hands together. They eat apart, work apart, and are divided at public worship. Celibacy is strictly enforced, and married people are not received into membership till they are lawfully released from the marriage tie. Persons of opposite sexes are not allowed to visit each other's rooms except upon errands, and then not for a period of more than fifteen minutes; an idea that, possibly, was borrowed from the old English conveyancers, who used to have a similar stipulation, though more limited as to time, in deeds of separation. The Shakers are both the oldest and largest of the Socialist experiments in America, and have flourished or existed there for over a century. The Oneida community of "Perfectionists," which was based upon communism in the relation between the sexes, as well as communism of property, only maintained its peculiar tenets for some thirty years, and then they fell back upon the old principles of marriage and property. The observation of these little experiments at their doors renders Americans incredulous as to the larger theories of Socialism.

A striking proof of the small hold that Socialistic ideas had upon the people here, at least a few years ago, is given by the nature of the proposals that the working people of California adopted in their hour of triumph under Kearney in 1877. There had been a violent and not unnatural outburst against the abuses of Government and the domination of the great Corporations. The Populists and the demagogues carried all before them. A State Convention was called, which undertook thorough reform in the interests of the people. Some of the delegates to it held the most advanced views. When framing the new Constitution, one member objected to the law that provides for the obligation of contracts, as he maintained that all jobs should be done by day labour. They all expressed their resolve that capital should be "cinched," or strapped up in an unpleasant manner; and they had power to adopt whatever proposals were most popular among the crowd. Yet in the result no suggestion of Socialism or Communism was adopted or even seriously made. The Constitution ratified by the Convention limits the powers of the Legislature and seeks to control Corporations, but it actually strengthens vested rights, particularly in land. It provides that "private property shall not be taken or damaged for public use without just compensation having been first made to the owner." I heard an eminent Labour leader, when addressing the London County Council, say that they intended to take the lands in England " with or without compensation."

Apart from the Socialist sect, yet for some purposes co-operating with it, there are various powerful Labour Associations in America. The Knights of Labour had at one time a great following, and won some local elections. That body proposed to unite in its membership all classes of labourers, whether organized under Trades Unions or unorganized, and also the members of professions and those who follow literary callings. But they excluded lawyers, gamblers, bankers, stockbrokers, and saloon keepers. Their journal, published in Philadelphia, is a well-written paper, which bears the truly just motto: "That is the most perfect Government in which an injury to one is the concern of all." Their programme embraces proposals for improving the conditions of labour, some of which all may approve. They have rapidly lost influence, and their numbers have fallen away from a million to 150,000, owing, it is stated, to the mismanagement of the cause by the leaders. The American Federation of Labour has its head-quarters in New York, but its organisation spreads through the United States and Canada, and includes in its ranks workers of every description. Its first origin dates from the close of the Civil War, when the power of great Corporations became marked; but its course for a time was a troubled one, once even threatening to develop into a secret association, pursuing methods that are alien to the instincts of the true workman of England and America alike. In 1881 it was reconstructed, and has since worked in the light of day for the practical improvement of the conditions of labour. It has over half a million members. Its motto is the old time-honoured one, "*Labor omnia vincit*," and, like the English Trade Unions' Congress, it yearly holds meetings in the principal cities of its country. An idea of its work may be had from the summary that its official report gives of the proceedings at the Thirteenth Annual Convention at Chicago. That was a gloomy meeting. The industrial depression throughout America was great. The unemployed were estimated to reach the appalling total of three millions. This, truly, is an astounding number, yet it is instructive to call to mind that it is small compared with the pauperism of England in the time of Elizabeth. It was computed that there were then not less than 350,000 beggars in a population of about 5,000,000.

Chicago itself, after the boom, was in a state of collapse. The President, Mr. Gompers, informed the Convention that he had walked through the corridors of the City Hall the previous night and seen hundreds of men lying on the stone flooring, on the iron steps, and some who could get no corner to lie in, had fallen asleep standing up. Yet Socialist proposals were not adopted, and the record of the work done at the meeting is moderate and unpretending. The Government ownership of telegraphs and telephones and the institution of Postal Savings Banks were urged; better food and quarters for seamen, the abolition of the sweating system and of sub-cellars for bakers were demanded, and an alliance with the farmers' organisation was urged. The decisions of the judges which were inimical to labour were denounced and an investigation by Congress demanded. A delegation of ministers visited the Convention and assured it of their good-will. A political programme was referred to affiliated organisations. Large sums of money previously loaned to "organisations engaged in disputes" were given to them absolutely. A magazine to defend the interests of labour was ordered to be published.

The object of this powerful association is indeed an admirable one. It is declared to be to "render employment and the means of subsistence less precarious by securing to the toilers an equitable share of the fruits of their toil." The means to secure this end are stated to be, the federation of all trade and labour unions, the establishment of unions where none exist, the formation of public opinion by platform and press, and the reduction of the hours of work. The President, in his opening address at Chicago, says: "From every country comes the cheering news of the growth and extension of trades unions and trade union sentiment. The conviction is fast gaining ground that political liberty with economic slavery is delusive and for all practical purposes valueless. The wage-workers are discerning that the road to economic independence, and thus to full and free exercise of political equality and freedom, can only be achieved by and through the trades unions." The preamble of the Constitution of the Federation states that a struggle is going on in all nations of the civilised world between the capitalist and the labourer, which will work disastrous results to the toilers unless they combine for protection, and that therefore they must unite to secure their rights. But throughout both their proceedings and their publications no countenance is given to the Socialist theories; though they adopt what the Socialist hails as the first step on the right road—the Government ownership of monopolies, particularly railways.

The vast railway system of America employs over 850,000 men, and 150,000 of these are members of the American Railway Union, which played such an important part in the great Chicago strike and riots of 1894. This Association proclaims the brotherhood of all railway *employés*, but confines it to those born of white parents. Its Constitution declares that "The protection of all members in all matters relating to wages and their rights as *employés*" is the principal purpose of the organisation. Railway *employés* are entitled to a voice in fixing wages and in determining conditions of employment. Fair wages and proper treatment must be the return for efficient services faithfully performed. Such a policy ensures harmonious relations and satisfactory results. The Order, while pledged to conservative methods, will protect the humblest of its members in every right he can justly claim; but "while the rights of members will be sacredly guarded, no intemperate demand or unreasonable propositions will be entertained. Corporations will not be permitted to treat the organisation better than the organisation will treat them. A high sense of honour must be the animating spirit, and even-handed justice the end sought to be obtained. Thoroughly organised in every department, with a due regard for the right wherever found, it is confidently believed that all differences may be satisfactorily adjusted, that harmonious relations may be established and maintained, that the service may be incalculably improved, and that the necessity for strike and lock-out, boycott and black list, alike disastrous to employer and *employé*, and a perpetual menace to the welfare of the public, will for ever disappear."

In each State there are to be found branches of these central organisations, and also independent associations for promoting Labour, Populist, Socialist, or Anarchist views. Naturally, there is a great similarity between the platforms of the respective propaganda throughout North America. The same arguments and illustrations are repeated. The only difference that one notices arises from the application of the general principles to the local grievance in each district, which, in so vast a territory as that of the United States, makes some variety. Often in these platforms a preamble of wide range and dark denunciation ushers in, as the great national need, the reform of the evil that most affects the district. Thus the manifesto of the "People's Party," adopted at Omaha in July, 1894, recites: "We meet in the midst of a nation brought to the verge of moral, political, and material ruin. Corruption dominates the ballot-box, the Legislatures, the Congress, and touches even the ermine of the bench. The people are demoralised; the newspapers are largely subsidised or muzzled; public opinion silenced; our homes covered with mortgages; labour impoverished, and the land concentrating in the hands of the capitalist; the urban workmen are denied the right of organisation for self-protection; imported pauperised labour beats down their wages; a hireling standing army is established to shoot them down. The fruits of the toil of millions are boldly stolen to build up colossal fortunes for a few."

From this formidable general indictment it goes on to emphasize the silver question as the pressing one. It says: "Silver, which has been accepted as coin since the dawn of history, has been demonetised to add to the purchasing power of gold by decreasing the value of all forms of property as well as human labour, and the supply of currency is purposely abridged to fatten usurers, bankrupt enterprise, and enslave industries. A vast conspiracy against mankind has been organised on two continents, and it is rapidly taking possession of the world."

It then goes on to set forth its platform, the first demand in which is for a new system of currency. "We demand the free and unlimited coinage of silver and gold at the present ratio of 16 to 1. We demand that the amount of the circulating medium be speedily increased to not less than fifty dollars per capita."

They denounce the issue of bonds by the President for the purpose of keeping up the Treasury supply of gold as "an act of treason and usurpation unequalled in the history of civilised Government." One of their pamphlets describes it as the "crime of all crimes." The whole document is full of very strong language; but one of their leading men assured me that the silver question was their real grievance, and that they only smiled at the ideas of Henry George and Bellamy.

When I was in Philadelphia the Socialist Labour party of that State put forward nominees for a coming election for all officers from that of the Governor downwards. Their platform also begins with a wide preamble,

in which they put the Socialist theory rather clearly:
"Whereas the time is fast coming when, in the natural course of social evolution, the old system, through the destructive action of its failures and crises on the one hand and the constructive tendencies of its trusts and other capitalistic combinations on the other hand, shall have worked out its own downfall," therefore we invite all to organise with a view to preparing for the coming co-operative commonwealth. But, coming down from the large scope of action thus suggested, they embody their present social demands in proposals for reducing the hours of labour, for the Government owning the railways, for the progressive income tax, revocation of grants of land to corporations, the conditions of which have not been complied with, and similar measures of a popular character. As is the custom here, the leaflet containing the platform has upon the outside a striking woodcut likeness of Mr. Grundy, the Socialist nominee for the office of Governor of Pennsylvania.

While many things in America tend to mitigate the keenness of the Socialist feeling, there are also some conditions of life and industry there that go to intensify it. The general wealth of the country is enormous, and while a large number share it, yet the extraordinary accumulations of a few, owing to the vast nature of the industrial operations carried on there, naturally challenge popular attention. A writer in *The North American Review* says: "We are, as a nation, peculiarly identified with money. The vulgar European belief in our worship of the 'almighty dollar' is undoubtedly more or less well founded. As a people, we unquestionably do think more of money than any other people of modern times. We love the possession of money in ourselves; we honour it in others. Our principal object in life is to make money, and for the last ten years we have made more money and have made it of more different kinds than ever nation did before."

It has been calculated that seventy persons in America own between them 540 millions sterling of money, or about seven millions and a half each. Five citizens own twenty millions apiece, one fourteen millions, two twelve millions, six ten millions, thirteen six millions, ten five millions, and fifteen four millions. In addition to these there are fifty citizens in the Northern States alone valued at two millions each. There are stated to be sixty-three millionaires in Pennsylvania owning sixty millions sterling, and sixty persons in three villages near New York whose aggregate wealth is a hundred millions. In Boston fifty families pay taxes upon an annual income of £200,000. *Chambers' Journal*, which summarises these figures from an American authority, points out that even in wealthy England there is nothing to compare with them. One Duke is valued at ten millions and another at eight millions, while only one hundred and four persons were returned as deriving an income from business profits of over £50,000 a year. Further, while statistics show that the wealth of England is becoming more distributed, it is alleged that in the United States it is becoming more concentrated. Mr. Shearman estimates the average annual income of the richest hundred Americans at about £300,000 and that of the richest hundred Englishmen at £90,000. The earnings of four-fifths of American families do not, he calculates, average £100 a year. "According to the estimates of the wealth of American millionaires, it seems that 25,000 persons own one-half of the entire wealth of the United States; and if the present rates of taxation and accumulation continue, it is computed that that great country will be practically owned by about 50,000 persons—say one-thousandth part of the present population." Such vast masses of wealth, won by extensive business operations and monopolies that were unknown in the time of our fathers, introduce new ideas into the old conception of private property, which entitles a man to keep what he earns. True, the millionaires only heap up for the public. They do not consume their hoards, but scatter them again in industries. And that computation overlooks the power of dispersion that rests in social causes as well as the power of accumulation. The possession of wealth by the action of inevitable influences, enfeebles the possessors who have not earned it, and reduces them or their children again to the ranks. " Three generations between shirt-sleeves " is how the Americans express it. But the dangerous side to the question is that this money-making, unless controlled by a firm Government, is one form of acquiring power in the State—wealth one phase of rule.

In the United States, too, unquestionably, the methods by which these vast accumulations are often made, by which some great companies and combinations acquire the monopoly of the means of production, and the manner in which they use their power, is a national evil that ought to have been long ago effectually grappled with by the Government. Rings, trusts, pools, combinations, enable enormous fortunes to be made, but only by the exploitation of the community at large. A railway company will refuse to let its trains stop at a considerable town on the prairies, and fix its station further on, where it has a grant of land, so as to compel people to begin a new town there and pay what price it thinks proper for the building sites. The old town is thus deserted and ruined. When I was at a rather large town the people told me that, some time before, they had been startled by a report that the company were going to have their station some three miles out, so as to compel them to buy allotments there. The discrimination in freight rates is another means of oppression and wealth-making by indirect means. Some rates are lower from San Francisco to New York than from Kansas City to New York. It was proved before the Railroad Committee of the Colorado Senate that coal was carried to Leadville and sold for seven dollars a ton, while the same coal, after 150 miles' further haulage, was sold at Denver for five dollars and a half. Professor Parsons mentions that between Minneapolis and Chicago the rate on flour and wheat is the same for a station eighty miles from Chicago as for one 420 miles distant. The practice was (I was told by those who had practical knowledge) for the railway companies to compute, as the harvest-time came on, the utmost that the farmers or other settlers could possibly afford to give to have their produce carried, to fix their rates accordingly and leave them the alternative of submitting to it or letting their crops rot upon the ground. A committee of the United States Senate thus reported upon these and other abuses:

"Unjustifiable discriminations are constantly made between individuals and between localities similarly situated. . . . . The effect of the prevailing policy of railroad management is, by an elaborate system of secret special rates, rebates, drawbacks, and concessions, to foster monopoly and enrich favoured shippers."

While I was in America the papers were busy discussing an incident that had been revealed during an inquiry into the accounts of a railway line that had become bankrupt. There was a sum of seven million dollars that had disappeared; where it had gone was difficult to trace. The services of expert book-keepers were called in, and ultimately it was ascertained that it had been secretly paid back to favoured shippers as rebates. The process was simple. The company wishes to favour some shippers so as, between them, to establish a monopoly. The shipper, to apparently comply with the law, pays the freight according to the published rates of the company, and after a while, in pursuance of the secret arrangement, gets the rebate agreed upon returned to him. Thus, while seeming to carry on business upon the same terms as his rivals, he is able to undersell them directly. A leading and reliable New York paper dealt with the matter under the head of "A Widespread Conspiracy." It said:

"It was by such conspiracy between railroads and favoured capitalists that enormous monopolies were built up to prey on the consumer and to corrupt politics with their ill-gotten money."

It was stated that this practice was a common one on the railroads, even on those that were worked by receivers appointed by the Courts. Another device resorted to was for the railway company to profess its inability to find the necessary trucks for the obnoxious trader, while amply supplying his rival. It was proved in one case that the parties to the monopoly divided the rebate between them. Some of the papers made urgent appeals to the Government to put the law in force against the offenders. The report of the joint committee appointed by the Legislature of Pennsylvania some years ago to inquire into the disastrous strikes and riots that had taken place in that State says:

"The citizens had a bitter feeling against the Pennsylvania Railroad Company on account of, as they believed, an unjust discrimination by the Railroad Company against them in freight rates, which made it very difficult for their manufacturers to compete successfully with manufacturers further west; and this feeling had existed and been intensified for years, and pervaded all classes."

These are great abuses and ought to be put down by the strong arm of the law, if the law has a strong arm. The extent of these social evils is an explanation of, if not a full plea of justification for, the occasional extravagance of proposed social reforms. These companies assume powers that would not be conceded to the Sovereign of a State. All such practices are criminal according to the principles of the old English (and American) common law. The Federal and the State Legislatures have also made laws forbidding them. Readers of English history will call to mind the horror that Englishmen ever had of all sorts of monopoly; and lawyers know how sternly our law condemned the tricks of trade. It is refreshing to turn from an organised system of scheming and sharp practice to the old ideas of commercial fair dealing as they used to be enforced by English judges. Some of their notions may be obsolete, but the ruling principles are sound.

It was, for example, held that it was contrary to the old English law for a merchant to buy up all the goods in one line in a particular place, and to induce others to hold, so as to cause a rise in prices, for the purpose of speculation. In the beginning of the present century an English merchant was convicted before the Court of Queen's Bench of this offence, and sent to gaol for several months. The judge, in passing sentence, said:

"The sum, then, of the offence is, that the defendant, a merchant of credit and affluence in Kent, having a stock of hops in hand, went to the market at Worcester, not to buy hops, for that he disclaimed, nor to sell them, for upon the evidence it does not appear that he offered any for sale, but merely to speculate how he could enhance the price of that commodity. And for that purpose he declared to the sellers that hops were too cheap, and to the hop-planters that they had not a fair price for their hops: and lest he should be defeated in his speculation to raise the price of a falling market, he contracted for one-fifth of the produce of two counties, when he had a stock in hand, and admitted that he did not want to purchase. . . . The freedom of trade, like the liberty of the press, is one thing; the abuse of that freedom, like the licentiousness of the press, is another. God forbid that this Court should do anything that should interfere with the legal freedom of trade. . . . But the same law that protects the proprietors of merchandise takes an interest also in the concerns of the public, by protecting the poor man against the avarice of the rich; and from all time it has been an offence against the public to commit practices to enhance the price of merchandise coming to market, particularly the necessaries of life, for the purpose of enriching an individual. The freedom of trade has its legal limits. No man under that liberty is permitted to dispose of his riches, in purchasing what and of whom he pleases, or when or where he pleases."

It was questioned by Adam Smith and the political

economists, as well as by those who were engaged in trade, with its rapidly growing spirit of speculation, whether the economic principle of cases such as these was sound. But at least they show that practices such as one finds rife here are crimes according to the law of England. There is no question that its principles have ever condemned all combinations against the freedom of trade and industry, inasmuch as they "discourage labour and industry and restrain persons from getting an honest livelihood, and put it in the power of other persons to set what price they please upon commodities, all which are manifest inconveniences to the public."

It was only to be expected that so intelligent and fair-minded a people as the Americans would be shocked at such abuses of power and try to put them down, and they have grappled with them in so far as they can, by passing new and stringent statutes to enforce the principles of the old common law. The Inter-State Commerce Act and the Anti-Trust Act forbid such practices. The Supreme Court of Illinois, by a most just decision, has declared that, while a Corporation can hold all the property that it wants for its own business, yet, if it buys competing properties merely for the purpose of shutting them up and destroying competition, it transcends its authority and forfeits its charter. The law against all conspiracies is clear. Yet the practices are said to continue. Professor Parsons says that the laws are a dead letter. He quotes Mr. Cator as saying, "It is well known that the law is systematically defied," and says that a President of one of the railway companies declared that, "if all who have offended against these laws were convicted there would not be gaols enough in the United States to hold them." An instance of how the law is evaded is given. One trader secured a rebate that gave him control of the market, having first become a stockholder of the railway that favoured him. When summoned before the Inter-State Commerce Commission he declined to appear, upon the ground that, being a shareholder in the offending company, he could not be required to criminate himself. This view was supported by the Courts, so that all an intending monopolist has to do to secure safety is to buy a few shares in the railway that he is going to work with. Some of the States have tried Government ownership and management, but it has failed, and a return has been made to private management. In Canada the Dominion owns one system of railways, but it does not pay, though the Minister who had control was said to rule independently of all political influence and to bravely insist upon pure business management. Some public men there, however, told me that his rule was exceptional, and that in the end political agencies would prove too strong for him. Government ownership, with leasing under proper conditions to private enterprise, has still to be tried.

Certainly what one observes here shows a want of power in the State Legislature to *govern*. The Federal Executive is strong when roused for a national emergency, but industrial and social life in the States drifts along and the people do as they please. No control is the order of the day. Money then becomes a great power, moving, perhaps quietly, but not the less effectually, many agencies of public influence. Each political party is struggling for votes, anxious to conciliate all interests, fearful to offend any. If the country could be thoroughly roused, war might be resolutely waged by some Dictator against these abuses; but in the quiet daily course of democratic government an active private interest often prevails over the public welfare. It is the old difficulty about governing in a popular Government. It is seen in an exaggerated form in the great cities, with their secretly growing abuses and their recurring periods of purging and vomiting. The same weakness was shown in the manner in which even the Federal Government dealt with slavery. The slave-holders were quite in a minority, but they were a compact party, united by self-interest, and for years they governed the Union. Jefferson, Madison, Marshall, Webster, Clay, Calhoun were all slave-owners. As far back as the

o

year 1779 it was proposed in the American Legislature to grapple with the slavery problem by declaring all children of slaves, born after a certain day, to be free, and then to transplant them in time to a new settlement. This would have also solved the Black difficulty which the sudden emancipation of the slaves during the war, has entailed on America. But nothing was done; the question was let drift. Whatever laws the slave-owners wanted they were able to secure, despite all the opposition of those who fought for principle. To the last the North offered them full security for their cherished institution if they would only remain in the Union. When Horace Greeley appealed to Lincoln to proclaim the slaves free during the war, he wrote in reply: "My paramount object is to save the Union, and not to either save or destroy slavery. What I do about slavery, I do because it helps to save the Union; and what I forbear, I forbear because I do not believe it would help to save the Union." Thus were some eight millions of Southerners able to dictate to some twenty millions of Northerners, until, fortunately for the cause of freedom, they went too far and were crushed. It is the imperfection of government, showing itself sometimes in one way and sometimes in another, that is the perennial difficulty in human society, and, until this can be mended, the plan of handing all industrial enterprises over to State management, would not get rid of the evils we suffer under, but would only alter their direction.

CHAPTER IX.

THE UNITED STATES (*continued*).

FACING the great corporations and unions of employers are the workmen combined in associations, some of which I have referred to. When open hostilities break out it is a serious matter. It is civil war limited in area. In the Pennsylvanian coal strike of 1894 there were, at a conflict that occurred at Connellsville, twelve rioters killed, and in a fight between the strikers and the deputy marshals in Alabama six were killed and twenty wounded. In Colorado 1,600 men fortified a camp, and only gave way when the troops approached with cannon. The great Chicago strike was going on while I was in Canada, and we daily read startling details in the papers of the events that were taking place in that city, at San Francisco, and along the railway lines. When in America, I inquired into the facts; they are worthy of a brief record, not alone because of the vast proportions of the labour-war, but also for the evidence they afford of the power of capital, under a popular Government, in the struggle. The Commission appointed by the President to investigate the "causes of the strike and the best means of adjustment" of the difficulties that existed, presented a carefully prepared report, the tone of which was decidedly sympathetic to the side of the *employés*. The Commissioner of Labour of the United States, Mr. Carroll D. Wright, whose interest in all that concerns the workers was acknowledged to me by several Labour advocates, was, in accordance with the terms of the Act under which the inquiry was held, one member of the board, and the two others were nominated by Mr. Cleveland. They were thirteen days at the scene of the conflict, taking evidence from all parties and interests concerned, and examined 109 witnesses. We get, therefore, from their report reliable details. The direct loss to the railroads in property destroyed during the strike, and expenses incurred, was estimated at $685,308; the indirect loss of earnings at $4,672,916. Some 3,100 *employés* at Pullman lost in wages at least $350,000. About 100,000 railway servants lost in wages $1,389,143. Besides this direct loss there was the indirect injury to trade and industry owing to the stoppage of the trains and of business, that could not be accurately estimated. There were employed in suppressing the riots and in protecting property 1,936 men of the United States troops; the State militia on duty numbered 4,000, while there were 3,000 of the Chicago police, 5,000 extra deputy marshals, and 250 extra deputy sheriffs—making in all 14,186 fighting men. The large number of men thus engaged is, however looked at, one of the most striking facts in the story. All had to be paid for, none were brought merely for the sake of show. We are reminded of the Duke of Wellington's estimate of the number of soldiers necessary to preserve civil order in any emergency. He informed the English Government, when riots were threatening, that 300 soldiers ought to be sufficient to cope with any mob. Twelve persons were shot and fatally wounded; 575 were arrested by the police. The intervention of the President in sending the United States troops was applauded by the public generally, but strongly censured by the Populist party. The framers of the Constitution, who never dreamt of such a state of things as in fact then existed at Chicago, declare as follows in the fourth article of the Constitution: "The United States shall guarantee to every State in the Union a republican form of government;

shall protect each of them against invasion, and on the application of the Legislature, or of the Executive (when the Legislature cannot be convened), against domestic violence."

In this case the Governor of Illinois not only did not apply for the troops, but warmly protested against their being sent. He declared that he wanted no assistance to suppress the riots. But his protests and the apparent meaning of the Constitution were disregarded, ostensibly for the purpose of protecting Federal property and preventing obstruction in the carrying of the United States mails, but really to make Chicago safe against pillage. That there was real danger of this, and that the local militia could not be relied on, I was assured by official people whose business it was to know. The Superintendent of Police at Chicago naturally speaks guardedly considering the action of his Government, but he says: "When the troops arrived the indications looked bad, and the arrival of the troops I think was opportune."

The report of the Commission says: "That the policemen sympathised with the strikers rather than with the corporations cannot be doubted; nor would it be surprising to find the same sentiment rife among the military. These forces are largely recruited from the labouring classes."

The press reported that at the riots at San Francisco, which arose from this strike, the militia, when drawn up before the railway station and ordered to advance and clear out the mob who had taken possession of it, broke their ranks and walked away. The President sent United States troops there also. I asked a resident who was describing the scene to me, whether the accounts in the papers were correct. He said that they were, and that not only did the militia walk away, but that they left their arms in the orderly-room for the mob to seize.

Public opinion justified the President in maintaining the people's peace and preserving life, whether with or without the sanction of the Constitution. It is an example of how the practical needs of a nation will modify a paper constitution, when events occur that were never thought of by its framers. In the Pennsylvania riots some years before, the aid of the central Government was not asked for nor given, and matters were left in the hands of the local militia. At the memorable rising at Pittsburgh they naturally sympathised with their fellow-labourers, stacked their arms, and fraternised with the crowd. When militia troops were brought from a distance, who would fight, things had become so serious that, sad to relate, in one conflict between the soldiers and the mob twenty-two people were killed. The troops were fired upon from the houses and even the police-stations of the city. Persons who were arrested for pillaging were at once discharged by the local authority. A part of the town was burnt down. The report of the Legislative Committee of the State says: "About 1,600 cars (mostly freight), including passenger and baggage cars, with such of their contents as were not carried away by the thieves, 126 locomotives, and all the shops, materials, and buildings, except one or two small ones, of the railroad company, from above 28th-street to the Union depôt, were burned on Saturday night and Sunday." Although Pittsburgh was the centre, rioting was also carried on at Reading, Scranton, Alleghany City, Altoona, Harrisburg, and Philadelphia. At Reading 200 soldiers were wounded by the brickbats and paving-stones of the mob. The damage done at Pittsburgh was estimated at $5,000,000. The report of the committee further says: "The large class of labourers in the different mills, manufactories, mines, and other industries in Pittsburgh were also strongly in sympathy with the railroad strikers, considering the cause of the railroad men their cause. This feeling of aversion to the railroad company and sympathy with the strikers was indulged in by the Pittsburgh troops to the same extent that it was by the other classes, and, as many of them had friends and relatives in the mob, it is not much to be wondered at that they did not show much anxiety to assist in dispersing the crowd and enforcing the law." The Commission upon the Chicago strike says: "The danger is growing that in strike-wars between corporations and *employés*, military duty will ultimately have to be done by others than volunteers from labour ranks."

These "strike-wars," as the Commission truly designates them, certainly show a want of executive power in the States' Governments. A strong Government would put down, by penal means if necessary, the illegal practices of the great corporations by which the people are oppressed and exasperated. But it would also promptly protect the public peace and suppress and justly punish outrage. At present safety is only ensured, at least in some States, when there is a President strong enough to act over the head and against the will of the local Government.

What possibly made Mr. Cleveland the more prompt to act in the case of the Chicago riots, was that the Governor of Illinois was believed to have owed his election to the Anarchist and Socialist vote. He had in the previous year granted an absolute pardon to three of the men who were convicted of complicity in the Chicago murders in 1886, when a bomb was thrown among a party of the police, and several of them were killed or wounded. This outrage, which illustrates the methods of one class of the foreign Socialists, made a vivid impression upon the public mind of America and the whole English-speaking world, for up to this time such methods of vengeance had found no countenance from the Anglo-Saxon race. Both the plan of the crime, and its perpetrators, were of foreign origin. A number of persons were arrested, and after the delays and rehearings which the American law provides in its anxiety to do full justice, eight of the prisoners were convicted, of whom four were hanged, one committed suicide, and three were sentenced to imprisonment for life or for a lesser term. It should be stated that the men were convicted, not upon the ground that it was proved they had actually participated in the throwing of the bomb, but that they had by speech and writing advised the outrage, and that it was perpetrated in consequence of their advice. Petitions were presented, which appear to have been numerously signed by all classes, praying for their release upon the ground that, though guilty, their punishment had now been sufficient. But some based their demand upon the ground that the judge who tried the case was prejudiced, "or else so determined to win the applause of a certain class of the community that he could not and did not grant a fair trial," and that the "jury was a packed jury, selected to convict."

There is no more delicate duty than that cast in English communities upon the executive, when it is asked to remit a judicial sentence; it is so liable to abuse, in which case it is so entirely destructive of the pure administration of justice, and the confidence of the people in it, giving, as it does, immunity to those who can command influence. Nothing can be of less real value than petitions in such cases. They may be signed from mere good nature, from indifference, through sheer ignorance; sometimes from fear, and specially so when the friends of the criminals are daring and the Government weak. In England and her colonies the Government is very slow to alter any judicial sentence, and never does so except after consultation with the judge. In this case the Governor not only pardoned the accused, but did so upon the express ground that the trial was unfair, disclaiming the grounds suggested in the other petitions. His reasons were published in a pamphlet of sixty-three pages, signed by him, which contained an elaborate statement directed to prove that the trial was a miscarriage of justice, from which it followed, as they were all tried together, not only that the men imprisoned should be discharged, but that their comrades who had been executed were murdered.

Concluding his long argument, he says, under the heading "Prejudice or Subserviency of the Judge": "It is further charged with much bitterness by those who speak for the prisoners, that the record of the case shows that the judge conducted the trial with malicious ferocity, and forced eight men to be tried together; that, in cross-examining the State's witnesses, he confined counsel for the defence to the specific points touched on by the State, while in the cross-examination of the defendants' witnesses he permitted the State's attorney to go into all manner of subjects entirely foreign to the matters on which the witnesses were examined in chief; also, that every ruling throughout the long trial, on any contested point, was in favour of the State, and, further, that page after page of the record contains insinuating remarks of the judge made in the hearing of the jury, and with the evident intent of bringing the jury to his way of thinking; that these speeches, coming from the court, were much more damaging than any speeches from the State's attorney could possibly have been; that the State's attorney often took his cue from the judge's remarks; that the judge's magazine article recently published, although written nearly six weeks after the trial, is yet full of venom; that, pretending to simply review the case, he had to drag into his article a letter written by an excited woman to a newspaper after the trial was over, and which, therefore, had nothing whatever to do with the case, and was put into the article simply to create a prejudice against the woman, as well as against the dead and the living; and that, not content with this, he in the same article makes an insinuating attack on one of the lawyers for the defence, not for anything done at the trial, but because more than a year after the trial, when some of the defendants had been hung, he ventured to express a few kind, if erroneous, sentiments over the graves of his dead clients, whom he at least believed to be innocent. It is urged that such ferocity or subserviency is without a parallel in all history; that even Jeffreys in England contented himself with hanging his victims, and did not stop to berate them after they were dead.

"These charges are of a personal character, and while they seem to be sustained by the record of the trial and the papers before me, and tend to show that the trial was not fair, I do not care to discuss this feature of the case any farther, because it is not necessary. I am convinced that it is clearly my duty to act in this case for the reasons already given, and I therefore grant an absolute pardon to Samuel Fielden, Oscar Neebe, and Michael Schwab this 26th day of June, 1893."

This shows how the wilder political developments chafe under the independent action of the judiciary, and it all seems strange and sad to those who are accustomed to the traditions of English justice. The Governor never seems to realize the dark crime that he imputes to the judge and jury of his State in slaying innocent men in response to a popular cry for their blood. Publishing his official reasons in a pamphlet that was sold for a few cents at the bookstalls, shows that public justice had degenerated into the sphere of party politics, if, indeed, sympathisers with crime can be looked upon as a party. It is stated in the press that in two years, 128 convicts have been pardoned in Illinois, twenty-two of them being murderers, and that respectable lynching parties justified their summary justice upon the ground that it was the only way that any justice could be secured.

The President's interference against the Governor's protest, while generally approved, was of course the subject of adverse comment in many papers. At a large public meeting in New York, his action was denounced as being destructive of constitutional rights, and a petition was sent to Congress demanding the impeachment of the Attorney-General of the United States for advising the action that had been taken.

In connection with these strike-wars, what most impresses one is the defiant tone that the employer corporations maintain throughout them. Society must take care of itself, and save the public peace as well as it can, but they will fight on till they conquer. In 1886, a voluntary unincorporated body was constituted at Chicago, in which the twenty-four railroads, centring in or terminating at that city, were combined. It is termed the "General Managers' Association," and acts unitedly when a dispute with the *employés* of any of the lines arises, and generally in matters of management. This body directed the conflict upon the part of the companies during the Chicago strike, and advised with the military authorities as to the disposition of the troops. One hundred and twenty thousand workmen, represented by 415 delegates, declared for the strike. When it was coming to an end, the American Railway Union, representing the men, sent through the Mayor of Chicago to the General Managers' Association, offering to declare the strike off if the men would be restored to their old positions, except those who had been convicted of crime. The General Managers' Association gave notice that they would receive no communication whatever from the American Railway Union, and returned the letter unanswered. I quote from the Commission's report of the evidence of Mr. John M. Egan, the strike manager of the association:

"A few days later I was out of the office for a while, and on my return I found the Mayor and Alderman M'Gillen talking to Mr. St. John. I went into the room, and Mr. St. John told me the Mayor had come there with a letter signed by the officers of the American Railway Union. I told the Mayor I thought he should not have permitted himself to be a messenger boy for those parties, and that I further considered that the General Managers' Association should not receive any such document.

"Questions by Commissioner Worthington:

"18. Was there anything in the document itself that was offensive or insulting to you?—*A*. The document was printed in the papers that afternoon and the next morning, and I think it speaks for itself.

"19. Did you consider it offensive or insulting?—

A. I considered that any party who attacked railway companies as the American Railway Union has done, and were whipped, as I considered they were, it was displaying considerable cheek to dictate the terms of their surrender.

"20. You do not answer my question. I asked you if there was anything in the document itself that was offensive or insulting to you?—*A.* I don't know as I would be the judge of that.

"21. What is your opinion about it?—*A.* I have not the authority to say whether it was insulting to the general managers, or anything of that kind.

"22. Did you return it on that account—because the terms of the document were offensive or insulting to you or the managers?—*A.* Well, the managers requested it to be returned.

"23. Was that the reason you returned it?—*A.* That was the reason I returned it; yes, sir.

"24. Is it not a fact that, instead of being offensive in its character so far as the composition was concerned, it was a document courteously composed, and looking toward the settlement of a great and destructive strike that was then in progress?—*A.* Well, as I said, the document speaks for itself. I considered that the matter was settled then practically."

Some corporations even claim the power of forbidding their servants from exercising their political rights. The Union Pacific Company issued a notice to their *employés* to abstain from all participation in politics.

While I was in Philadelphia an incident happened which also illustrated the independent stand that is taken up by the corporations. A suit was pending before the United States Circuit Court between the Brotherhood of Railway Trainmen and the Philadelphia and Reading Railroad, in which the men sought to have the governing body of the railroad restrained from discharging any of their members where the sole reason for the discharge was their being members of the brotherhood. The Attorney-General of the United

States, conceiving that the public were concerned in the determination of the important question that was thus raised, forwarded to the judge a statement of his views upon the public aspect of the dispute, and sent copies of it to the counsel upon both sides. He stated that he intervened " merely as *amicus curiæ*, and by express leave of the Court." In his paper, which fills two closely printed newspaper columns, he urgently pleads for arbitration as the true means for settling labour disputes.

Whether this interposition of the Attorney-General came within the principle of suggestion by an *amicus curiæ* may be doubted, but one would have expected that the company, from prudential reasons alone, would have shown some respect for this high official, however strongly they combated his opinions. But their leading counsel, an eminent member of the bar, spoke of both the official and his argument in terms of contempt, said that he had committed a grave official impropriety in intervening at all, and added : " I hope it is superfluous to say that neither my clients nor myself care a button about this paper."

The absolute tone of these corporations, and the consciousness of power which it reveals, makes us realize the fact that there is in modern society an industrial rule, as well as a political one, though they operate in different ways, the one directly and the other in a manner more subtle, but not less effectual.

While in Canada we had heard much of what was called Coxey's army, which was then marching through the United States, and which even threatened, it was said, to come on to Canada if it did not get justice in America. By the time that I had reached Washington the movement had met with an inglorious end, and I found people indisposed to say much about it, and apparently regarding it as beneath serious attention. Yet the novelty of the project, and the proportions that it had at one time assumed, entitle it to notice by any one inquiring into social phenomena, the more especially as its leading idea was to compel the Government to find work for every one who said that he wanted it. There had been great industrial depression, and honest men in many parts of the Union found it difficult to get employment. Jacob Slecher Coxey, of Massilon, Ohio, had always sympathised with the poor, though he himself fully reached the old English test of being a substantial man in that he kept not only a gig, but a carriage, owned a number of horses, and also possessed "a stone quarry." He may be classed as one of those who have greatness thrust upon them, for at first his simple idea was to walk to Washington at the head of the unemployed, and to require the Federal Government to provide for them. His plan for finding work was as simple as his original idea. The national debt was to be repudiated and the country relieved of paying the interest on the bonds, and then greenbacks to the value of $500,000,000 were to be issued, which were to be loaned to the municipalities to be spent upon labour in making internal improvements, the municipalities giving bonds to the central Government for the advance, which were ultimately to be paid, and not repudiated. In support of this project there were at one time 7,250 men marching on Washington from different parts of the Union. As for Coxey himself, his objects were as harmless as could be those of any one advancing such a silly proposal. But no sooner was the idea announced, than the unfortunate and the idle and the restless of all districts hailed it with a ready response, and would doubtless have risen in vast numbers had any success attended the pioneers. As it was, separate detachments of the "Commonweal Army" marched from Ohio, from San Francisco, from Los Angeles, and from Rhode Island, thus representing the length and breadth of the Union. Coxey was all for peaceable means, but, as is always the case in such movements, hardier men soon came to the front. The leader of one division thus addressed a crowd of 2,000 labourers: "My comrades, we may have trouble before we reach Washington. Some of us may never return. It may be you; it may be me. All revolutions have received a baptism of blood, and I don't expect this one will be an exception to the rule." Another general— for they had military designations—spoke thus: "We will go right up to the Capitol and demand our rights, and we will insist upon them in spite of Mr. Cleveland or of any one else. If we get there and find Coxey's army has been prevented from entering Washington, we will join him and help him to get his rights, even if we have to fight for them." Parties left from most cities in the Union to join the army. When I was in Boston they told me that a contingent had gone from that staid and intellectual city. Inspiring songs, as well as fiery eloquence, were not wanting. One was modelled after the address of Bruce to his army, and began thus:

> Tramps who have with Coxey bled!
> Tramps whom Browne and Frye have led,
> Welcome to your gory bed
> Or glorious victory.
>
> Now's the day and now's the hour,
> See the front of battle lour,
> See your foe—"the money power,"
> Resolved to make you slaves.

Necessarily, a large number of the army were of the ordinary, hapless class of tramps. Mr. Morton, the Secretary of Agriculture for the United States, thus describes them in *The North American Review*: "If a life history of each individual of the 'Coxey Army' could be truthfully written, it would show, no doubt, that, with a few honourable exceptions, the multitude now following the reincarnation of John Lowism, Greenbackism, and all the other isms of ancient and modern times have, each one of them, paid out, from birth to date, more money for tobacco, whisky, and beer than for clothing, education, taxes, and food, all put together." But the most scathing description of the Coxeyites comes from the Superintendent of the New

York Police Department, that was undergoing such an exposure just about this time. He says: "The men who compose these so-called armies are, so far as I can learn, what are ordinarily called tramps—that is, they are men who do not earn and have not earned a living and supported themselves. They have banded together —a menace to the communities in which they were— and they propose to demand that Congress pass certain laws. Their avowed object is to assemble in front of the Capitol in Washington, and there, by their presence and numbers, to so intimidate the Congress of the United States as to force that body to pass certain laws dictated by them. Think of it for a moment. These idle, useless dregs of humanity—too lazy to work, too miserably inefficient to earn a living—intend to 'demand' that Congress shall pass laws at their dictation. 'Demand,' that is the word they use in their so-called proclamations. . . . It is easily understood that a tramp, to whom all places are alike, would find a pleasurable excitement in the march. He is supported as he walks, which is all he cares for. To him, the army movement is a vast picnic. . . . I think this movement is the most dangerous this country has seen since the civil war. . . . The movement is illegal, un-American, and a disgrace, and should have been stopped long ago."

This officer's indignation against the army of tramps gives colour to the view that I have before adverted to, that the Americans tolerate some evils to be protected against others—excuse what they term "boodling" for the sake of protection against violence. Ex-Senator Ingalls, who is well known in America, declared that the Coxeyites were merely the Jack Cade men of our time, trying to delude people "with the same vagaries, chimeras, nostrums, and panaceas that have cheated mankind since the flood, and will perhaps continue to cheat them till the final conflagration."

But the army of tramps was not without its defenders. The Socialist and Labour journals stood by them, as indeed their objects were similar, though the method of the tramps was new. The Coxey petition to Congress demanded that the State should provide farms and factories for the unemployed; should affirm the right of every one to have work; should find immediate employment for the unemployed; should abolish all interest-bearing bonds and nationalize the railroads, mines, and telegraphs. "The evils of murderous competition and the supplanting of manual labour by machinery" were denounced. An extract from a lecture given at the "Church of Humanity," Philadelphia, may be taken as an example of some of the panegyrics which the Populist party bestowed upon the followers of Coxey:

"What is there in it? There is this in it: It will accomplish more than the war of the Revolution; that war achieved the political freedom of the country, this movement is the beginning of the industrial freedom of the people. What is there in it? There is this in it: An army armed only with protests against wrong, equipped only with the weapons of justice, equity, and mercy, goes forth to win victories that sword and bayonet, and artillery of war, have never yet won. There is this in it: It marks an epochal period—the dawn of a brighter day, the foreshadowing, if not the commencement, of the reign of peace and righteousness. . . . With all reverence for Christ and all due respect to Coxey, I claim that they both belong to the class which the big firm that owns the universe—the firm of Mammon, Capitalism, Religio-Philosophia, Christiano-Politico, Robbery, and his harlot mistress Charity, modern Pontius Pilate and Company — denounces."

However, on they marched. As for food, they billeted themselves upon the farmers and townships as they passed along. No violence was used for this purpose as indeed none was needed, for the scared people were only too glad to pay the cost of passing them on to another district. Unlawful billeting was one of the grievances that helped to bring about the Revolution in England.

P

The Constitution of America is careful to provide that no soldier shall in time of peace be quartered upon any one without his consent, nor in time of war except according to law. But the States' Governments were unable to vindicate their law; indeed they were unable, or not ready, to do anything to meet the emergency. When occasion offered the Coxeyites captured trains, and so sped along their way; once 500 of them were brought 400 miles in this manner. In Montana they seized a train and fought the United States' marshals, wounding some and ultimately capturing them all and holding them as prisoners. In Indiana they captured another train, and, with revolver at the engine-driver's head, made him carry them along.

But when all this came to be known and the weakness of the States' Governments was apparent, the strong man at the head of the Federal Executive soon took steps to protect the public. The United States troops recaptured the trains, and, as Coxey was hurrying on with his division to Washington, arrangements were quickly made to confront him, and to show the other contingents that nothing was to be gained even if they did reach the capital. The army approached the city and camped a few miles out, while Mr. Coxey in his carriage, with his daughter mounted upon a cream-coloured pony, and representing the "Goddess of Peace," advanced to interview the President. Unfortunately, in going up to the White House, he walked across a grass plot, in contravention of the city bye-laws, and he was thereupon immediately seized, and, upon conviction, sent to prison for twenty days. The military broke up the camps in the neighbourhood of the capital. The only blood shed was that of a poor cat that, with the instincts of its kind, clung to the vehicle it had travelled in. Some of the army were sent to the Maryland House of Correction, but most were hurried back to the different States that they had come from.

This movement showed the great restlessness that was pervading the people. More fully developed or less firmly met, it meant a general rising of the unfortunate and the discontented. Most certainly the movement ought to have been stopped in each State at the start, as the project to overawe the Government at Washington was illegal and destructive of the public peace. But the social conditions of America are too stable to be shaken by such a demonstration. Reference has been made in connection with it to the march of the Marseillais upon Paris at the beginning of the Revolution. But the condition of the two countries was different. That march ended in terror, this one in laughter. Still, like the strike riots, it showed the weakness of the local Governments and the need of a strong central power, or, at least, some power, to protect the public; for the State fails in its primary function if it does not protect its people from invasions, whether internal or external. The Constitution declares one of its chief objects to be " to ensure domestic tranquillity."

The same value of the Central Government was shown in dealing with the, at one time portentous, but now nearly forgotten, plague of Mormonism. A firm administration of the law, aided by any special legislation that the novel nature of the evil required, would soon have suppressed the Mormons, at least as a separate body with a distinctive creed. But no such wholesome remedy was available. In Missouri and at Nauvoo they were merely handed over to a mob violence that cemented them into a band of martyrs. At last after they had taken refuge at the Salt Lake, where the United States had power, wise legislation backed by bayonets soon limited the evil and weakened its spell.

Thus, in dealing with the strike-wars and with social difficulties, such as Mormonism and Coxeyism, the weakness of the States' Governments and the power of the Federal executive was shown. It gives matter for reflection to us in Australia, who hope soon to be framing our Federal Constitution. In Canada the militia is in the hands of the Dominion Government, and is ordered from place to place at its direction. When we drafted a bill for the Federal Government of Australia at Sydney, in 1891, the Constitution of the United States was simply copied. The clause ran: "The commonwealth (of Australia) shall protect every State against invasion, and on the application of the Executive Government of a State, against domestic violence."

The Populist party in America, like the Independent Labour party in England, represents that discontent of the people, which is often the parent of progress. It disclaims allegiance to both the great political parties, and adopts a large portion of the Socialist creed, while disavowing its ultimate design. Its direct power in general politics is small (though it claims to be yearly growing in numbers), and is lessened by the fact, which has been before referred to, that its immediate objects are influenced by the varying local feelings of the vast continent that it operates over. In one State the crying need of the hour is held to be the nationalization of the land; in another, that of railways; in a third, the reform of the currency on a silver basis. In a few States they have been able to exercise a determining influence, as in the election of the Governor of Illinois, whose pardon of the dynamitarders I have referred to. In Kansas they have carried the government, and not with the best results, if one may credit the vigorous denunciation of their rule by a prominent ex-Senator, that I read in the *New York Herald*. He says: "If the sworn, specified, detailed, and documentary accusations of their own leaders are to be believed, the Populist administration in Kansas has been the most profligate, debased, degraded, and disgraceful Government ever known in any State in the Union. Before it Tammany pales its ineffectual fires." Its influence is chiefly manifested in its effect upon the action of the two governing political parties, each of whom are ready to enlarge their platform so as to give standing place to as many Populists as they can secure. The passing of the income tax in 1894 was claimed as their victory, and opponents of the measure admit that neither the Republican nor Democratic party really desired it. In one respect, certainly, it bears the impress of the Socialist creed.

In all the Socialist and Populist platform, both in England and in America, an income tax, exempting smaller incomes and increasing progressively towards the extinction of the larger ones, stands prominent among the immediate measures of relief that are claimed. And this, not for financial, but for political objects, as an apt and ready means of redressing the inequalities of fortune, in so far as preventing accumulation can do it. One of the features of an income tax that enables us to judge whether it is a true tax or not is its limit of exemption. Its limit is its principle. As Tom Paine in his "Rights of Man" says, "If a nation choose to pay ten times more taxes than it has occasion for, it has a right to do so; and so long as the majority do not impose conditions upon the minority different from what they impose on themselves, though there may be much error, there is no injustice." This tax exempted, among other objects, all whose income was less than $4,000, or £800, a year; that is, it was made to apply to only some 86,000 people out of 70,000,000 in the United States. Thus out of every 1,000 people in America 999 imposed the tax and one paid it. The one who paid had practically no voice in imposing it. The 999 who imposed did not pay it. The vast mountains of wealth accumulated in America afford some excuse for such taxation, till one considers not so much the case of those who pay as that of those who do not. It is right to exempt from such a tax the small incomes of the poorer classes, but it must be demoralising to the sense of citizenship and the responsibility that ought to accompany the taxing power, for the mass of the people to levy imposts, that leave themselves untouched, upon a handful of citizens who for this purpose are practically disfranchised. The only principle of taxation and representation is discarded. Those who pay have no representation, and those who have all the representation do not pay.

I have before referred to the fact that the Constitution of the United States rests upon the written document which all the States agreed to in convention, and which can be altered only by the same authority acting in the manner the Constitution prescribes. The Supreme Court possesses the transcendent power of declaring, when appealed to in due course of law, whether any Act, either of Congress or of a State Legislature, is or is not contrary to the provisions of the fundamental compact. If it is, it is void, as it is forbidden by the voice of the whole people, who are supreme over all laws and constitutions. This, indeed, is a transcendent power for nine or ten lawyers sitting in their chamber to exercise. There is nothing like it in England. No Court there could venture to declare any Act of Parliament bad. They must accept it, whatever it is. Some of the politicians regard the Supreme Court with jealousy, and I saw it stated in publications of weight that this feeling was increasing. But if dissatisfaction is to be, it ought to be directed against the Constitution. There it is—"a piece of paper," as the malcontents express it. The Court only acts under it in maintaining, until altered by the whole people, rules that the whole people have laid down. The Court, when appealed to, cannot help itself. It is the distinguishing feature of the judiciary that it never acts till it is invoked; once invoked, it must act. With the Legislature it is just the other way. It moves when and how it pleases, and, if it do not like, will not move at all, however much it may be importuned to do so. But there has been all along in America a feeling of irritation with some against this paramount control of the Court. As long ago as the time of General Jackson, we read that that hero used to chafe under the rulings of Chief Justice Marshall, the eminent jurist, and when he thought that he had checkmated him by some of his strong executive acts, would exclaim, "We will see now what John Marshall can say to that."

The Supreme Court has since been appealed to, and after hearing powerful arguments upon both sides from leading members of the bar, who seem to have presented the question in every aspect, has decided—by, however, only five judges to four—that the income tax law is void because it imposes a class tax upon a few, while the Constitution requires that all direct taxes shall be uniformly borne by the whole people. It would require an intimate knowledge of political conditions in America to estimate truly all the results of this momentous decision, by which the will of President, Senate, House, and people is set aside. It is a striking illustration of the power of that judicial authority in the Constitution which has so often engaged the attention of Englishmen. It will give a plausible topic to those who object to the control of the Court and asperse its judges as being under the domination of capital.

There is a good deal of this feeling with regard to the States courts. It surprises a stranger, and that not agreeably, to see the tone adopted towards them by men who cannot be classed as mere demagogues. When I was in Massachusetts the address of the candidate for Hampden county to the electors induced me to look at some papers that he had shortly before published. In one he thus describes the judiciary of his country: "The courts of law—no longer courts of justice—have become the instruments of tyranny and oppression, controlled by the rich and manipulated by them for the subjection of working men. The courts of law are now subjects of contempt to the people, so much so, that if all who are guilty of this offence were to be punished, there would be none left to inflict the punishment; because no one, not even the law makers or the law administrators themselves, with their owners — the wealthy—can have any other feeling than contempt for such contemptuous objects as these courts of law have become."

One would think that this must be the utterance of a mere ranter. The writer, however, was a well-known business man, and had been assistant editor of a reputable paper. We would stand amazed to hear such language applied to the judges in England. They, no doubt, have an advantage in the separation of the two branches of the legal profession. The counsel, from whom the judges are selected, have no direct personal relations with any great client corporations. No one can be identified as having been all his professional life the trusted attorney of any of them. They all stand upon a high personal level in doing their professional work. But the judges of the higher courts in America, though just as honourable as their English brethren, can be more plausibly attacked, as the custom of their country does not allow that strict professional demarcation that provides a class of select men for the position of judge.

The Supreme Court of the United States, sitting at Washington, justifies the expectations that one forms of it as the most powerful judicial tribunal in the world. The English judicial committee of the Privy Council has a jurisdiction over an even greater area, but only between subjects. That at Washington adjudicates between States. The judges display a broad grasp of principle, as well as great learning. Their integrity is such as we are accustomed to in English judges, their manner judicial. They sit only from twelve o'clock to three o'clock, and devote the rest of the day to considering their judgments, which they always write out at length, giving generally a full history of the facts of each case. All the previous proceedings in the causes are printed in pamphlet form before the argument comes on. The statement for each side contains full details of the grounds of appeal and the authorities relied upon, and an elaborate and often forcible epitome of the reasoning that counsel is going to submit orally. This appears to lessen the importance of the argument itself in ordinary cases. At least, in two or three cases which

I heard there was not that interchange of thought between the bench and the bar that sometimes takes place in England during arguments. But the Court was a pattern for calm judicial attention to all that was brought before it. It has become the practice for the local advocates in the tribunals, whose decisions are appealed against, to attend the Supreme Court and argue their own cases, not confiding them to the management of the bar at Washington, as was the habit in earlier days when travelling was more difficult. This sometimes detracts from the importance of the legal debate. It has become the practice not to give the arguments at all in the authorised reports, unless in special cases. In the older English reports the arguments at the hearing used to be fully given, but the Transcript of Record in each case here, and the written judgment, give all that can be wanted, both of the facts and of the arguments.

During my stay I had not the opportunity of hearing any of the leaders of the American bar, but they are known by their reputation to English lawyers everywhere. The arguments upon both sides of the income tax case are said to be worth studying as part of the literature upon the subject of taxation. The professional emoluments of the prominent men appear to be larger even than those of leaders in England. In both countries the fiction that the advocate's reward is honorary, or at least to be only according to a fixed professional scale, belongs now only to the forgotten past. He now claims whatever price his position can command. It is said that Lord Mansfield, when he had been sent a retaining fee of 1,000 guineas, returned 995, stating that the professional fee was five guineas. No barrister would be expected to do this now upon either side of the Atlantic. The *honorarium* sometimes paid to American counsel appears to be very high. The papers state that one eminent lawyer received a fee of close upon £1,000 for advising a railway company as to the proper wording of a notice to warn the public at a crossing. The old notice was " Beware of engines and cars," and in some actions against the company this was alleged to be insufficient. Counsel advised them to paint up in future, "Railway crossing. Stop, look, and listen," and was paid that handsome fee for a suggestion that, simple though it seems, may save many an adverse judgment. I have given some particulars about the Supreme Court as, owing to its unique power over the Government, it may be said to be the highest political authority in the Union.

The position of women forms an important branch of any inquiry into Socialism and labour subjects, but so much has been written upon it by those who had better means of observation than I had, that I will only refer to some points that I find suggested in my notes. America is, as has been said, the land of fearless experiment. For a century past the presumption there has been in favour of any new idea, at least to the extent of giving it a trial, and society has been so young and strong that it could afford to try experiments. Like a young man, it could afford to take liberties that would be dangerous for an older constitution. But experience reveals weak points in many notions that look plausible at first. And America is in the position of having tried to some extent and got experience upon proposals that older communities are only talking about or just beginning to take up. In time they will get their own experience.

This applies to the woman question. Years ago in America the liberation of woman was announced; politically it was promised, socially it was commenced. Experience seems to be defining the practical scope of this movement. In so far as it opens to women new and suitable means of earning a living, it works well and all approve of it. Bolder experiments have not been followed by satisfactory results. State school teaching is almost entirely in their hands, and a large proportion of clerical work. In the Supreme Court at Washington a female clerk came upon the bench and arranged the books and papers for the judges before they took their seats. They do a good deal of reporter's work, both for the press generally and officially for the Court. This leads to inconvenience when a case of an offensive nature has to be dealt with. The papers mentioned one instance where the official reporter informed the Court that she declined to take the next case owing to its disagreeable character. The judge emphatically lauded her resolution, and ordered a man to be sent for. The respect that Americans show to women and their readiness to assist them, is one of the most pleasing features in the national character. There are nearly 1,000 women who live by writing for the papers in the States. Three hundred and thirty are reported to be dentists. Over 200 women are lawyers, some of whom practise in court. In one case the counsel for the plaintiff were a lady, who was leader in the cause, with her husband as her junior. Barristers, who understand the subordinate position that a junior counsel occupies and how liable he is to be snubbed by his leader, may think that this is a mere story, but I can assure them that it is a fact. It was, however, quite exceptional, and caused only laughter. Women will never do much as advocates in court. Some women preach in America, as elsewhere. There are said to be 200 female ministers who disregard the injunction of St. Paul. I heard one, but she was not, I think, one of the leading preachers. She was ladylike in her manner, and faultlessly dressed, and desired to prove that there was no such thing as the transmission of qualities or vices from parent to child. She cited several texts from the Bible in support of her view; especially the statement that "God is your Father." The congregation listened attentively, and appeared to be satisfied. There are as many as 4,555 female doctors in the States, but they do not appear to have succeeded in doing as much practical work as it was expected they would. Even with women they do not seem to be largely successful. A leading doctor told me that he had often advised his lady patients to go to one of their own sex, but that he could not overcome their disinclination to do so. When a married lady follows the profession, if she has children, she has to engage another lady to take charge of them. I met an instance of this. Generally, it may be concluded, that what work women can do as well as men—or better, as they do some things—they will hold their own in; but both they and the public will get tired of their trying to do what they can only do at a disadvantage.

The women's suffrage movement is an instance of how experience tells upon the public mind. A generation ago its prospects looked brighter in the United States than they do now. It was the watchword then, never to rest till the suffrage had been secured, and also a woman elected President of the United States. America has the advantage of being able to try experiments in one or more of its numerous States, while the rest look on and take note of them. Female suffrage has been tried in Wyoming, Washington, Colorado, and Utah, where, strangely enough, the women supported polygamy by their votes. In Colorado, their victory was owing to the Populist party carrying that State. The friends of the movement do not claim that it has achieved any great results in those States. Women who have homes and children do not vote at all. The Governor of Colorado, who supports it, says: "It must be admitted that the effect which equal suffrage will produce upon the States and nation is a matter of conjecture. In Utah, the right of women to vote under the Territorial laws did not injuriously affect polygamy. . . . In Wyoming and Washington, to my knowledge, no extraordinary progress has been made that can be traced to female suffrage; and in Colorado, sufficient time has not elapsed to speak understandingly of the result. Certainly there is little hope of the future, unless women, admitted to the suffrage, acquaint themselves more thoroughly than men with political affairs." The Socialist and Labour parties in England were all for "women's suffrage and the absolute equality of woman with man in all things." But some of the most advanced platforms in America, such as those of St. Louis and of

Omaha, reject it. In Nebraska, several years ago, the Legislature passed an Act submitting the question to a convention of the people, and the National Women's Suffrage of the Union had a special gathering in Omaha, the capital of the State, and worked vigorously to secure a favourable vote. But out of nearly 90,000 who polled, only 25,756 declared for it. The Dominion Parliament in Canada rejected the proposal for woman's suffrage last year by 105 votes to 47. In New York the Constitutional Convention rejected it, and Bishop Doane, of Albany, who is a representative man with his party, declared that he was "sick and tired of the way in which the talk of woman's vocation fills the air." Certainly one of the city election fights would not be a wholesome exercise for any woman to join in. I may mention that, in New Zealand, the Bill to admit women as members of Parliament was carried in the House of Representatives in 1894 by the casting vote of the Speaker; but in 1895 it was rejected by 35 votes to 26, though the example of Colorado with its three lady legislators was invoked. In intellectual Boston, where there are a great number of talented women, who make their usefulness felt in directions many and various, I was told by some advanced men that women desired the right of suffrage, not that they cared to vote, but as a tribute to and recognition of the worth and standing of woman. The idea seemed to be that women were too good and valuable to be confined to merely the domestic sphere. Some in America, and more in England, supported female suffrage from a point of view that was quite different to that commonly taken. More or less directly expressed, their creed was this: Now that you have got manhood suffrage, you may just as well get the other, too. If one man is as good and better than another, a woman is at least as good as a man. Either they will do nothing in politics or do some good, so it will be either no change or a change slightly for the better. Their reasoning is like that which Dr. Johnson says makes many of the utterly poor marry. "I cannot be worse off than I am, so I'll e'en take Peggy."

One does not hear or see so much of the New Woman in America as in some other lands. At Philadelphia I was present at a meeting of a women's association there, which was attended by over 200 ladies. The president gave an address, and speeches were made, but the topics and their manner of treatment were such as, according to old ideas, came quite within woman's province. At Boston there appeared to be much intellectual activity among the ladies of the city, which, however, expended itself upon the old lines of woman's usefulness. When I was at Washington, upon a festive occasion, one of the President's Ministers responded to the toast of the President's wife, and, while justly lauding that lady's virtues, emphatically declared that her sphere was the drawing-room of the White House, where her rule was supreme. This seemed to be the tone of much of American society. It is curious to note that at Chicago a city law was proposed prohibiting women from wearing leggings and short dresses. But the age is one of new ideas, and for giving new ideas a trial. Woman's rights may be fated to come, and fated also to bring some unexpected consequences in their train. If it were to be a reality women would govern the country, as there are always, in any given locality, more women available for voting than men. In small, young communities, surrounded by fertile land, experiments may be tried with impunity. They can live with any Government or no Government. But in old, densely populated countries woman suffrage would in time force a reconsideration of the suffrage question as a whole, while in the graver periods of national life, as when the arbitrament of arms is appealed to, it would necessarily be brushed aside. No female votes would have stopped the Germans from springing on France in 1870. Not all the women's votes in America would have stayed the men from crushing the South in the civil war. The Americans have a phrase which declares that behind every ballot is a bullet.

The Commissioner of Labour has given special attention to the task of ascertaining the condition of the working women in the large cities of the United States. One volume of his interesting reports, which contains over 630 pages, is wholly devoted to this subject. The inquiry was conducted almost entirely by women, and no less than 17,427 workwomen were separately met and questioned as to their condition. Particulars are given from twenty-one great cities. In the more crowded of these, things appear to be no better than they are in England; in some cases not as good. The work-girls of Boston are declared to be intellectual in their tastes. They attend lectures and oratorios, and contribute to the magazines. They are wise indeed if they understand truly "the dignity of labour," as the phrase was in bygone days, and are not raised above it by a little book-learning. Burns, after he had written verses that will live as long as the language, used to boast that he could still earn his bread at the plough, and drive as straight a furrow as any man in Scotland. In a cigarette factory in Richmond an excellent library is provided for the *employés*. But the American girls, like most other girls in our time, object to household service, and prefer in San Francisco to work at the benches of a cigar factory side by side with Chinese. A strict moral tone pervades these reports. When, in dealing with the moral character of the workwomen, a reference is made to men who lead loose lives, they are designated with a tone of reprobation that is not often found in official reports.

The great facility for obtaining divorce that exists in many States of the Union is in accordance with the Socialistic sentiment, though it did not originate with the desire to sanction the view of any new creed, but simply from a natural longing of men and women for freedom from restraint. In the end this looseness must impair the position of women. A man can better afford to go on changing his wives than a woman can to go on changing her husbands. The evils growing out of the prevailing laxity, and the differences between the marriage laws of the States, were so great that in 1887 an Act was passed by Congress appropriating money to enable the Commissioner of Labour to make full inquiries into the subject of marriage and divorce, and to report to Congress. The result was a most searching investigation under the direction of that officer, and a report that gives complete information as regards America, and an accurate summary of the marriage laws and statistics of other countries. It is published in the form of a bulky volume of 1,074 pages. It shows that in twenty years 328,716 divorces were granted in the United States. The records of the courts were searched, and the causes upon which divorces were granted are taken from the plaints in ninety-nine cases. They are often so trivial that it only amounts to the wife being tired of her husband, or the husband of his wife. These are some of them.

"Plaintiff alleges that the defendant does not wash himself, thereby inflicting upon plaintiff great mental anguish."

"When defendant suffers financial loss he lays it to plaintiff and censures her in bitter terms. He treats her as a child, claiming the right to do so because of his age and sex."

"Plaintiff says that she is subject to sick headaches that grow worse when she smells tobacco. Defendant uses tobacco and thus aggravates her headache."

Divorce granted because husband enlisted in the navy.

From plaintiff's testimony: "During our whole married life my husband has never offered to take me out riding. This has been a source of great mental suffering and injury."

"Defendant was cruel in this. He caused a letter to be written saying he was dead. Plaintiff ordered a mourning garb and grieved a long time, but at last learned that the letter was a fraud and that defendant was not dead."

"Plaintiff says defendant will not work during the week, but on Sundays he puts on his old clothes and works hard all day, which conduct sorely grieves the plaintiff." Upon grounds such as these divorce was given. The report mentions that in the State of Utah, the divorces granted were as follows: In 1874, 149; in 1876, 709; in 1877, 914; in 1878, 298; in 1879, 122. The fact being that in 1876 and 1877 the divorce lawyers in the eastern cities used the State as a handy place for working the "divorce mill," which caused legislation to be passed, checking the practice. Such a travesty of marriage and the divorce jurisdiction excites the indignation of all thoughtful Americans, and the experience of loose marriage laws is teaching the nation a lesson, the effect of which is seen in a gradually increasing stringency of the legislation upon the subject. Some influential associations have been formed to assist in promoting a reformation.

The United States have been forced to depart from the attitude of welcome to all strangers that they maintained for the greater part of the century. Immigration has had to be restricted by the State, and the Labour bodies expressly demand the exclusion of foreigners—Canadians are often named—from employment upon public works. A commission had been appointed in Massachusetts to inquire into the question of the unemployed. I met the members of it in Boston, and they appeared to be highly intelligent men, well qualified for the work, and conscientiously anxious to arrive at a just conclusion. I see that they have since presented their report, and in it they say: "It appears to us that the evil of non-employment is in a considerable measure due to ill-responsible, ill-advised, and ill-adapted immigration." Attention is also being called to this difficulty in England. In the colonies we used to assist immigration by State grants of money; but this is stopped now. At one time we were in real danger from a promiscuous immigration of Chinese. As there are 400,000,000 of them quite near to a part of our coast, and we are only 4,000,000, they would soon have swamped us. Two distinct civilisations—and they have a civilisation of their own—cannot exist together. What we learnt of the condition of San Francisco with its Chinese settlement made us the more resolute. While Attorney-General of Victoria I advised my Government that they could lawfully prevent some Chinese, who were aliens, and who claimed the right to land in Melbourne, from disembarking, by virtue of the Queen's prerogative power to prohibit aliens from coming into her dominions. A Chinese who was kept out brought an action and recovered damages in the colony, but we appealed, and after a full argument before the Privy Council, in which I had the honour of taking part, the Court allowed the appeal, and sanctioned, though not in its entireness, the position that we had asserted.

The constitution of California provides that "every citizen may freely speak, write, and publish his sentiments on all subjects." The people of America generally, apart from any specific leave, have long exercised this right. The varieties of religious teaching have ranged from the most orthodox forms of the old churches down to the abuses of Mormonism and the extravagancies of Spiritualism. At a Spiritualist Church, at which there was a considerable congregation, I heard a long sermon, which questioned all material things and raised doubts as to whether we were sitting there at all or not. The press is a wonder. The reviews take place among the first in the world for tone and ability. The daily papers of the great cities surprise one by the union of great merits with faults of tone that jar upon the stranger. Nothing can exceed the enterprise with which news is gathered from every quarter of the globe, and the ability displayed in the editorial columns is often marked. As an instance of enterprise, the report of an interview with an English statesman, which appeared in a Philadelphia paper while I was there, may be referred to. It was published only a few days after the statesman had been seen in England, and consisted of nearly three columns of matter, sent by cable, giving his views as expressed in the course of the conversation upon many matters of great interest, Socialism included. It was accompanied by four different portraits of the gentleman, fairly done on wood blocks. These were respectively entitled: " A. B., the mountaineer, age 23; A. B., the historian, age 42; A. B., the statesman, age 52; A. B., from his latest photograph." One of the ablest arguments that I have seen against the merely materialistic view of life was in a leading article of a New York paper. Yet side by side with valuable matter you have details about people's private affairs or comical references to serious things. Cleverly pointed headings in large striking print attract attention. " Her Bones are Breaking " introduces the details of the case of some young lady, whose name and place of abode is fully given, who is suffering from some peculiar malady. When a murderer who is executed dies penitently, the large heading announces that "He is Jerked to Jesus." Some of those who were plundered by the New York police complained aloud, while others paid quietly. The first were designated in big letters as "Victims who Squeal." We are informed that the Archbishop preached an impressive sermon to such a crowded congregation that a little dog who got in was so squeezed that he could not bark. "Blank *has* the Needle!" in large print is followed by a full account of how the person specified, who lives in such a street, had a needle in his leg for some months after the doctors had thought they had extracted it. Ample details are given concerning the turkey which the President is to have for dinner on Thanksgiving Day; and so on. This peculiarity of tone rather impairs the effect of the really valuable matter in these papers.

The Americans join the frankest condemnation of the evils of their country to the most perfect confidence in it and its future. The papers were teeming with denunciations of the corruption in New York, and also in other great cities. No outside observer would care to use language so strong as comes under his eye every day. It was the same a few years ago when the general politics of the country had certainly got into a bad case. The whole press, from the best reviews downwards, were filled with bitter imprecations against the politicians, and, indeed, against the whole system of the Government of the country. An extract from the *New York Tribune* may be taken as a sample. It describes the then public life of America as an "era of such official corruption and dishonesty, such selfishness and shamelessness, such low aims and base purposes, such grasping avarice and eager over-reaching, such speculating in official information, such bribery, and such barter and sale of offices, and such degradation of all things which the nation has held to be high and holy, and worthy an honest pride, that, to-day, the country hangs its head and holds its nose."

In conversation, too, people will condemn public men and give a bad account of institutions with great frankness. I have given some examples of this in a previous chapter. One is always meeting with it in America. When going over a large State school, where black and white children were taught together, I asked the head mistress if mixing them worked well. "Not at all," she said, "it works badly every way. It is bad for both the blacks and the whites. The parents don't like it, and I have reported that it makes the discipline bad and does harm." "What continues it, then? Why is it not changed?" "Politics," she replied, with a contemptuous smile.

Even when there is no suggestion that anything is wrong one is often surprised at the low tone taken. In an important argument before a Supreme Court judge, the leading counsel is reported as saying: "It was truly said of one of your predecessors, in a tablet upon the wall before us, that 'no influence or interest could touch his integrity or bias his judgment,' and that can happily be said with equal propriety of every one of his successors." An English judge would be rather surprised at such a reference to his integrity. It is something like, though not so marked as, the words of a judge some years ago to the jury in a Californian case, which I take from the shorthand writer's reports. He said : " I have been censured somewhat for keeping you together as I have done, but I hope you do me the credit of believing that I acted conscientiously. By doing so I have guaranteed that no one can insinuate that a bribe was employed to influence your verdict." In the Transcripts of Record in cases before the Supreme Court one meets remarks such as this : " We earnestly insist, while conceding absolute sincerity to the learned justice of the Supreme Court of Florida, that his opinion is wrong."

Yet, while disparaging and severely critical of themselves to themselves, they combat criticism from outside, and when they admit evils it is with the air of men whose position is so strong that they can afford it. Their country is so great that a little depreciation does not matter. And this tone is not without justification. The magnitude of their evils is partly owing to the vastness of their community ; coping with them as they do, shows its strength. A New York merchant, while he gave an ill account of the politicians, yet resented any general bad conclusion, saying that things were improving, that, whatever they might be, they were all patriotic, and whenever there was any real danger for the country the politicians stood as one man for it. A Chicago resident, who had no sympathy with strike-wars, when he heard some hostile comments upon what had happened in his city, disputed the gravity of the whole situation, and declared that the accounts that we read were worked up and exaggerated by the papers. An official who admitted the corruption of their city Governments said that at any rate they were no worse than many of the cities of Canada or England. Some whom I met laughed at the Coxey movement as a joke, and said that no country could have afforded to treat it as lightly as they did. I saw a scathing article in a review, which made specific statements as to corruption in a certain State Government which were rather more striking than usual. I inquired whether I could accept the facts stated as accurate. The editor, however, made little of the matter, and replied that there had been undoubted irregularities, but that, as to the particular article, they always gave their writers free scope to choose their own language.

This patriotic pride in their country, and unwillingness to concede anything against it, at least to the stranger, was illustrated by a story that is related of the experience of the late Chief Justice Coleridge, during his visit to Washington. Walking along the banks of the Potomac with a distinguished American friend, he alluded to the tradition that Washington in his youth was possessed of such athletic vigour that he could throw a dollar from bank to bank over the broad waters of the river, and asked his companion if this was true. The distinguished American replied: "Well, my lord, it is not for me to belittle the father of my country. Whether the hero shot a dollar across the Potomac I could not say, but I do know that he tossed a sovereign across the Atlantic."

Early Liberals had nothing but admiration for America, and they never seem to have thought that it would alter from what it was in their time. One of the most eminent of them declared that there was less to deplore and more to admire in that land than in any country under heaven, not excepting England. The philosophical Mackintosh proclaimed that the authors of her Constitution had constructed a permanent answer to the sophisms and declamations of the detractors of liberty. It is in truth a country where great experiments are freely made, and intelligence gained from them. Serious evils are developed, and are checked, more or less effectually, as soon as the people come to realize them. Mormonism, strike-wars, the domination of wealth, the oppression of corporations, Coxeyism, public corruption, currency crazes—all have tested the strength of the community, which ultimately rests in the discernment and common sense of the people taken as a whole. It is not to be denied that this test will present itself under more serious conditions as the country fills up. America's trial will be more formidable when it is as densely populated as Europe—indeed, its real trial will be then. But as its difficulties increase, its experience accumulates. All flippant or despondent criticism is silenced by the consideration that her cause is the cause of our civilisation. If she fails, it fails. She is leading the way that we all are following. Her dangers are ours, and the safety that she will achieve remains also for us.

Una salus ambobus erit, commune periculum.

I should mention that I got much information from the comprehensive reports of Mr. Carrol D. Wright, the Commissioner of Labour of the United States, whose reputation as an expert in the subjects he deals with is known to us in Australia; from *The Journal of the Knights of Labour*, the "Report on the Chicago Strike" by the United States Strike Commission, "The Reasons for pardoning Fielden, Neebe, and Schwab," by the Governor of Illinois, *The North American Review*, and the press generally.

CHAPTER X.

SOCIALIST LITERATURE.

The literature of Socialism is immense. Like a religion, the new creed has its standard writers on the faith, its popular tracts, plenty of controversial pamphlets, and its Labour Church publications, down to Socialist lessons for children at its Sunday Schools. The official reports of England, the United States, Canada, and the colonies on Labour questions are voluminous and continuous. The Report of the Royal Commission on Labour, that was published in London in 1893-4, represents in several volumes the work of some years, and the thoughtful conclusions of able men, several of whom were experts in the subject with which they were dealing. As is well known, these experts in the end were not able to agree. The majority considered that the State had nearly exhausted its power of legislative cure for industrial ills, and that what was wanted now was better administration of the law. The minority, in a report that ably represented the Socialist view, contended that we had only come to the threshold of State action, that eventually the State must take all into its own hands, and that meantime it must accept the immediate proposals of Socialism as an instalment. There are, in addition, some thirty Blue Books, containing evidence or reports upon industrial questions. In the United States, the Commissioner of Labour publishes elaborate statements on the condition of the people and their industry, which appear to be as accurate as they are comprehensive. He did me the favour of sending me one set, which consisted of four large volumes, containing together 2,764 closely printed pages. To strikes were given 1,172 pages, to railroad labour 888 pages, to the subject of marriage and divorce 1,074. The general condition of working women filled, as I have before mentioned, one volume. Canada had its Commission upon the Relations of Labour and Capital, which sat for several years, and presented a report dealing with the whole subject, and giving the results of their inquiries into forty-one distinct branches of it. It fills seven volumes, and the total number of pages is 4,971. I am indebted to Mr. Griffin, the Parliamentary Librarian at Ottawa, for this useful series. The Massachusetts Bureau of the Statistics of Labour presented in 1894 a comprehensive volume upon "Unemployment"; the report itself occupied 267 pages. It also publishes a "Labour Chronology" for each year, giving the notable labour events for each day of the year. All our colonies have published reports giving information upon every aspect of this vital subject. It is a hopeful sign of our times that such pains are taken at least to throw light upon the state of the wage-earner and his grievances. The whole evidence taken before the Select Committee of the House of Commons in 1825 on the Combination Laws is comprised in one volume of 421 pages, and much of it was directed merely to showing the evils of trade combinations. In earlier times there are no direct accounts, whether official or popular, as to how the poor and the worker lived and died. Historians have to grope to conclusions by inferences from general information.

The general literature of the present phase of Socialism derives its inspiration from the German writers, several of whom were Jews. They showed an insight into the evils of society, and whatever we may think of the different remedies they proposed—for they were not identical—the power they displayed is undoubted. Nor can any one question the ability shown by several of the later writers, many of them belonging to England. My object, however, is not to attempt any digest of these, but to give my impression of the Socialist literature that is based upon their speculations, and is supplied in cheap form to the common reader. What he reads is the matter of immediate importance. He translates the theories of the closet into the maxims of the pavement. What he thinks leads to action.

The supply of this literature is, as has been said, vast. If this knowledge is not freely partaken of, it is not for want of ready access to the tree. The Fabian Society publish a pamphlet containing a list of books to read. It fills thirty-two pages, which enumerate some five hundred chosen books, pamphlets, or reports. There is a Bellamy Library, and a Social Science Series which contains some eighty volumes. The Fabian Essays are read everywhere, and the Fabian Tracts circulate largely in England. They are full of facts and figures, and like other Socialist publications, are not wanting in diagrams and drawings to illustrate in a striking manner the inequalities in the distribution of wealth. Nothing can exceed the cheapness of this light, skirmishing literature of pamphlets, leaflets, songs, stories. A hundred of them can be got for a few pence. " Merrie England," a clever and attractive discourse in favour of Socialism, which fills 206 pages, is sold for one penny.

The most popular of all the Socialist series, and indeed the most effective, are the imaginative sketches, such as Bellamy's " Looking Backward." These sell by the thousand all over the world. They are just what suits the struggling man, for they give in a clever way the sketch of exactly what he wants. Difficulties can be easily veiled by a ready pen in this sort of composition. It is like a skilfully constructed play; the impossible may be plausibly put so as to seem more probable than the possible is if awkwardly related. More than one worker whom I met told me to read

Bellamy, as his book showed just what he looked to. If you want to think the matter out, nothing can be more unsatisfactory than writing of this kind. You never know where you are, when you are standing or when you are swimming. It is like going to the historical novel to verify the facts of history. It certainly has been the method often adopted by great authors in past times, when they wished to be free to speculate as to what they might fancy human life to be in some future unknown age; and it is no more to be subjected to logical criticism than are the pious hopes of the Christian millennium. Yet they have great effect. Their ideal being accepted as a coming reality, its votaries regard the present conditions of life as bad, beyond remedy by any ordinary means, and are thus led to support anything that will destroy existing conditions, and so clear the way for the new era. These sketches have less weight in their own land, America, than at a distance, partly owing to the common sense of the people, sharpened as it has been by experience of quite a variety of similar romances, dealing with all possible subjects, from the currency downwards, and partly perhaps owing to the fact that the prophet gets least honour in his own country. When Henry George published his book it attracted little notice in America. It was only after its popularity abroad that it was taken up at home; and now it has less weight and is more sharply criticised there than in any other land.

In so far as this literature forces attention to the condition of the poor, and to the need of having improved conditions of industry wrought out, it is doing good work, but work that is common to many reformers, though the writers often appear to assume that they are alone in it. The ills of poverty, and the evils that the institution of property develops, have been powerful topics to conjure with from the earliest ages. These they forcibly urge, but not more forcibly than they have often been urged before. They do not want thinking over; they force themselves upon common observation. In none of the Socialist tracts is the apparent injustice of property put in a more striking way than it is by Paley in his Moral and Political Philosophy, where he pictures men as a flock of pigeons surrounding a heap of grain that they have all collected, jealously guarding it for one to gorge or waste, and picking to pieces any hardy or hungry bird that dares to touch it. But he spoils his vivid picture for Socialist use by going on to remark that there must be some very strong reasons in the background that have driven men in all ages to support such an institution.

A full discussion of these publications would add another volume to the long list; but some points that suggest themselves to the man at the bookstall may be noted.

They commonly describe those who have property as robbers and evil-doers, owing to that fact; and the more vehement of them declare that they will take vengeance on the delinquents. Intelligent Socialists disclaim this conclusion, though at the same time it is the natural outcome of their teaching. Some gloomy philosophers have declared that the violent consummation threatened is the necessary result of that teaching. But to condemn individuals for the alleged fault of a system is obviously wrong, and is felt to be so by the man in the street, particularly if he happens to have some small property himself. This tone impairs the practical effect of some of this writing. Then they ascribe all the ills of life to the one cause—Henry George to the private ownership of the land, the rest to the ownership of any property. The one remedy is to remove the cause. But the problem is too complex a one to be really solved in this way; these single exact methods for setting up fallen men are delusive. Human nature, with all its twists and defects, the causes that make a certain proportion of men poor and shiftless under any conditions, the difficulty of unlimited population in the new state, and the loss of freedom that is involved, how to maintain production, energy, inventiveness—on these things little thought is bestowed.

This loss of personal independence is what appals any thinking man who has seen political life as it develops in the management of industrial affairs—for example, in some of the American cities. He cannot reconcile himself to the prospect of having the industry of himself and his family under the direction of a Ward Boss. But such feelings are ignored or only touched lightly. Indeed, some writers appear to quite relish the idea of all being marshalled in the ranks under Collectivist discipline. If they cannot exalt those of low degree, at least they will put down the mighty from their seats. Co-operation, small holding of land, any effort at self-help, nay, thrift itself, is decried. One of the best writers, indeed, puts it thus: "Instead of converting every man into an independent producer, working when he likes and as he likes, we aim at enrolling every able-bodied person directly in the service of the community, for such duties and under such kind of organisation, local or national, as may be suitable to his capacity and social function."

While this is proclaimed, the attempts to grapple with the enormous practical difficulties of working it out are fanciful. When reference is made to that aspect of the subject, a want of knowledge of the wayward ways of men is shown. Thus in a tract dealing with the restoration of the land to the people, the work of a competent author, and published by the English Land Restoration League, the question of how to parcel it out anew, and with the improvements of generations upon it, among the many applicants, is dealt with as quite a simple matter. We read that "each community, each town or parish, should elect its own land board or council to settle the terms upon which each block of land, or each house and its appurtenances, may be assigned in permanent occupation to those who need and have the best claim to them." Those who have had experience of the comparatively easy task of distributing the waste lands of Australia will smile at this.

The enunciation of half-truths marks much of these publications. Thus it is true that the worker often now does not get his fair share of the wealth that he produces, and by some means—co-operation and profit-sharing, systems of progressive wages, or plans known as the "good fellowship" plan, or the "reference rate" plan, first suggest themselves; but let experience, if it can, teach better—a fairer division must be secured for him. But it is not a true representation of the case to display a small square as showing the receipts of labour, and a large one to indicate the profits of capital, and to argue that all that labour does not get goes as a mere oblation to capital. The ability and skill to direct labour is as necessary as labour itself; it is a rare quality, and its services must be rewarded by a share of the produce, or else the mere toiler would labour in vain. When we hear of some new venture in industry failing, it is not for want of labour, but for want of head—because the projector has not been able successfully to judge the conditions of success. The thinker in the office has miscalculated, and muscle and sinew are strained to no purpose.

Again, one finds frequent reference to the people as being oppressed, "exploited," ground down by the "ruling classes." This, again, is not a whole truth. They have had middle-class government in England for over sixty years; household suffrage and the ballot for some thirty; general education, and popular statesmen, continuous attention to social wants by inquiry and legislation. Yet the people are addressed as if they had no voice in the Government, and were ignored in the political world. It is just the same in the Socialist literature of the United States, where the people have had power over their local Governments and over industrial legislation for a century. There, too, the workers are addressed in language such as was used in past times to peoples who were groaning under despotism and looking for a ray of liberty to light their lives. It is so all the world over. The party that aims at absolute power declares there is no freedom until it gets it. In my own province of Victoria the people rule. The Lower House is elected by universal suffrage and the ballot. The members are paid; the Ministries are what the people wish them to be. Education has been free and compulsory for a generation. The Upper House, too, is elective; the ratepayers of the colony being, substantially, the electors. Yet when I was in America I was given a copy of the organ of the American Federation of Labour for July, 1894, which contained a letter from one of our Labour leaders to Mr. Gompers, the President of the American Society. In this letter the Americans are informed that "we in Victoria are cursed with as bad a Government as in any part of the world. It is a Government of men who restrict the franchise of the labourer and increase the franchise of the employer and the wealth-owner." If this condemnation of the institutions of England, the United States, and the colonies be just, it goes to show that popular government, so far, is not a success. At whosoever's door the blame be laid, the fact would remain, and render us doubtful whether its further development might not also produce unexpected evils. But the truth is that this style of writing is not meant to be taken seriously.

While on this point, it is but fair to add that it was not only depreciation of Australia that I saw in the American Labour papers. In the *Journal of the Knights of Labour* for July 26th, 1894, I read "that the railroad men receive twenty-five to thirty per cent. more wages for eight hours of labour than they are paid in this country for ten; and that in Victoria, where these rates prevail, the net income from the roads last year was sufficient to pay all the Federal taxes." Another writer tells us that "Australia, which has the most extensive railroad system in proportion to inhabitants of any country on the face of the globe, has paid for her railways from the earnings of the roads in ten years, and for the last three years has appropriated their net earnings to the support of the Government, reducing national taxation nearly one-half. This has been done with a reduction of freight rates to one-half of the former rates, and the reduction of passenger rates to one-half cent. per mile, or one guinea for a thousand mile ticket. Fellow-citizens, how would you like to be able to ride a thousand miles for five pounds? And to know that the biggest part of that is profit, going to reduce the taxes. It can and will be done, if you will put the people's party in power."

This is good news to us in Australia, but it is news!

Another thing that we learn from this current literature is how rapidly social questions develop in these days. Proposals that a few years ago were disclaimed, are now accepted absolutely as if no one ever could have questioned them. It is not so much a mental process as a social growth. Thus from the Report of the International Trade Unions' Congress in 1888, it appears that the English delegates by a large majority disapproved of the State regulating the hours of labour, and decided "to rely upon their own strength to obtain their freedom."

In 1890 the proposal for an absolute eight hours law was generally disclaimed. The Fabian Society drafted a Bill which provided for a limitation of hours in employments already regulated by the State, and in monopolies and as regards other employments enabling the workers to arrange as they pleased for themselves. Sir Charles Dilke at that time wrote that it must be conceded that the eight hours system was not applicable to all trades. In 1892 Mr. Chamberlain, in his sketch of a Labour programme, said that it would be waste of time to consider it, as there was no evidence that the workers would accept it. But in 1894 scarce a voice was raised in the Trade Unions' Congress for any limitation of a general absolute law, and the Secretary was ousted from his office for voting in Parliament in favour of allowing districts to decide whether the law should be extended to them. The latest Socialist literature declares for an absolute eight hours law.

The effect of new and vast machinery upon the dispossessed workers has often perplexed reflecting men. True, what benefits society is the thing produced, not the work of producing it. Yet if by the continual expansion of machinery the workers are edged out, where will they get wages to buy even the cheap new things? The old way was at least a means of dispersing wages, which now are lost to them, whoever else may gain. The ultimate remedy for this state of things that the Socialist press proposes is simple. When the Government owns everything, and employs everybody, the more machinery the better. Enough will be produced for all; two or three hours' work a day will suffice. But until then, in several leaflets and pamphlets one finds it stoutly contended that we should cease from using machinery extensively and enlarge rather than curtail hand work, the true end to be sought being not production but employment. On the same principle many advocate short hours of labour, not so much to ease the workers as to provide work for the unemployed.

It is an admirable feature of the English Socialist tracts, that they display confidence in the law of their country. There are no such attacks upon the honour and impartiality of their judges as one finds in a similar class of publications in the United States. Upon every needful occasion the Courts are appealed to to vindicate any rights of labour that may be questioned; and their decisions are accepted as honestly declaring what the law is. The Red Van Report records with triumph how, when summoned in the country for obstruction, the Red Vans won in court. "A barrister from London appeared for the defence, instructed by the Hon. Solicitor to the League. The charge of obstruction broke down hopelessly under cross-examination, and the summons was promptly dismissed. After the report of the case appeared in the country papers, nothing more was heard of the other threatened prosecutions."

The Report of the Poplar Labour Electoral League mentions that some question was raised as to the decision of a Police Magistrate regarding street meetings, and that the Home Secretary had been questioned upon the subject in Parliament, and it goes on to say: "'Mr. Asquith said it would of course be presumptuous of them to criticise the exposition of the law. All he had to do was to take the administrative question, and in his opinion the police ought not to interfere with a meeting unless it created a serious obstruction.' The foregoing reply practically establishes the legal right of free speech, provided no obstruction is caused thereby." It is a great quality this Saxon respect for the law. Were it not for it an army would be required to enforce the numerous decrees that daily issue from the English Courts. The only exception to this wholesome tone that I observed was in a paper that claims to be the "Organ of the Social Democracy." It derides the notion that "this capitalist society can be transformed into a co-operative commonweal by the simple process of slipping votes into a ballot-box," and advises the resort to force.

But this respect for law does not extend to the politicians. They are condemned throughout these papers, and general distrust of them expressed, though not in as absolute a manner as is the case in the United States. Even Mr. Gladstone is referred to contemptuously. When they wish to describe an evasive speech, it is declared to be "Gladstonesque." It should be added that some publications that are called Socialist are only charitable. A "Grammar of Socialism," that was said to have a large sale, states merely the religious principle of charity, and ends by referring the reader for all details to Cruden's Concordance of the Bible.

The number of Socialist and Labour newspapers and periodicals is considerable. The *Workman's Times, The Clarion, The Labour Leader*, the *Labour Prophet, Brotherhood, The Church Reformer*, are among these, while the *Torch* represents the Anarchists, and *Shafts*, a monthly magazine, claims to speak for women. "Its editor believes," we read, "that the grand procession through which each individual soul passes in its earthly development culminates in woman, sex being one stage, and feminine the highest and last. It demands an equal standard of morality and an equal measure of justice for both sexes, and throws its influence steadfastly to the upholding of the 'New Woman.'" There are several books of songs "Of the Social Revolution," with or without music, and serial stories in which Nihilists, Secret Society men, and capitalist villains figure. Certain words and phrases, such as Collectivism, Spurious Collectivism, Exploiting, Unsocialism, Incidents of Capitalism, Free competition, Economic struggle, Acosmic warfare, Atomism, are current in all this writing. Sets of questions for candidates and directions how to work Local Government Acts are plentifully supplied.

Some of the papers are translated into other tongues for the use of those who are not familiar with English. The general reader need not be told that the leading Reviews of England and America frequently devote their pages to Socialist discussions. In the year that I was in England over two hundred articles upon such subjects appeared. In the few places where Labour Churches are established, they have Sunday schools for instilling right principles into the children. Outline addresses for the use of teachers are published after the manner of the Orthodox Churches; as for example: "Bees—One bee gathers a little honey. Many gather much and store it. As winter approaches, the workers kill the drones. Will not support those who do not work. All workers share honey." "Children walking in the fields. *Trespassing!* Ground *not* free to all."

"Pigs feeding. Enough for all. But greedy pigs take more than their share. Others must therefore go short." Among the lighter means for scattering the winged words are packets of stamps sold for a trifle "for sticking on letters, papers, books, doors, everywhere." These bear appropriate mottoes, such as "Let civilisation perish if it can bring only ruin to the workers, pomp and luxury, and breed pauperism, degradation, and crime."

The Socialist and Labour literature that the man in the street meets with in the United States is marked by the same essential features as that of older lands; but it has some characteristics of its own. Much of it has a tone of moderation and common sense. The diverse local wants of so vast a territory give some variation to its expression. There is at times a display of erudition and scientific precision in propounding startling theories; also, frequently, the grave humour, and, occasionally, the tendency to "tall talk," which, of old, has been observed in the Americans. Notwithstanding the disturbing element of the foreigner, the political education of the workers is more advanced than in Europe, or even in England. They have gone further in making political experiments, and in some respects have fared worse. This makes the more thoughtful of them sceptical of new proposals for righting directly all social wrongs. The deep-seated distrust of politicians is also, as has been said, an important factor with many.

Before dealing with the popular prints of America a word may be said about the power of the platform there. The press and the platform are institutions that possess many points in common. They both treat subjects with a warmth and colouring that produces an immediate effect and fades with the using. Marked power is in our day displayed by both, but it is of a different kind from that of the solitary thinker who comes first and manufactures what the others afterwards retail to the public. They appeal to the crowd in the street that is always passing along and always changing, and do the daily work of educating this crowd. They come in at the stage when theories have to be reduced to practice and thoughts put into action. More is made of the platform in the United States than in England, certainly more than in the Colonies, and greater use has developed its powers, though some Americans maintain that it has not improved its tone. Lecturing in the States is a paying business and a serious one. In the list of forty-five lectures announced for the season by what is described as "the oldest lecture and amusement bureau in America," the Lyceum of Boston, there is only one announced as humorous. I went to a political meeting of the Republicans in Philadelphia, and was impressed by the ability of the speaking, the vastness and good order of the crowd, and the good style in which everything was carried through. It was held in the Opera House of that city. The gathering was large. Policemen regulated the incoming crowd. The building was filled from the pit to the top galleries. The ample stage was occupied by some two hundred chairs for those who had platform tickets. A semicircle of arm-chairs for the more prominent men occupied the front line. The orchestra discoursed music, national and other, at fit intervals, "God Save the Queen" coming in as part of a general melody. The only ladies that I saw were a few, apparently connected with some of the speakers, who occupied a side box. The greater part of the large audience held little flags of the right party colour, which they waved enthusiastically while they were cheering the orators, and thus produced quite an exhilarating effect. I was much struck by the orderly character—almost the business-like character—of the meeting, and their good-humoured patience. The party of speakers were late in coming in, and the crowded benches were kept in expectancy for some twenty minutes. But there were none of the cat-calls, stamping of feet, or exclamations, humorous or otherwise, that we are accustomed to in England under similar circumstances. All was taken seriously and attentively, relief being afforded at intervals by the music. There was no trace of the "larrikin" or "hoodlum" element. At last the men of the evening appeared, including some of the leaders of the party from adjoining States. They met with a great reception, the whole of the vast audience cheering and waving their flags with an enthusiasm that somewhat surprises a stranger who has heard "the politicians" so ill spoken of. This was a party demonstration, however, and chiefly a middle-class one, and they were supporting the leaders of their cause. The speaking was excellent, but mainly possessed a local interest, as it was directed to demonstrate the wickedness of the Democrats. I gathered that there had been a slight "bolt" from the Republican party previously, for one of the younger spokesmen urgently appealed to the bolters to return to the legitimate state of life, and illustrated the position by some humorous stories drawn from the conditions of married life "out west." The audience cheered, waved, and laughed in a grave manner. This meeting enabled one to realize how effectually the platform can be made a twin worker with the press in influencing the public mind, and when the press reproduces its appeals, it combines the powers of both agencies. It also manifested the strength of the great parties here in all the machinery for working politics. The meetings of the Socialist, Labour, and Anarchist parties were insignificant in comparison. Capital is the power here, too, for both the Republicans and the Democrats spend large sums in such demonstrations.

I will give a few examples from among many that one meets with of the moderate tone that the American Labour organs often take. The constitution of the American Federation of Labour declares its object to be to "secure National Legislation in the interest of the working people, and influence public opinion by peaceful and legal methods in favour of Organised Labour." The President, Mr. Gompers, a well-known advocate of the rights of Labour, says in a paper that he read before the International Labour Congress, "The Trade Unions have deprecated the malevolent and unjust spirit with which they have had to contend in their protests and struggles against the abuse of the Capitalist system; yet while seeking justice they have not permitted their movement to become acrid by a desire for revenge. Their methods were always conservative, their steps evolutionary." The First Nationalist Club of Philadelphia in its declaration of Principles says: "We advocate no sudden or ill-considered changes; we make no war on individuals; we do not censure those who have accumulated immense fortunes simply by carrying to a logical end the false principle on which business is now based." The Journal of the Knights of Labour gives prominence to a sermon that Cardinal Gibbons had just preached, under the heading, "The Cardinal on Labour. Dignity and Rights of Labour. He favours Arbitration." In it the preacher, while laying down that Labour has its rights, declares that "Labour societies have many dangers," and that they are in need of leaders "who will aid the *employés* without infringing upon their employers."

The elaborate preamble to the constitution of the society of the Knights of Labour contains little to which any thinking man will take objection. The American Federationist publishes a paper upon Professor Ely's "Socialism and Social Reform," which disclaims Socialism, and shows that the Professor is not, as is sometimes supposed, a friend of the new system. It says, "The fact is, he holds aloof from the Socialist party, he discredits the scientific basis of Socialism, and he upholds principles in social reform totally at variance with Socialist principles. All this after a patient, sympathetic, and thorough study of the history, methods, and expositions of Socialism as given by Socialists." The Journal of the Knights of Labour also prints, with apparent approval, an argument against Socialism, from which I make an extract:

"The fundamental contradictions in modern society are the result of a failure to recognise and apply the natural law of social justice. The Socialism so eloquently praised will fail to solve the problem, because it proposes to perpetuate in the economic world the errors that have been made in the political world. It proposes to use the political power in the hands of those not prepared by personal fitness to use it honestly or intelligently, to establish equality of economic conditions by legal enactments, regardless of equality of merit. It does not teach that all political and economic betterment, individual or social, is dependent upon the honesty and intelligence with which each member of society uses his own resources. It does not teach that there is no social salvation apart from individual reformation. How is this much-praised Socialism to remedy the evils caused by those who will not work when they can; by those who are viciously or ignorantly dishonest; by those who are intelligent and dishonest; by those who are shirks and slighters of work; by those who are governed by prejudice and evil passions; by those who spend their earnings to satisfy the demands of vice; by those who waste their time in useless repining or indolence? These are the evils to be overcome. All efforts to relieve a person responsible for them from the results of his own acts, to the extent of permitting him to continue in his evil course without suffering the consequences, are a subversion of the requirements of moral and economic law."

The *Commonwealth* is a Socialist paper, the motto of which is "From each according to his ability, to each according to his needs," and it strongly condemns the present industrial system, but in its issue for September, 1894, it writes: "We must not be too hard on the Capitalist. He simply conforms to the system under which we are living. I do not blame the landlord. He also is a product of his age." Lyman

Abbot, while supporting much of the Socialist indictment says: "The just reformer will not condemn these makers of great fortunes. He may even commend their sagacity and their generosity in so using their advantages as to make the public real sharers of their wealth. But he will condemn the system."

It would be hard to collect many such extracts from the Labour papers of England or Europe. Compare with these even the Fabian Essay on "Transition to Social Democracy." It gravely announces that private property has been "convicted of wholesale spoliation, murder, and compulsory prostitution; of plague, pestilence, and famine; battle, murder, and sudden death. This was hardly what had been expected from an institution so highly spoken of." While the American press depicts forcibly the ills of the worker, and supports in part the Socialist proposals, it points rather for the full remedy to some plan of profit-sharing, joined to a general amelioration of the conditions of life.

The Single Taxers have a little literature of their own, of which Henry George's book and pamphlets by various writers in explanation and support of it are the mainstay. It can claim a more select class of readers than the direct Socialist publications attract. There is an exactness and completeness about the Single Tax theory, and also a simplicity, that has a charm for some social scientists, but which bewilders the common man, while it renders the business man and the political man sceptical. And as rent forms only a small part of the income of the propertied classes, any plan that touches it only necessarily seems imperfect to those who desire an all-round change. The ingenuity of Mr. George is undoubted, as also, I may add, is his sincerity and fearlessness. While seeking popular support, he condemns in an outspoken manner many ideas that are dear to the toiler. In addressing a great Populist meeting in Chicago, after denouncing protection as "blackmail," and "under pretence of protecting labour, robbing labour," he continues: "There is no such thing as a real conflict between labour and capital. There is nothing really wrong with the wage system. Competition in itself, so far from being an evil, is that which brings about the largest, widest, and most delicate of co-operation. All that is necessary to give labourers their true earnings, is to make labour free to the element without which labour cannot be exerted—to give to labour access to land."

Single Taxers have their lighter moments too. At the bookstall I got a sheet that showed in nine rough illustrations, with appropriate footnotes, the conversion of a portly clergyman, who must have belonged to the Established Church, if there were an Established Church in America, by a rather starved-looking Single Taxer. He "just drops in" to ask the clergyman if he believes that God made the earth for all His children alike, and upon a ready assent being given to this proposition, he draws on the unsuspecting Churchman, through the remaining eight illustrated stages, to admit that if any one took for himself any portion of the land, he should at least pay the rest its rental value. Says the cleric, "Young man, there is Christianity and sound reason in these ideas. Now, if these crank Single Tax people would devote themselves to something of this sort——" Single Tax Man: "Sir, these are the doctrines that the Single Tax men advocate. Good morning, sir."

Many writers who do not accept Mr. George's theory exclaim against the vast extent of land that is possessed by railway and other companies, the great power over the industry of the country that this ownership confers, and the despotic manner in which it is exercised. They contend for a law that will not abolish the private ownership of freehold, but limit it to what is actually used by the holder. Specially with regard to land, but generally upon the whole question, the position of the great corporations of America and of some wealthy individuals affords not merely the most plausible, but the most real arguments for such controlling legislation over land tenure, as the special conditions of each country may require.

John Bright used to say that no one in England understood the currency question; but in America many believe that they do, and in several States the Socialist energy is mainly turned in that direction. The tracts which discuss this perplexing matter are often equally learned and positive in their statements; all the wrongs of the wage-earner being laid at its door. One of these, published in Minneapolis, is entitled, "Why are we Poor? How the Money Power has made Wage Slaves of the American People." It gives particulars of the value of gold relatively to silver in Greece at the time of Herodotus; among the Romans; in the Arab States in the 7th century; in England in the 12th; France in the 14th, and Japan in the 17th; in Portugal and in Spain. The definitions and descriptions of money and credit, given by Aristotle, Herbert Spencer, Professor Browning Price, Stanley Jevons, Webster, Benjamin Franklin, and several other authorities are given. The intricate legislation of the United States upon the subject is discussed, and the question is asked in large print, "Do you begin to see why we are poor? The People Bonded to Shylock for 30 years." It concludes by declaring that the different Currency Acts ought to be entitled, "Acts to place the Yoke of European Bondage upon the People of the United States," and to provide for the closing down of all the industries of that country. The Populist politician who gave me this pamphlet assured me that the silver question stood first in the social group. In a Socialist book of some consequence, the money power is referred to in this crudite manner: "The Capitol at Washington should be torn up from its double miasm of Potomac catarrhal fever and worse infectious land and real estate rings that have corrupted the moral atmosphere with the sickly effluvia of their lobbies. When the conscript fathers planted the city here it was in the nation's centre. But Rome outgrew the den of the wolf that suckled the king, and was glad to transplant from the Tiber to the more charming shores of the Bosphorus, in a geographical centre of her dominions. It is not an idle fancy, but a stroke of wisdom, with many an argument, and of statesmanship with a mighty following. Already, as at Rome, the hideous money power is settling like an incubus over the city of Washington, Franklin, and Jefferson. Like the scaly boa of Pliny and Suetonius, stealthily crawled within the gate, with recurved fangs and greedy appetite, it coils to spring upon and constrict and swallow the unwary children of this nation."

In the "Socialist Annual," published by the Central Committee of the Socialist Labour Party at Boston, one finds a metaphysical account of the Philosophy of Socialism, dealing with Human Organism, Divine Economy, the Relation of God to Man, Interdependent Relation, and so on. There is a class of readers who like a philosophical style of treatment of the most revolutionary theories. The same number contains attacks upon the political powers of the State of Massachusetts, struck off in the usual lurid colours. It gives part of the speech of one representative who was opposing some vote in the Legislature which it describes as the "Telephone Grab." Many members, it states, quailed under this speech.

The speaker says: "And I warn you that the people's thunderbolts are hot, and that their indignation, when you have to face it, will be fierce and blasting and pitiless. The people are long-enduring, and much-forbearing. Errors of judgment, though wrong be done, they may pardon, but for a betrayal of their trust they will show no mercy. The storm is coming. You can feel in the air, even now, the ominous and portentous stillness that tells of the coming of the storm in its fury, as the people learn of what you propose to do, and wait and watch and listen for your action. Bend your ear to the ground, and you can hear the low thunder of the approaching tempest, before whose mad sweep this Legislature must bow its head."

It has been stated that the public press of America of all parties gives but an ill report of the people's representatives. But the lower down you go in the Socialist line, the fiercer becomes the denunciation of the Government, the judiciary, the politicians. This is the most striking feature in the penny Populist press. That this should be the result, even among a minority of the people of a century of popular government, is subject for thought, more of a grave than a cheerful character. It matters little that these papers may not be of the highest type, and that the people who believe them may not be the wisest of men. And it matters little, too, who is to blame for it—there is the result of the forces that have been at work for a century in a country that is politically the freest in the world, and materially the most happily situated. They think, write, and speak as if they were slaves living under a Government in which they had no voice. All the old complaints of the oppressed against the tyrant reappear. In a pamphlet entitled, "Breakers Ahead," which bears the impress of the Commonwealth Company, New York, the condition of the Federal Executive, the two great parties, and the churches, is painted in the blackest outline. Formal proofs in the shape of affidavits are given of large bribery transactions, and other particulars which one does not care to reproduce are referred to. The remedy is declared to be for the people to take everything into their own hands, to have the right to initiate laws by petition to the President or the Governor of a State, to enact them by direct popular vote, and at any time to dismiss public officers or members of the Legislatures whose conduct has become unsatisfactory. Such ideas are of consequence as showing that as far as this party is concerned, faith in representative government is waning. What they want is a despotic Government—upon their own lines.

President Cleveland has long favoured arbitration as the best means of dealing with Labour difficulties, and his Message to Congress upon the subject some years ago is referred to with approval by the Labour journals —though for the purpose of condemning his action now. He declares that the relations between Labour and Capital are far from satisfactory, and that while the men are sometimes to blame for "causeless and unjustifiable disturbance," the discontent of the employed is largely due to the "grasping and heedless exactions of employers." He recommended the establishment of a State Board of Arbitration, and it was under the legislation that followed upon his suggestion that the Commission which inquired into the Chicago strike was appointed. Its report, which I have before referred to, was claimed by the Labour press as a victory for their side.

The respect paid by the Americans to the platform, and the patient attention that they give to it, may account for the length of the speeches that are made here. When I was in New York the press reported the speech of a Labour leader. It was headed "General Master Workman Sovereign speaks to D A 49," and filled five columns of close print. The speaker does not absolutely endorse the principles of Socialism, but he condemns the evils of the present system unsparingly, and as to the politicians, he says that "there is nowhere in all the murky nooks of the past a lurking monster of depravity whose life parallels the iniquity of our two old parties." (Applause.) He is even more emphatic in his denunciation of Wall Street, the bankers' quarter of New York.

"Wall Street, with its commercial pirates, sordid harlots, and mercenary knaves, who prolonged the rebellion, gambled in the life of the nation, defiled their sacred temples, sold their conscience and their God for gold; and, like the fabled Atlantis, wrote in the blood of careworn widows and innocent babes the song of death on the face of a fair land, as redundant in production as the fabled gardens of Elysium. (Applause.) Wall Street, where a perfidious moneyed oligarchy canonises robbery as business success and legalised fraud as righteous law. Where they clip coupons, gamble in bread, open banks with prayer, and lie to tax assessors. (Applause.) Where they marshal lobbies against Legislatures, convert wealth into interest-bearing bonds, overawe the people with threats of bankruptcy, rob labour through stock gambling and usury, and drive the common people into poverty and crime. Where the great money power puts its iron heel on the neck of labour, and with its icy hand darkens the window in the watch-tower of national hope, and moulds for the future a dungeon of despair, and obscures the last star in the canopy of heaven, which God designed to light the weary pilgrim on his pathway to the tomb. (Applause.)"

Carlyle mentions that he got his earliest encouragement from America. Socialist writers there make frequent use of those passages in which he graphically touches off the evils in the state that most impress them, and some of them even seem to approve of his scornful condemnation of popular government as at present constituted. In the *Commonwealth* we read:

"Thomas Carlyle was a great man. A little acrid, perhaps, but profound in his judgment of men and things. Thomas said some years since: 'England contains twenty-seven millions of people—mostly fools.' If Thomas were alive to-day, and living in America, and reading the election returns, he would murmur gently: 'The United States contain about seventy million people—nearly all of them the most unreasonable idiots in Christendom.' Carlyle said the American people were rushing over Niagara. Wise Carlyle. They are going over the falls, boots and breeches, while the Populists are trying to hold them back by the shoddy fabric of their rotten coat-tails. Let us build a monument to Carlyle."

And a Populist writer in *The National Labour*

Tribune, Pittsburgh, cites with approval this gloomy prophecy "of the eminent Philosopher, Thomas Carlyle":

"The Republic west of us will have its trial period, its darkest of all hours. It is travelling the high-road to that direful day. And this scourge will not come amid famine's horrid stride, nor will it come by ordinary punitive judgments. But it will come as a hiatus in statecraft, a murder bungle in policy. It will be when health is intact, crops abundant, and the munificent hand open. Then so-called statesmen will cry 'over-production,' the people will go to the ballot-box amid hunger and destitution (but surrounded by the glitter of self-rule), and will ratify (by their ballots) the monstrous falsehood (over-production) uttered by misstatesmen and vindicated by the same ballot; the infamous lie (over-production) will be thrown upon the breeze by servile editors through a corrupt press. And this brings ruin upon his country, serfdom upon himself, and oppression upon his children."

In this literature one comes upon certain sayings of remarkable men that are often referred to. Mill, Carlyle, Ruskin, Cairnes, Herbert Spencer, and even Bismarck are cited when they express some opinion that fits in with the writer's view, though their authority upon every other point is defied.

There are twenty-one leading Socialist or Populist newspapers in America, several organs of the German Socialists, some of the destructive wing of the Anarchists, in addition to the pamphlet literature that I have been referring to. The American sense of humour is not wanting in these. Even when they are most indignant, the writers never appear to be so much in earnest that they cannot have a joke about it. Thus you will have a mock trial of the monopolist reported, in which Colonel So-and-so for the people brings a crushing case against the defendant, and General Blank says what little can be said for him. The judge—this time a just one—charges the "ladies and gentlemen of the jury" in a manner that leaves little hope of escape for the criminal. If they convict they are instructed, according to the law in their State, to fix the punishment, "which must include a restoration of the twenty-one billion dollars or more of which the robber has robbed the people." When heavy taxation of land was urged years ago, it was in this fashion: "Tax these lands till they perspire great clots of coin; tax them till the owner shall so groan beneath his weight of land that the grave shall be a welcome resting-place from his burthens; tax them for a school-house upon every mile square, though there be not a shepherd's tow-headed urchin within ten miles of the site. Open through these tracts great broad highways, and build, wherever gulch or stream or rivulet crosses them, splendid bridges of cut granite. Let the Legislature tax them, and the country supervisors tax them, and the township and village authorities tax them."

The first great strike on record is thus described in the Journal of the Knights of Labour: "The first strike on record was led by an agitator named Moses, and took place in Egypt over three thousand years ago. This Moses was a Jew, and it is a singular fact that this race has furnished all the great Socialists. Moses was not only an agitator and leader of strikes, but he encouraged the strikers to borrow a lot of gold and jewellery, which was never returned to the owners; and he caused the death of a number of deputy marshals and 'Pinkertons' by enticing them into the dangerous fold of the Red Sea." One of the most popular of the ephemeral class of writings is entitled, "The Dogs and the Fleas," by "One of the Dogs," which is announced as an entirely new departure in Reform Literature. It is declared by the Socialist press to be a "vitriolic, side-splitting satire" on society, and the Populist Governor of Illinois recommends it as "one of the most striking books of the period." But its chief recommendation to the American mind appears to be its fun.

The press here freely opens its columns to adverse criticism, much in the same way as in conversation people will admit great evils to exist in their country, with the air of men who can afford to do it. I saw in many papers the letter that Herbert Spencer wrote to an American friend concerning the Chicago strike, in which he declared that they were rapidly advancing towards a "military despotism of a severe type." To be sure, it was only what he had said of England already: "We are on the way back to the rule of the strong hand, in the shape of the bureaucratic despotism of a Socialist organisation, and then of a military despotism that must follow it, if indeed some social crash does not bring this last upon us more quickly."

It cannot be said that these papers of the bookstall assist one much in arriving at a just conclusion of the subjects dealt with. Their value is in showing the manner in which the theories of the closet are served up for common acceptation. They also have the merit of forcibly calling attention to defects in the social state that must and will be, in some way, mitigated. They may do this in an exaggerated and a bitter style. The spirit that actuates some of them may be mainly destructive. Yet among a people who are fairly intelligent they do useful work all the same. Some whom I met with made little of them all, said that nobody minded them, and that their ineffectiveness was proved by the few representatives of the cause who were elected, either in England or America. But their influence, so far, is felt not so much in the number of members that they can return, as in the manner that they affect the ideas of the wage-earners, and thus indirectly the views of the two parties that are struggling for power in each country. In England we know that many of the Liberal measures, from Catholic Emancipation to Household Suffrage, have been passed by the Conservatives. In America the Income Tax is credited to the Populists; and in the Old Country what are called the half Socialist tendencies of some of the Rosebery Ministry, are ascribed to the influence of the Labour party. But too much weight must not be given to the bookstall either. The very quantity and the variety of aim of much that is printed dissipates its strength. The extravagance that sometimes marks it carries with it its own corrective. We think of a thing printed as given to all the world, but in fact only a few of the people may read it; of those who read less may attend to it. Many Americans seemed to regard the "tallest" of writing (and speaking) as only so much business to be got through for the cause in hand, and not to be taken too literally. Behind all is the common sense of all the people, and the older they are in political experience, the more wary they become. Nearly twenty years ago, Fawcett prophesied that if Socialism in the United States continued to advance with the same rapidity that it had lately shown, the day was near when it would control the legislation of the country. It has been speaking and writing ever since, and that day appears to be still distant.

CHAPTER XI.

THOUGHTS OF THE MAN IN THE STREET.

It may seem labour in vain to discuss the possibilities of the Socialist ideal, since the most intelligent Socialists admit that its complete accomplishment is far distant, some saying that it will take generations, and others centuries, before men are ready for it. Yet the inquiry is a practical one, for it influences the aspect in which you will regard remedies that are now proposed, the length that you will be ready to push them to, and particularly the direction that you will give them. When you are treating the patient it is important to know whether his constitution only wants strengthening and improved tone, or whether his case is so desperate that you must, at the risk of his life, adopt a kill-or-cure method. Many now become Socialists without in the least knowing where they are going to.

There has been much philosophical discussion upon this subject, and many learned arguments concerning the modified attitude of the newest school of political economy towards it. Twenty-one pages of one number of *The Fortnightly Review* were occupied while I was in England with an erudite answer by Professor Karl Pearson to Mr. Kidd, in which evolution, Darwin's theory, intra-group struggle and extra-group struggle, physical selection, and panmixia were deeply considered, and the argument as to panmixia was represented symbolically by a series of equations. Such are the problems that lie at the core of this subject. I desire, however, rather to suggest some of the difficulties that occur to the man in the street, and some of the reasons that lead him, though perhaps at first attracted by the humane spirit of Socialism and the grand prospects that it holds out, to see that it cannot become a fact.

The first, and indeed the main, postulate of the Socialists is that the State should own the land and all the instruments of production and exchange. This was resolved unanimously, though inadvisedly, as the lawyers say, at the Norwich Conference. I never heard any suggestion as to how the State was to get these except by the spoliation of the present owners, and this course is approved by representative Socialists. This would mean revolution. Further, I never heard or read of any plausible justification for such spoliation. People have bought and improved, not only with the sanction of the present law and industrial system, but at its invitation; for men have been encouraged by their fellow-men to save and invest for centuries. A Labour leader told me that the people now were not bound by laws that they had no voice in making. This doctrine would upset all continuity of national life, and reduce a State from being one entity, with generation knit into generation, to become a series of dissolving crowds inhabiting one part of the earth's surface. But, besides that, England has had some popular government for sixty years at least. It has had household suffrage and the ballot for thirty years. In the United States they have had popular government for a century. Most of the existing conditions of property-holding have taken effect within the last thirty years, either by purchase or succession. New conditions are happening every day. Admittedly a large majority of the people at present approve the industrial system now in force. The plea, therefore, that a people are not bound by laws not of their own making is unsound in theory and untrue in fact. The proposal to tax away gradually only adds an element of cunning to the spoliation. It may be that Socialists are impelled to such a proposal by the impossibility of finding the funds to purchase honestly—for that is impossible; also by its incongruity to the new departure; for what would be the use of giving men money to-day when it is all to be taken from them on principle to-morrow? But such tactics would produce even more serious consequences to the spoilers than to the spoiled. What would be left fixed after such an unsettling? Where would public faith be in the new community? It is a principle with some professors of the creed to allow the future citizen to keep and save what they term "the rent of ability," the fees paid to a Paget for operating, or a Patti for singing. But for how long? Only till a majority again voted away these personal accumulations. The effect of deliberate national dishonesty upon a people's character is lasting. An individual may do an unprincipled act and recover himself. Not so easily a community.

There is another consideration that suggests itself on the threshold of inquiry. Voluntary association for Socialist enterprise can at any time be undertaken by those who believe in it, and be backed by the support of philanthropic people outside. There is plenty of room to try it in England itself; or vacant spaces, apart from human settlement, are still to be readily found the world over. The experiment can be made upon whatever lines appear to be best from time to time to those who undertake it. If successful, the example would be followed. But any such attempt is repudiated by the Socialist. His object is, having got possession of government, to compel all the people to submit to the proposed industrial system. The fact that nothing like a large community remaining subject to such a *régime* has yet been seen in the course of the world's history, makes the man in the street sceptical. But the success of the scheme is assumed by its followers, who are thus led to regard the present condition of society as hopeless, and any means useless for reforming it, and justifiable for upsetting it. If difficulties are suggested, they say that

they are matters of detail that will settle themselves
when we come up to them, that they for their part do
not care to puzzle over the future, or that things are so
bad now that any change would be for the better.

Let us, however, consider a few points. The teachers
of the new system assume as its broad foundation a
radical improvement in human nature—so radical, indeed,
that if it could be secured we would get on very
well with the present system, or with any system.
Sometimes they express it that "human nature will
take a new direction." Some races of men have improved
in the past four thousand years; others have
deteriorated. In the better races men are less fierce;
when influenced (often indirectly) by Christianity, they
are what is termed more altruistic, more feeling for
suffering in others. It was Christianity that gave
charity a world-wide application. With the Jews it
had a limited scope; among the Greeks and Romans
it did not exist. But it is surprising how little we
have got away from our human nature in all that time,
and in particular from that cardinal instinct in it that
makes us first regard ourselves and those near to us.
Good men have ever struggled to curb this impulse,
with more or less success. In some saintly characters
it is suppressed by, or concealed under, a passion for the
good of others, that is with them a noble form of self-gratification.
Languages die, civilisations pass away,
religions decay. A thousand years passes over the
world, new forms of life, manners, and literature appear,
and all the while man remains each with the impulse
fixed and rooted deep inside him to take care of himself
and his children. And it would be adopting the tone
of Joseph Surface or Pecksniff to affect to condemn this
impulse as all bad. It is old Nature's way of preserving
men and improving the world. It wants regulating
and elevating, not extinguishing. Extinguished it will
not be, whatever social state may be imposed on men.
The ship is anchored to it, and however the currents
may make it swing first one way and then another, it

all the while does swing round the one holdfast. Why is this to change under the new system? If all private property were abolished, there are still longings for many things left in the human heart. But unless the love of self is changed it would soon produce a discord in men's wants and desires that would be increased by their being thrown together, and that could only be suppressed by force.

But the most striking of the new manifestations of nature must be in the rulers. All the evils under which the nations of the world now groan arise, not from the want of good systems of government, but from the want of good men to work them. The earth is full of excellent forms of polity. Nothing can be better than the system by which in China the poorest peasant lad, if he shows merit at the examinations, can win the position of mandarin. But how does it work in fact? It is the custom for the neighbours to subscribe towards sending forward any promising youth to his studies. They regard it as a fair speculation, for if he becomes a mandarin he plunders and swindles his province to pay them back with interest. The visitor from Mars, reading the statutes of New York, would declare that they must be a most virtuously governed people. And so they would be only for human nature. Honesty, truth, respect for others' rights, sobriety, purity, charity—not to speak of exactness in accounts and absolute rectitude in electioneering—are all straitly enjoined or provided for. But systems cannot work themselves, and this noble ideal comes to be spoiled because of the men who are to give it effect. Not that these are all bad, but that the friction of affairs, operating upon imperfect men and in many unexpected ways, prevents the straight progress in its designed path of any human institution or contrivance. In all ages and under every possible form of government, from the days of the Pharaohs to the present time, and from the despotism of Russia to the republic of America, the followers of the political calling, the instruments by whom government is worked, have been imperfect enough, and have, further, been regarded by people with perhaps even more distrust than they deserved. This is only saying that they are men acting in a sphere of difficulty and temptation. But all this is to change. Yet experience shows that, as we might expect, the more politics become a matter of industrial details, the less lofty is the type of the politician. Exercised upon the great, broad issues of his country, he is a statesman ; managing the local business of his district, he is an agent. The proposed Socialist system would give opportunities for favouritism in matters most vital to the citizen and to the life careers of his family ; for grants or concessions to particular industries and localities; for promotions to office; for exemptions from service ; and generally for jobbery such as even the politics of a bad city government could not give us a foretaste of. The city government may do public evil, but it leaves men to follow their careers in private as best suits them. The sort of public men that you would require to manage such affairs as these would be the ideal member which a political optimist sketched a century ago :

> The legislator, the representative of a great people, the true man of the commonwealth, does not intrigue ; he has no creatures ; he does not procure places for any one ; he seeks consideration for virtue only. For him individuals have no existence : the general good absorbs all his attention, and to that he sacrifices every passion. The pride of a statesman ought to be noble, like his functions. He is identified with the common weal, and nothing that does not injure it should have the power to wound him.

The people must, as one of the ardent spirits of the American revolution insists, elect only the virtuous :

> "Virtue," he declares, "ought to be above all other considerations at all times and on all occasions. Besides the danger that a man void of principle runs in betraying his trust and bringing affairs into confusion, the evil example of placing a bad man in an honourable station tends to damp all desire of keeping up a character. And what can be imagined more ruinous to a State than to kill emulation in the people—the noblest of all emulation, the emulation of being virtuous ? "

These are lofty ideals, but can we calculate upon reaching them when politics become a personal matter and appeal to the sordid part of human nature? And, as the American workman, whose conversation I have previously recorded, remarked to me, if, when the Socialists come in, the politicians do *not* vastly improve, what a mess they would all be in!

Personal independence must be given up in the Socialist state. Some that I spoke to seemed rather to enjoy the prospect. But the idea in their minds was that they and their friends would govern the rest. They never contemplated what it would really be like to live under an industrial despotism. They would be the very people who would resent it. Much is submitted to now, under trade organisations, because they are fighting their cause against the capitalist. But when the system became a Government, with all men subjects beneath it, the love of liberty, which is so indestructible in man, and which has played so large a part in his history, would reappear —divine discontent, with the longing for change, would be present as it was in the beginning and has been ever since, and the old cause of personal freedom, now neglected because securely achieved, would again stir the hearts and rouse the energies of men. It would again have its poets, heroes, martyrs. That would then be the line of progress.

For the obvious difficulties as to how work is to be apportioned, and how, when apportioned, enforced, when the motives that now direct and impel the individual are paralysed, no reasonable solution is suggested. People, we are told, will volunteer to sweep the gutters or dig in the mine, or a short time at unpleasant labour will be pitted against a long day in the shop or the office. No such compensation influences people's choice now. A boy or girl now will prefer the most grinding service in the bank, or behind the counter, to three hours a day at the plough or the wash-tub. Some have ability and no strength, others have strength and no ability. Who is to discriminate? And the idle? Some say that they are to be let starve. But is compassion, even for the worthless, to become extinct in men's hearts? And if there were a good many of them, as there always has been, what then? Others say that they will be subjected to penal discipline. Is this to be after a legal adjudication or at the word of the overseer? Is it confusion or the slave-driver? Seeing the futility of all this, one or two authorities say that, in some unexplained way, people are to be allowed to select their own work, and even to have the " rent of ability." If so, we need no revolution. We can work towards improved conditions of life upon the present lines. The truth is that if you take away independent exertion, with the stimulus of rivalry, from men, you can only find an adequate motive power to keep things going in the compulsion of slavery.

Socialists hold out the hope of two or three hours' work a day producing all that we need, and the rest of the time being spent in intellectual cultivation or innocent pleasure. This is surely a welcome prospect for poor man, upon whose brow the sweat of toil has ever stood. When one thinks of the cruel effect of overwork now, who can help longing for such a deliverance? It is impossible not to sympathise with workers when they tell you that they look forward to this rest. But can production be indeed thus maintained? Can accumulation for bad cycles be secured? Can the rivalry in the world's business of non-Socialistic states be fought, or is foreign commerce to be disregarded? How is the influx of useless foreigners to be met? And what would be the effect upon a people of going to the other extreme, and having no work to do for twenty hours out of the twenty-four? To few of even the highly educated and trained is given the aptitude to occupy a leisure life in a healthy manner. The failure of young men who are exempted from the discipline of labour by a competency is the commonplace of observation. It is in vain that, oppressed by the evil of overwork, men take refuge in the vision of a general rest. Nature will not have her plans upset in that way. Quite apart from the Darwinian theory, or the details of the learned article in *The Fortnightly Review* that I have referred to, experience teaches us that industry is necessary to keep human nature sweet. The idle races spoil. The iniquity of Sodom was declared in part to consist of "fulness of bread and abundance of idleness." National decay would be the penalty of national inactivity.

Jefferson, the father of American democracy, when arguing for a wider distribution of the power of government among different organs, says: "Were we directed from Washington when to sow and when to reap we should soon want bread." No such fear disturbs the Socialist speculator. The individual being suppressed, the State or the local government is to supply the directing power for managing the intricacies of commerce, the hazards of agriculture, the methods of manufacture, the infinite complexity of the details of distribution. Surely these things are the chimeras of the closet. They are like the assumption that there is to be no more war either by or against the Socialist State—apparently because it would not accord with the then fitness of things, or that if one country adopted this system all would follow. Cobden, with more reason, though in vain, prophesied that all nations would tread in England's free-trade footsteps.

Finally, Socialism is incompatible with fixed marriage and separate family life. These are inextricably mixed up with individualism, with allowing a man to work for his own people and keep what he earns, and so are condemned by advanced Socialists in an absolute manner, while others hesitate at the conclusion to which their principles naturally lead. I will deal with this topic later.

So far, then, as the complete Socialist system is concerned, the conviction forced upon the mind of the man in the street is that it cannot be successfully established. If imposed upon men by force it would not long be submitted to. If one nation did submit it would soon be thrown behind by the others and left to decay. If all the advanced nations adopted the principle—were this possible—it would show that this cycle of civilisation had run its course, and that Providence was preparing means for its gradual decline. No means could be better adapted towards the end.

But though the final stage proposed by the Socialist be unattainable, it by no means follows that nations may not take some steps on the way to it; for it is a peculiarity of the situation that many lines of progress seem all to run on the one track, like the rails at a railway junction. It is not till you pursue them awhile that you find that of several, which are side by side at first, some would ultimately take you to the east and others far away to the west. Thus all will agree in promoting a better distribution of wealth, in securing higher remuneration for the worker, and in destroying the dominant position of monopolies; but some do all this with the object of subverting the present social system, others with a view to improving and preserving it.

It would be outside the scope of these pages to discuss fully the various schemes of social reform that are advanced in our time, either in concert with Socialism or in conflict with it. Obviously one of the first things that meets us on the onward road is the just demand of the worker to get a larger share of the value of the production in which he takes part. This has long been recognised by fair-minded men, and a generation ago high hopes were entertained of its being secured by profit-sharing in co-operative work. This principle of co-operation has enlisted the support of the most eminent men, from Gladstone, who pronounced it "most excellent," to the political economists like Mill and Cairnes, who declared it to be the true way for the labouring classes to emerge from the mere hand-to-mouth way of living. Pronounced advocates of the working man used to applaud it. At the Co-operative

Congress held at Newcastle in 1873, Mr. Holyoake submitted these resolutions:

1. To regard capital not as the natural enemy of anybody, but rather as the nursing mother of production, and accord it adequate interest.
2. To secure the workman a fair share of profits, and protect his share by giving him adequate representation on the directory of the company for which he works.
3. To credit the customer with the share that remains when justice has been done to all producing agents concerned in serving him.
4. To set apart, as the stores do, funds for educational and journalistic purposes.

Since that time co-operation has grown, though not as it was expected it would, a good deal owing to the Socialist diversion to other and wider aims, and also to the fact that it takes time to educate men up to the higher tone required for successful co-operation. Yet there are in the United Kingdom nearly 1,800 co-operative societies, with over 1,280,000 members, a capital of more than £18,000,000, and making yearly profits of nearly five millions sterling. They sell goods to the value of fifty millions a year. The difficulty has been with co-operative production, partly owing to the want of management, and partly from the common difficulty of want of market. Yet what would seem more feasible, or could be more admirable, than that a number of men should join together to cultivate the cheap land, say in our colonies, and divide the produce or profit among them? In 1873 I passed a bill through the Victorian Legislature giving friendly societies the power to trade, and facilitating, among other things, co-operative settlement on land. But men's minds have been somewhat diverted from efforts in directions such as this by the large scope of employments and the expectations that the State holds out.

Many, indeed, who have no faith in Socialism advocate the Government owning and working all monopolies. Unquestionably there is both justice and expediency in the State having control over great industrial agencies, that for their operation require the assistance of State laws, and often the monopoly of public advantages. The railways of America are an example of what unrestrained private ownership leads to. It is no new idea, but, as I have said before, as old as our Common Law, that no set of men are entitled to monopolise public advantages to the detriment of the common weal. If in any case, for industrial reasons, it be for the public good to allow it, it should be on such conditions and under such control as best secures the interests of the whole people. It must be admitted, as a charge against popular government in America, that it has been so feeble in grappling with the rings and trusts and aggressive combinations of capitalists. If public opinion was strong enough to support a resolute administration of the law against such abuses, there would be less demand for the alternative of State ownership. There is now a considerable body of opinion among the working classes in England and America in favour of extending the sphere of State ownership, and experiments will probably be made in this direction. Holders of stock who get small profits, and classes of the public who suffer exploiting, favour the movement. If a domination such as we have seen in America can be prevented in no other way, the State may have to substitute itself for private ownership in this class of undertakings. The objection to this course is that State ownership of the monopoly is apt to be followed by State management of the industry, though it is by no means its necessary complement. The State might own and lease under such general conditions as would be necessary to protect the public interest. But what the Socialist party want is for the political Government to be the employer of the workers and the manager of the works. To this many Americans, socially inclined, demurred. As I heard the Boston lecturer, Dr. Joseph Cook, express it, they felt that they were between the devil of monopoly and the deep sea of Government management.

Their objection to Government management is well founded. It never has been a continued success. It can only avoid mercantile failure by absolutely excluding political influence; and the more democratic Governments become, the more difficult—indeed, the more impossible—it is to do this. Some of the American States that made the attempt failed, and had to hand over their railways to private management. Italy also was forced to renounce Government control and to lease her railways. The experience of other countries is the same. The conditions developed by politics are antagonistic to those wanted for industrial enterprise. The ballot-box is adapted to express public policy, not to indicate business capacity. Democracies do not organise well. The American general, Sherman, in his letters, deplores the waste of life in war, in which he took so brilliant a part, owing to the incapacity of the Government management. Under it there would be no necessity for economy; for if the undertaking does not pay, the alternative is not bankruptcy, but the open public purse. Old countries, already weighted with their heavy taxation, could not stand the strain. Discipline would be impaired by the fact that the *employés* would be the masters of their masters. The incentive to push, to inventiveness, to striving to please and attract the public, would be weak. The indispensable condition of success is to have able men at the head, and these can only be secured by large rewards and assured position, which democracies object, on principle, to give. The plan of paying all well and none much can produce only mediocrity. At election times the State *employés* would exercise a determining influence, partly owing to the cogent force of private interest as compared with the general sense of the public good, and partly owing to the generous feeling which induces the outside working classes to make common cause with their fellows.

The Americans will experience all this if their Government ever undertakes the management of the railways, with its million *employés*. Some advocates of State management there told me, in a confident manner, that they would easily meet any difficulties such as these by disfranchising all the public servants. This only shows how proposals are adopted without being thought out. Others proposed to have an independent board to manage, as it would a private business. The difficulty is that the business is not a private one. If the board is really independent it is also irresponsible to the political body, and this is apt to produce friction. If there is to be public patronage, where, it is asked, can it more properly be trusted than in the hands of the people's representatives? If the political authority indirectly controls it, then the board is only a screen. If Governments are forced to take the ownership of monopolies, experience will teach them to avoid the management.

The privileged position and liberal payment of Government *employés* is lauded by Socialist leaders in England as establishing a high standard of wages. And there can be no question that if the Government is an employer it should be as liberal as the most liberal private employer can be. But the more State business is undertaken the more it will be found impossible to stop at this. The result would prove to be the establishment of a privileged caste under Government, which the outside community, and particularly the tillers of the soil, for whom the State can do little, must be taxed to support. Thus private industry is discouraged, particularly farming, and all strive to enter the safe and highly paid ranks of Government employment. A middle class of State functionaries is constituted in the name of the poor man, in which, however, in fact he has small share. Indeed, when the State enters into business the more it does employ the more it may employ; and to be just it should complete the Socialist circle and employ all. And if it will be found bad for business to be mixed with politics, it will be found equally bad for politics to be mixed with business.

T

Public spirit would be dulled in the State *employé* by a natural regard for his own weal, and public issues would be determined by the activity of a number of private interests. I do not know that we could reasonably expect this to be otherwise. Yet it disappoints the old prophecy as to the value of the franchise in taking a man out of himself and possessing him with a noble concern for the public. This anticipation would not only be unfulfilled but reversed. Some thoughtful American writers realize these difficulties, and propose that the Government should own and then lease, under proper conditions, to private management. Experience will probably drive them to this, or to a real control and strict regulation of private enterprise.

If the communities, then, that I have been visiting are not likely to adopt the full creed of Socialism, neither are they likely to go very far on the road of the State management of industries, though State ownership may be necessary if, in any country, the people and the law are not strong enough to cope otherwise with the abuses of monopoly. State ownership and independent management by co-operative private industry may come about in the future. In this way the wage-earner would cease to be a mere wage-earner, and would be, as he ought to be, a participator in the profits.

It is unfortunate that the Socialist plan for a general upturning is pressed on while, as yet, the system of freedom has had no fair trial. Socialists appeal to the evils of the past and to the bad conditions of the present, as if it must be always thus, and things were never to improve. But this is not so. Struggling out of feudal conditions, the better off classes having government in their hands in England till as late as 1832, then the rampancy of individualism having been maintained for a generation by the Manchester school, the true principle of individual industry has hitherto had to contend there with unfavourable surroundings. It has also had to cope with disadvantageous conditions in other lands.

It never, indeed, was part of that principle that every one was to be allowed license to do what he pleased with any industrial agencies that he could get hold of, and that there was to be no Government interference to help those who had fallen and were in danger of being trampled on, or to restrain those who were abusing social powers. Adam Smith, starting from the premiss that "no society can be flourishing and happy of which the far greater part of the members are poor and miserable," justified many phases of Government intervention on behalf of the people, from State education down to laws for suppressing the truck system. Mill, while, like Henry George, strongly defending the legitimate principle of competition, worked during his whole life to secure for all fair conditions under which to carry on the contest. Mr. Goschen did not consider it at all inconsistent with his pronounced devotion to freedom in industrial affairs to warmly support Government intervention to secure decent dwellings for the poor. The Socialists fall into the error of accusing the advocates of liberty of being the champions of license. But there remains the old solid distinction between the two. The writings of some economists may give colour to this mistake; but the masters of the science are not open to the cavil, and certainly not the English Government for forty years past, which has often thrown the shelter of its laws over the workman, and striven by just regulation to make that personal freedom in industry, which it has so far maintained, a reality and not merely a name.

It takes time to modify the conditions of social life, yet that, even under disadvantageous conditions, a marked improvement in the state of the poor has been going on in the past, gives hope for what may be won in the future. Sixty-two persons in every thousand were paupers in England in 1849, but only twenty-five in a thousand in 1892. Wages have risen, and also the purchasing power of wages, and thrift has increased. Investigation shows that the number of fairly well off people increases faster in England than does that of the rich. There are more people rich, but not more very rich people. And now the conditions of the struggle are being altered all in favour of the weak, and the improvements that we witness are only the beginning of a great onward movement of general amelioration. The education of all, which is not so much a mere question of book learning as a guarantee that none shall grow up outcast of the community, is only beginning to do its work. Taxation that will deal generously with the poor, strict control of monopolies, facilitating small holdings of land, provident regulation of industries, arbitration for labour disputes, the proper housing of the people, and, in the near future, co-operation and profit-sharing in industry—all these belong to normal progress, and do not depend on Socialism nor require revolution. The details of a plan for State aid to pensions are still unsettled, but the principle of the State assisting the worker in his effort to make adequate provision for old age is so just that, if progress upon the present social lines is not diverted into the new track, it must succeed. There is no measure which should be more earnestly undertaken, and none for which the better off should be more willing to submit to any taxation that may be found necessary. One of the evil results of the Socialist crusade is that it turns men's minds from useful reforms that are now possible, leading some to contemn them as only postponing the revolution, and others to be lukewarm about them, fearing that the attitude of the extreme party may render them unpalatable to the people, and therefore of little value in the end. For the ablest of the Socialists condemn unsparingly all efforts at individual help. Mr. Sidney Webb says:

> I should have thought there would have been no doubt as to the side that we Socialists should take in this controversy. It may be all very well for a little group of thrifty artisans to club together and set up in business for themselves in a small way. If their venture is prosperous, they may find it more agreeable to work under each other's eye than under a foreman. Co-operative production of this

sort is at best only a partnership of jobbing craftsmen, with all the limitations and disadvantages of the small industry. From beginning to end it is diametrically opposed to the Socialist ideal. The associated craftsmen produce entirely with a view to their own profit. The community obtains no more control over their industry than over that of an individual employer.

Further on he writes:

I suppose no Socialist desires to see the land of the country divided among small peasant freeholders, though this is still the ideal professed by many statesmen of advanced views. . . . The same spurious Collectivism runs through all forms of leasehold enfranchisement—a thoroughly reactionary movement which, I am glad to think, is nearly dead.

Mr. Belfort Bax writes:

As I have said, co-operative experiments reflect what are, from a Socialist point of view, the worst aspects of the current order. The trade co-operator canonises the *bourgeois* virtues, but Socialist vices of "overwork" and "thrift." To the Socialist, labour is an evil to be minimised to the utmost. . . . Again, "thrift," the hoarding up of the products of labour, it is obvious, must be without rhyme or reason except on a capitalist basis.

Thus Socialism represses independent energy, and by impairing the ceaseless and all-pervading principle of self-help would promote a general habit of leaning, in the hope of its justifying and ensuring in the end the adoption of its full scheme. But these represent the conclusions of men with a propaganda to enforce, not the aspirations of the average man. He still longs to get a piece of land for his very own. Emphatically, it will be found, when the test time comes, that he still wishes to remain free.

Simultaneously with the improvement of the condition of the poor, there is also going on a reforming movement at the other end of the social scale. Capital is losing its importance and some of its value. The fall in its productiveness is world-wide, and the best authorities say this fall must continue with its increasing accumulation. The tendency is for rent, interest on money, and trade profits to decline. Here natural causes are quietly, and in a legitimate way, working a revolution. Money no longer gives true social position or political authority. All vulgar display or conscienceless use of it is sharply condemned by an increasingly active public opinion. It is true that in some of the American States it influences politics in an underhand manner. But this is only a passing phase arising out of exceptional industrial and, let us hope, exceptional political conditions. Entails and the feudal tone of society that promote the continued holding of property do not exist out of England, and thus the powerful natural causes that scatter accumulations have full play. In democratic communities nothing is more striking than the rapid way in which families rise from the crowd and then fall back again into the crowd, sometimes in one lifetime. All idea of fixed or privileged classes is happily gone. Whatever may be said for an aristocracy of intellect—if you only knew how to find the best men—or even an aristocracy of birth in past times, when social conditions favoured it, no people could endure an aristocracy of wealth. Property, too, is now enfeebled by being divorced from public duties that in past times were not only allowed to it, but required from it. Each generation of a family must vindicate itself by its own merits. We learn from history that all privileged classes, even under the old social conditions, have died out in a few generations. In our time the wealthy and their families have no individual continuity; they only exist as a set that is constantly changing its personality by replacement from below. Society is like some of the substances that philosophers tell us of, with the atoms constantly darting up and down, and none remaining fixedly either in the upper line or the lower. The political and industrial agencies that are now active, evidently go not only to facilitate this dispersion of wealth, but also to slacken the causes that would promote its continued concentration in the hands of a few. We are growing naturally towards equality under the present system, and the agencies that in the past have produced an unfair depression of the masses, which is no necessary condition of the method of freedom, are now working with renewed energy to secure an open field for all.

There is always a fascination about the methods of revolution. The remedy proposed appears to be so complete and so prompt as compared with the slow progress of gradual reform. But the best and most lasting ameliorations in the condition of the human race have not been accomplished by violent dislocations with the past. The French Revolution and the civil war that freed the American slaves are no examples to the contrary. The most effective advances have been made by the help of many various causes, each of them perhaps small in itself, working slowly and often unnoticed by contemporaries. It is hard to point to the exact date when the English peasant became a free man, so quietly was the change accomplished from villanage to liberty. Things move faster now, and the next stage, from the wage-earner to the profit-sharer, is already well advanced, and will be accomplished as effectively, and without the loss again of personal freedom, unless progress should be violently turned into some backward track. Time, the great innovator, is ever producing change by the condition of growth and the continual dropping off of the dying parts. The people of communities sprung from the Saxon stem will prefer to assist this process rather than cut down the tree, marked though it be with some blighted spots, in the vain expectation of there springing up in its place some wholly new growth that is to be free from the natural imperfections of the forest and not subject to decay.

CHAPTER XII.

RELIGION AND THE FAMILY UNDER SOCIALISM.

The attitude of Socialism to religion and the family engages the attention of any one who desires to know whether it is ever likely to permanently influence human life and government. The amiable and even religious feelings of many who call themselves Socialists, and perhaps think themselves such, does not alter the principles that the new system really rests upon, nor the results that would come from the adoption of those principles. Men are free to choose their own line of action, but not the consequences that naturally follow upon it.

The present phase of Socialism is imported from Germany, and there can be no question that there it distinctly rests upon Atheism. This is not an incident of the new creed, but its foundation. Mr. Brooks, in his "Industry and Property," gives some pointed references, out of many that could be had. Karl Marx is regarded by English as well as German Socialists as the high priest of the system. No one is more frequently referred to by Socialist authors of repute in both countries. He says: "We are content to lay down the foundation of the revolution. We shall have deserved well of it if we stir hatred and contempt against all existing institutions. We make war against all prevailing ideas of religion. The idea of God is the keystone of a perverted civilisation. It must be destroyed. The true root of liberty, of equality, of culture, is Atheism." Feverbach thus explains the new idea: "Man alone is our god, our father, our judge, our redeemer, our true home, our law and rule.... Man by himself is but man, man with man, the unity of I and Thou, is God." The following was the first resolution adopted at the Socialistic Alliance of Geneva:

"1. The Alliance declares itself Atheist; it demands the abolition of all worship, the substitution of science for faith, and of human justice for Divine justice; the abolition of marriage, so far as it is a political, religious, juridical, or civil institution." Bakunin shortly puts it: "We declare ourselves Atheistic; we seek the abolition of all religion, and the abolition of marriage."

These may be taken as samples of German thought upon this subject. Some English writers express themselves with equal directness, at least against all the existing forms of belief; others express the same thing inferentially, or quietly assume the negation as true. A few seek to join Socialism to Christianity. Mr. Belfort Bax, who is always outspoken, and whose works are recommended in the Fabian Tract entitled, "What to Read," puts it in his "Ethics of Socialism" thus: "It is useless blinking the fact that the Christian doctrine is more revolting to the higher moral sense of to-day than the Saturnalia or the cult of Proserpine could have been to the conscience of the early Christians.... 'Ye cannot serve God and humanity' is the burthen of the nobler instincts of our epoch.... The higher human ideal stands in opposition at once to Capitalism, the gospel of success, with its refined art of cheating, through the process of exchange, or in short to *worldliness*; and to Christianism, the gospel of success in a hypothetical other life, or in short, to *other worldliness*." He goes on to urge that if we want an object of personal reverence, we should look not to Christ, but to some of the modern martyrs of Socialism. The Fabian Essays may be considered the text-book of the school in England. In the paper entitled, "Economic," the basis of belief is analysed thus: "It was pleasant to believe that a benevolent hand was guiding the steps of society; overruling all evil appearances for good; and making poverty here the earnest of a great blessedness and reward hereafter. It was pleasant to lose the sense of worldly inequality in the contemplation of our equality before God. But utilitarian questioning and scientific answering turned all this tranquil optimism into the blackest pessimism. Nature was shown to us as 'red in tooth and claw.' If the guiding hand were indeed benevolent, then it could not be omnipotent, so that our trust in it was broken; if it were omnipotent, it could not be benevolent, so that our love of it turned to fear and hatred. We had never admitted that the other world, which was to compensate for the sorrows of this, was open to horses and apes (though we had not on that account been any the more merciful to our horses); and now came Science to show us the corner of the pointed ear of the horse upon our own heads, and present the ape to us as our blood relation. No proof came of the existence of that other world and that benevolent power to which we had left the atrocious wrongs of the poor. Nature knew and cared no more about our pains and pleasures than we know or care about the tiny creatures we crush under foot as we walk through the fields." Here is the old problem of the Atheist school, and not better told than before. Mr. H. M. Hyndman describes Christianity as seen in England as "merely the chloroform agency of the confiscating classes." Gronlund, in his "Co-operative Commonwealth," which is also recommended to students by the Fabian Society, says: "If, however, by religion you mean dogmatic theology, Socialists do propose to drive it out. Socialism *is* the inveterate foe of theology—a fact of which our ecclesiastics are well aware, wherefore they are consistent in damning Socialism. . . . Theology is being driven out of human life by that 'Titanic laughter—that terrible, side-shaking, throne and altar shaking laughter' which Rabelais started." He would, however, allow an undefined religion of his own, which might or might not include the belief in a life beyond the grave, the longing for which "has been fostered by creeds whose whole strength consists in offering a consolation to people who feel miserable here. It is possible that when men live to a good old age, and enjoy during life all the delights which nature permits, this longing will disappear." This touches the keynote of Socialism.

What one learns from personal converse with Socialists quite accords with the ideas thus expressed. In England they do not make a profession of Atheism, and many, I doubt not, have religious feelings of their own; but the majority break absolutely with the existing Christian religion. Such was the statement to me of a clever and sincere Labour Socialist leader. Another leader put the same thing, only not so directly. His position, in effect, was that he knew this world, but not another, and that one world was enough to deal with at a time. The American workman, to whom I have in a previous chapter referred, told me that what drove him out from the Socialist ranks was the blank Atheism and free-love principles that he found were being developed there.

Where they can, they establish Labour Churches and Sunday Schools of their own. But the idea of their Church is defective; its message being avowedly addressed to one part of the people only. There are a few of them in England. These are not in one sense irreligious, for they propound a religion of their own, a religion, if it may be so called, centred in this life, and adapted as a counterpart to the secular principles of Socialism for remoulding it. In the Sunday School they teach the children everything about reforming society, but nothing about reforming themselves. *The Labour Prophet* is their organ. It explains their creed thus: "The message of the older Churches is that 'God was in Christ Jesus, reconciling the world to Himself.' The message of the Labour Church is that God is in the Labour movement, establishing His kingdom upon earth." We are also told that "we must cast away all the conceptions of God which we have been taught to regard as true." The Bradford Labour Church has its "object" printed prominently upon all its papers. It is: "The realisation of Heaven in this life by the establishment of a state of society founded upon justice and love to our neighbour." "In this life" is put in capital letters. Books are recommended "which throw an entirely new light upon the Bible." Certainly these Labour Churches make little progress, for reasons that I have referred to before; but they, or no form of the worship of God, are the reasonable outcome of the Socialist position; as is also the "rational" education for children, which one can see advertised in the Socialist papers. In the *Fabian News* one reads this among the advertisements: "Rational education for girls.—Park, Cromer. Ethical and moral training are substituted for so-called 'religious' teaching. The education of the body, for health and skill, is systematically carried out under the care of a specially-trained health mistress. Manual work has its proper place in the school curriculum. Competition is absent. For particulars apply to the principal, Miss ———." The coarser version of these views is to be found at some of the meetings that I was present at, where plain, rough men denounced in abusive terms religion and marriage. Even at the Kensington meeting that I have described, one of the songs sold there warned the people to avoid, above all things, "the Gospel Grind."

Socialists, from as far back as Robert Owen, have pronounced against fixed marriage and the family. Several whom I met, particularly in England, did not accept this position; neither, however, did they deny it. They left the question to the future, as they are quite entitled to do. But the more thorough exponents of the Socialist view, carried to its necessary outcome, admit and proclaim as much in England as all do upon the Continent, that the individualism of marriage and family ties must be put an end to. As Mr. William Morris, known in Socialist circles as "the eminent poet and art worker," puts it: "The present marriage system is based upon the supposition of economic dependence of the woman on the man. This basis would disappear with the advent of Socialism, and permanent contracts would become unnecessary." I cite Mr. Belfort Bax again, as he is one of the most active members of the Socialist League, and the author of many works upon Socialism. He says: "I should observe that we are concerned not with the Civilised man, but with the Socialised man, which makes all the difference; for Collectivism is undeniably a *reversion*, if you like to call it so, to primitive conditions. . . . The fact that group marriage obtained in early society should rather be, as far as it goes, a presumption in favour of something analogous to it obtaining in the future." The same author, in his "Religion of Socialism," says: "We defy any human being to point to a single reality, good or bad, in the composition of the *bourgeois* family. It has the merit of being the most perfect specimen of the complete sham that history has presented to the world. There are no holes in the texture through which reality might chance to peer. The *bourgeois* hearth dreads honesty as its cat dreads cold water." Further on he writes: "The transformation of the current family form, founded as it is on the economic dependence of women, the maintenance of the young and the aged falling on individuals, rather than on the community, etc., into a freer, more real, and therefore higher form, must inevitably follow the economic revolution which will place the means of production and distribution under the control of all for the good of all. The *bourgeois* hearth, with its jerry-built architecture, its cheap art, its shoddy furniture, its false sentiment, its pretentious pseudo-culture, will then be as dead as Roman Britain." Another Socialist authority refers to the "cant talked about family life—

man, after all, being but the highest animal, and there being no family life among cats and dogs." Mr. Bernard Shaw looks forward to the "happy time when the continuity of society will no longer depend upon the private nursery." Mrs. Besant and Mr. Belfort Bax would take the education of the family away from the parents. "*Bourgeois* liberty of conscience" is to give way to true liberty. The core of the matter is to make motherhood a business, arranged and paid for by the State, and to root out the institution and the very idea of the exclusive family. All this, however, is based upon, and only follows upon, the previous carrying out of the other proposals of Socialism. At present it is of importance only as showing to what these necessarily lead. As Karl Pearson, a gentleman whose authority is frequently invoked, puts it, the change in the mode of possessing wealth must connote a change in the sexual relationships.

This subject was discussed in all its aspects while I was in London, at a meeting of men and women who met at a Socialist club, to hear a paper by Mr. Levy upon the danger to women involved in the spread of Socialism. The report of the debate, in which a number of ladies took part, filled a column and a half of *The Sunday Times*. In it much appears about the old "*bourgeois* sentiment," "group marriage," Jean Jacques Rousseau, equality of women with men, Individualism, civilised man, and Mrs. Lynn Linton. Mr. Levy, who is an able champion of Individualism, rightly understood, showed that the Socialist movement had for its object the abolition of fixed marriage. A Socialist who replied to him declared that "what all true Socialists desired was that marriage should be an ordinary contract, to be dissolved by notice by either party." Several of the ladies who spoke were, wisely we must admit, not prepared to accept, even to this extent, the new creed, and contented themselves with strictures upon marriage conditions as they are now.

As I was desirous of seeing how this subject was

presented to the man in the street—which is, after all, the practical question—I got a pamphlet which had just been published by the Labour Press Society. It was entitled "Marriage in Free Society," by Edward Carpenter. The author is a well-known writer upon the Socialist subject, and has published several pamphlets upon its political aspect, and several more upon the manner in which the new principle will deal with the relation between the sexes. A prominent Labour leader told me that Mr. Carpenter was an excellent man, and one who spoke with authority in labour circles. I would repeat, however, that I do not infer that his views are necessarily accepted by all the labour Socialists. I only glance at the contents of this pamphlet, as showing the moral philosophy of the proposed revolution as it is presented, under reputable auspices, at the bookstall. The writer first devotes many pages to the condemnation of the present system of marriage, by which one man takes one woman for life. The young people "marry without misgiving, and their hearts overflow with gratitude to the white-surpliced old gentleman who reads the service over them. It is only at a later hour, and with calmer thought, that they realize that it is a life sentence which he has so suavely passed upon them—not reducible (as in the case of ordinary convicts) even to a term of twenty years." Once married, however, the slavery of the woman begins, and "willing or unwilling, they have to bear children to the caprice of their lords, and in this serf-life their very natures have been blunted." Even where the "*bourgeois* marriage"—the reader will have noticed this expression before; it is supposed to carry its own condemnation with it—is quite happy, and "just in its most successful and pious and respectable form, it carries with it an odious sense of stuffiness and narrowness, moral and intellectual, and the type of family which it provides is too often like that which is disclosed when on turning over a large stone we disturb an insect home that seldom sees light." The "modern monogamic marriage," as it is accurately termed, is further condemned as either "a thing obviously and by its nature bad and degrading," or at least condemned by "a fatal narrowness and stuffiness." As far as it is concerned, the only cure is declared to be "the abrogation or modification of the present odious law which binds people together for *life*, without scruple, and in the most artificial and ill-assorted unions." So far, there have been censures on the present system of marriage, with many oblique references to the "true marriage," "real love unions," and so on. Coming to the remedies for this bad state of things, we are told that there must be greater familiarity between the sexes in youth. This would not lead "to an increase of casual or clandestine sex relations. But even if casualties of this kind did occur, they would not be the fatal and unpardonable sins that they now—at least for girls—are considered to be." There must also be greater freedom for married people, for "it seems rash to lay down any very hard and fast general laws for the marriage relation, or to insist that a real and honourable affection can only exist under this or that special form. It is probably through this fact of the variety of love that it does remain possible, in some cases, for married people to have intimacies with outsiders and yet to remain perfectly true to each other; and in rare instances, for triune and other such relations to be permanently maintained." After this ambiguous explanation, which rather puzzles the man in the street, the reader is prepared for the conclusion that in real marriage there should be no contract at all. "Perhaps the most decent thing in true marriage would be to say nothing, make no promises, either for a year or for a lifetime." "It would be felt intolerable in any decently constituted society, that the old blunderbuss of the Law should interfere in the delicate relations of wedded life." This all puts in a tentative manner what more fearless writers, like Mr. Bax, assert directly and unequivocally.

The conviction left upon the mind by the literature

of Socialism, and by what one hears from its exponents, is not only that it does declare against religion, marriage, and the family, but that it must do so, if it is to prevail. It cannot succeed so long as they are in the way. The antagonism between them is absolute and lasting. Religion forbids us to centre all our hopes in this life, and declares that men cannot find full contentment here. Marriage of one man to one woman for life gives to each some of the most sacred attributes of property in the other. The family unquestionably means some exclusiveness, so long as good men think first of the happiness of wife and children, and prefer it to the pleasure of others, or even to their own. It would be futile to allow the old domestic institutions to continue while you condemn the economic conditions upon which they rest, and the virtues—as they have been considered—upon which their value and usefulness depend. Two writers of authority represent, as it seems to me, truly, what the Socialist position leads to. M. Emile de Laveleye says: "Herein is summarised the entire doctrine. Man is desirous of family joys and the supreme charm of liberty. Instead of these he is allotted compulsory labour and promiscuity of intercourse." Mr. Hepworth Dixon, cited by Mr. O'Brien in his "Socialism Tested by Facts," says: "The very first conception of a Socialist state is such a relation of the sexes as shall prevent men and women from falling into selfish family groups. Family life is eternally at war with Socialistic life. When you have a private household, you must have personal property to feed it; hence a community of goods, the first idea of a Socialistic state, has been found in every case to imply a community of children and to promote a community of wives. That you cannot have Socialism without introducing Communism is the teaching of all experience, whether the trials have been made upon a large scale or a small scale, in the old world or the new. All the Pentecostal and Universal Churches have begun their career with a strong disposition toward that fraternal state in which private property is unknown. Some have travelled along that line, adopting all the conclusions to which the journey led them, while others have turned back in alarm on seeing that the fraternal was at war with all the sacred traditions of home. . . . All the social reformers who have striven to reconcile the family group with the general fund have failed, though some of these reformers, like the pioneers at Brook Farm, were men of consummate abilities and unselfish aims."

Such being Socialism, how do the Christian bodies regard it? The position of the Roman Catholic Church is clear. It sympathises with all the Socialist's concern for the poor and the unfortunate, but disputes his right to be considered their only champion, and unequivocally condemns the measures that he declares to be necessary for their relief. The utterances of more than one Pope upon this subject are unmistakable. "Avoid," said the Pope to the French pilgrims, "perverse men, especially when they come in the name of Socialists, to overthrow social order to your detriment." So also is the teaching of lesser clerical authorities. When visiting the Church at Brompton, I found inside its precincts a bookstall, from which suitable literature was sold to the people. One pamphlet which I bought was entitled, "Why no good Catholic can be a Socialist." It was written by a priest, and, on the front page, stated to be published under the authority of Cardinal Manning, whose lifelong sympathy with suffering is the common knowledge of London, and indeed of the world. It demonstrates upon ecclesiastical lines how Socialism is irreconcilable with Christianity. A Catholic gentleman in America, who was well informed upon the subject, assured me that, as indeed might have been expected, there was in the voice of his Church there absolute unity upon the subject. That Church, indeed, while not disdaining policy at some times, and for some purposes, can claim this credit, that upon matters which it considers vital, it hoists an unmistakable signal, nails it to the mast, and if need be, is ready to go down with it. The writings of the Fathers are by some referred to as supporting Socialism; and they do so, in so far as denouncing selfishness, rapacity, the want of brotherly love, and the conscienceless use of riches, may be said to give that support. But they assume as their standpoint the truth of the Christian doctrines and of the Ten Commandments.

The attitude of the Church of England and the other Protestant bodies is also hostile to the essential doctrines of Socialism, while they are not behind the Catholic Church in their concern for the poor. But the position of the Church of England is peculiar. It is an Established Church. Its Bishops are Peers. It has for centuries been identified with the landed and propertied classes. It possesses vast endowments itself. It cannot say with the early Apostles, "Silver and gold have I none." Though it has always enclosed within its fold many truly Christian and merciful men, its attitude as a Church in England has in past generations been indifferent and hard to the suffering masses. It is a fact that the spiritual Peers in Parliament have been hostile or unsympathetic to the humane reforms that are the glory of our century, from that which freed the black slaves abroad to those which rescued the white slaves in the factories at home. Any other Churchmen, or men similarly identified with the Government and the ruling classes, would doubtless have been the same. It constitutes a striking warning against planning new social states, the buttresses of which are to be unselfishness, when we find that it was impossible to wholly banish that frailty from even a few select men, who had all the improving influence of high education, joined to which was often intellectual power and religious principle.

But this unsympathetic attitude of the Established Church has for many years past roused the indignation of an active and progressive party in her ranks, who are eager to show their affection for the poor, to disconnect her cause from that of rank and wealth, and link it to the people. Their main motive, and probably the only one they are conscious of, is the wish that the Church may rightly fulfil its divine mission among the masses, which obviously it never can so long as it is mixed up only with the well-to-do. Behind this is the Churchman's concern at the people slipping away from their control, and the determination to accept whatever may be necessary for keeping hold of them. They do not want to lose the people. They want the Church of England to have in reality that supremacy in every parish in England which technically it claims. For more than a generation the tone of the Church has been liberalised, and its efforts to relieve and elevate the poor have been unsparing. It is to further this object that a new development has taken place among the younger clergy. Socialism having undoubtedly a strong hold upon the masses, and the clerical estimate of its strength being possibly even exaggerated, many of them, from the time of Kingsley, have earnestly set themselves to see how far they can go with it. He and his friends vehemently condemned the Manchester school. In "Socialism in England" this attitude is contemptuously described as the Church "timidly turning to the rising sun." Finding that, to start with, they have much in common with the Socialists, as all wish to help the poor, and all condemn the abuse of wealth, they gladly call themselves Socialists. As is the wont of suspected people, they protest strongly. But their real purpose is religious, rather than economical. They become seeming Socialists in the hope of making the people real Christians. This was the attitude of the young clergyman whose views I have recorded in a previous chapter. He and all his friends were Socialists, but gave no sanction to, and indeed had no knowledge of, the real proposals of Socialism. They were Socialists in the same sense that their bishops are, when they pledge themselves, in the consecration service, to be examples of self-denial, and to show compassion to the poor and needy and to all who are destitute of help. Affecting to give a new name to the exercise, however fervid, of old Christian virtues and duties, is a weakness in their position, and certainly imposes upon no one outside of themselves.

How far removed these worthy men are from the Socialist who means business, we can readily learn by a glance at their "Church Socialism" publications. The Lambeth Conference of Bishops appointed a Committee to report upon the Social problem. It, after due deliberation, reported in favour of the extension of the system of small farms, of co-operation, Boards of Arbitration for labour disputes, the acquisition by municipalities of town lands, and the abolition of entail. It states further that "it does not doubt that the Government can do much to protect the proletariat from the evils of unchecked competition." The Bishops also declare themselves for a peaceful solution of social problems "without violence or injustice." Most of these proposals not only would not satisfy the Socialist, but would be tenaciously opposed by him. A paper by the Bishop of Durham on Socialism is apparently regarded as a declaration of Faith by the Socialist Church Guilds. It begins by stating that the Socialism that the Bishop contemplates has "no necessary affinity with any forms of violence, or confiscation, or class selfishness, or financial arrangement." It is obviously, therefore, not the movement with whose champions I have been conversing. The "Guild of St. Matthew" is declared to be the true Socialist organisation in the Church. Its principles are stated to be two, each equally obvious and just: that all should work, and that the produce of labour should be distributed on a more equitable system than at present. Sermons and papers of excellent tone are published by the Christian Socialist School, which deplore social inequalities and reprobate the selfishness of many. They proclaim no more than the truth, but do not do it as vigorously as Hugh Latimer did when he hurled

Christian anathemas against the wealthy Londoners who allowed the poor to languish at their doors.

But an impassable gulf yawns between the true Christian and the true Socialist. A man can be either, but not both. None proclaim this in louder tones than do the outspoken Socialists. I quote Mr. Bax again, because he, as usual, speaks directly:

"Lastly, one word on that singular hybrid, the 'Christian Socialist.' Though the word Socialism has not been mentioned, it will have been sufficiently evident that the goal indicated in the present articles is none other than Socialism. But the association of Christianism with any form of Socialism is a mystery, rivalling the mysterious combination of ethical and other contradictions in the Christian Divinity himself. Notwithstanding that the *soi-disant* Christian Socialist confessedly finds the natural enemies of his Socialism among Christians of all orthodox denominations, still he persists in retaining the designation, while refusing to employ it in its ordinary signification. It is difficult to divine the motive for thus preserving a name which, confessedly, in its ordinary meaning is not only alien, but hostile to the doctrine of Socialism."

If Socialists thus regard the Christian religion and morality, and religion thus looks upon Socialists, what is the impression left upon the man in the street by the controversy? As to morality, it is easy enough to see that Socialism, when developed, is inconsistent with the marriage of one to one, and with the exclusiveness of family life. From amid the decent veil of learned discussions and technical terms, and many references to primitive man and early group marriages, there emerges Free Love and State nurseries. The evils of the present system are obvious and are considerable. But it is plain that the advanced nations have been, by slow degrees, growing out of a state of more promiscuous living to the higher condition of Christian wedded life. The restraints that it imposes upon men and women, and particularly upon men for the benefit of women, are apparent. Bacon, whose wisdom will live when the controversies of to-day have long been forgotten, truly describes it as "the discipline of humanity." In one aspect, indeed, men and women are only animals, the woman obviously being enfeebled by her special functions. It has been the glory of religion and civilisation to equalize the relationship between them, and also to dignify it, mainly by the means of the institution of the family, as we know it. Keeping intact the intercourse and progeny of one wedded pair, with its necessary adjunct, the separate family, has long appeared to thinking men an admirable means for ennobling the relation between man and woman, and also for securing stable continuity to States, the true unit of which is the family, not the individual. To cast all this aside at the bidding of some recent but not new theories—for they have been advanced and discarded in times past—and to revert rather to the condition of the flocks and herds, certainly seems to the man in the street to be retrogression. It is not progress for the State, for man, or for woman, and particularly not for woman. The more you revert to mere animal conditions, the worse it is for the weaker animal.

As to the religious side of the controversy, it is to be observed that the question is not between one form of religion and another, but between some principle of religion and no religion. The idea of the Socialist is founded on sympathy for the poor and the unfortunate, and all credit to him for it; but it rests there, and has its ideas and aspirations so centred in this world that it cares not to look beyond it. The Socialist, while his nobler conceptions are the offspring of Christianity—for where, among men, outside the range of Christianity, is Socialism to be found?—yet stretches forth against the parent principle an unnatural hand. His system would inculcate in the place of what we term "religion," a noble love of humanity. But its creed is circumscribed by the outline of this globe on which successive generations of us men appear and disappear. Its idea is expressed by the motto of one of the Continental associations, "The earth is man's and the fulness thereof." Its philosophy is exemplified in the sentiment that one world is enough to look after at one time.

This philosophy contains within itself the seeds of failure. It is good-natured, but not strong enough for the place. It is doomed to decay, and to make the human race decay if they adopted it. Life is too grave a matter to be disposed upon these lines. If it is a serious thing to die, it is also a serious thing to live, and experience shows that to guide and support men effectually in the needs and stress of this life, you want sanctions drawn from beyond it—at least if you are to preserve the better type of mankind. Only a few of the more debased savage races are destitute of these higher aspirations. You must have the fulcrum of the power that is to influence civilised men, fixed outside. It is quite true, as a thoughtful Socialist remarked to me in answer to this view, that there is now among many little living religious belief. In every age the mass of people have taken but small interest in the religions of their day, and probably have not had much active belief among them. The few of higher aspirations bore aloft the ark of the faith, and were thus trustees for the rest. Some among the many turned now and then fitfully to religion for its consolations in the emergencies of life. But this state of things is widely different from a proclamation of national Atheism, a formal declaration that men's hopes and fears alike are to be centred in this world, and the announcement of a new creed, the principle of which is exactly expressed by the ancient exhortation; "Let us eat and drink, for to-morrow we die." What would be the effect on a nation's character of such a creed as this? For peoples do reflect their religion in their character, or what stands in the place of a religion to them. If it is fierce, they are fierce; if it is base, so are they.

Socialists demand for the new state a change of man's nature, or at least that human nature shall take a new direction, and empty itself of selfishness. But they reject the only religion that has made this sacrifice of self a living principle among men. The few Socialist communities that have had any success have been based upon this sublime and unworldly doctrine of Christianity. Where they have rested upon merely secular principles they have failed; for no one earthly motive has been found strong enough to subjugate all the rest. But the principle of Faith, and the support of hope beyond the grave, has nerved men during many generations to face cheerfully all the evils and terrors of this life. In truth, this divine element in the animal man is itself a standing miracle and a living proof that he is not designed to be all earthy. Whence comes it? It is a powerful instinct which is able to transform his nature, and to make him superior to all the pleasures that this world can give and the evils that it can inflict. If we can get so far as to concede a Creator to the universe, can we conclude that He is selling His creatures by implanting in them such aspirations while all the time He designs them only to grovel to the earth? Is this impulse alone among all our instincts delusive and purposeless?

This concentration, then, of the philosophy of Socialism on worldly phenomena only, lames it for dealing effectually with men even in the world. It lacks power to control, and scope to satisfy humanity. Obvious facts that other moral schemes endeavour to grapple with, it quietly ignores. The doctrine of some original fault in man may be held to be an invention of priests, but at least it is an invention to explain a fact. Universal experience, from the dawn of history till to-day, has revealed a defect in human nature that takes different directions in different ages, and in different circumstances, but shows little sign of thinning out altogether. Various races have their own legends for explaining it. It eludes the influence of the most diverse social conditions, and appears in every variety of human character. Poverty does not cause it, nor affluence cure it. The highest education may modify it, but by no means eradicates it. Could we get rid of it, the face of the world to-day would soon be changed. We could then throw off the burthen of standing armies, police, gaols, law courts, and the greater part of our public charities. Side by side with this moral frailty, and partly connected with it, though partaking also of nobler elements, is the discontent of mankind. This certainly induces progress, but no progress appeases it. No fact in the inner history of men is more certain than that this life does not satisfy them. All the good things that it can afford are vain to secure permanent contentment. Experience shows that wealth, ease, distinction, do not make the possessors personally happier than those in a humbler lot. The truth of the old story about the Fates remains. As the web of our lives is being spun, the envious sister stands by to slip the black thread into every coil. It is something coming from within us, not imposed from outside. From this imperfection and this discontent come the difficulties of human government. To them are due the failures of life. The Socialist triumphantly waves all this aside, and fastening upon men's industrial conditions, some of which are undoubtedly defective, imputes to them all human ills and dissatisfactions, and promises relief for all by a revolution that is to bring in material prosperity. But were all done and all swept away as he desires, man himself would still remain, and with him the weakness and the perplexity of human life. These cannot be charmed away by essay or manifesto. The final feeling of the man in the street, after listening to all the wisdom of the Socialist, is that there is more in heaven and earth than is dreamt of in his philosophy, and especially more in heaven.

APPENDICES

APPENDICES

APPENDIX A.

The following Despatches contain the best summary that is to be had of the views of the Imperial authorities upon the question that we considered at Ottawa, of trade relations within the Empire—a question that many of us believe has a future before it.

OTTAWA CONFERENCE, 1894.

No. 1.

The Marquess of Ripon to the Governor-General of Canada, the Governors of the Australasian Colonies (except Western Australia), and the Governor of the Cape.

MY LORD,

Downing Street, June 28, 1895.

SIR,

In my despatch of the 13th of December last I transmitted to you copies of the Report of the Earl of Jersey, G.C.M.G., on the proceedings at the Colonial Conference at Ottawa, together with copies of the proceedings of the Conference.

2. Since then the questions discussed at the Conference have been under the consideration of the various Departments specially concerned, and I am now in a position to place you in possession of the general views of Her Majesty's Government on the questions which formed the subject of the three Resolutions classed together by Lord Jersey as dealing with trade relations.

3. The first two of these Resolutions have for their object the repeal of legislation and the cancelling of treaty stipulations which, in the opinion of the delegates, obstruct the realisation of the policy indicated in the third Resolution, and it may be convenient that I

should in the first instance explain the views of Her Majesty's Government with regard to that policy before discussing the first two Resolutions.

4. The third Resolution declares that : "Whereas the stability and progress of the British Empire can be best assured by drawing continually closer the bonds that unite the Colonies with the Mother Country, and by the continuous growth of a practical sympathy and co-operation in all that pertains to the common welfare : and whereas this co-operation and unity can in no way be more effectually promoted than by the cultivation and extension of the mutual and profitable interchange of their products :

"Therefore resolved : That this Conference records its belief in the advisability of a Customs arrangement between Great Britain and her Colonies by which trade within the Empire may be placed on a more favourable footing than that which is carried on with foreign countries.

"Further resolved : That until the Mother Country can see her way to enter into Customs arrangements with her Colonies it is desirable that, when empowered so to do, the Colonies of Great Britain, or such of them as may be disposed to accede to this view, take steps to place each other's products in whole or in part on a more favoured Customs basis than is accorded to the like products of foreign countries.

"Further resolved : That for the purposes of this Resolution the South African Customs Union be considered as part of the territory capable of being brought within the scope of the contemplated trade arrangements."

5. With the preamble of this Resolution the feeling, not only of Her Majesty's Government, but of the entire population of this country, is, I need not say, in hearty sympathy—a sympathy to which no proposal clearly tending to promote the stability and progress of the Empire can appeal in vain.

6. The unanimity of sentiment which prevailed throughout the Conference on this point has been noted with pleasure by Her Majesty's Government, and it is with regret, therefore, that they feel compelled to express a grave doubt whether the fiscal policy the principle of which was adopted by the majority of the Conference, as a means of securing this object, is really calculated to promote it.

7. The Resolution does not advocate the establishment of a Customs Union comprising the whole Empire, whereby all the existing barriers to free commercial intercourse between the various members would be removed, and the aggregate Customs revenue equitably

apportioned among the different communities. Such an arrangement would be in principle free from objection, and, if it were practicable, would certainly prove effective in cementing the unity of the Empire and promoting its progress and stability. But it was unanimously recognised by the Delegates that the circumstances of the Colonies make such a union, for the present at any rate, impossible; and it is, therefore, unnecessary to discuss the practical difficulties which stand in the way of its realisation.

8. The actual proposition is something essentially different, namely, the establishment of differential duties in this country in favour of Colonial produce, and in the Colonies in favour of the produce of the Mother Country. Commercial intercourse within the Empire is not to be freed from the Customs barriers which now impede it, but new duties, confined to foreign goods, are to be imposed where none exist at present, and existing rates of duty, now of impartial application, are to be either increased as against foreign trade or diminished in favour of British Colonial trade.

9. It was generally recognised at the Conference that this policy involves a complete reversal of the fiscal and commercial system which was deliberately adopted by Great Britain half a century ago, and which has been maintained and extended ever since. By a consistent adherence to this system one duty after another has been swept away in this country, until, at the present day, the few import duties remaining are retained, either for revenue purposes alone on articles not produced here, or in order to protect the Excise revenue.

10. A differential duty is open to all the objections from the consumer's point of view which can be urged against a general duty, and, while it renders necessary the same restrictions on trade, it has the additional disadvantage of dislocating trade by its tendency to divert it from its regular and natural channels.

11. These general objections to the policy advocated are sufficiently serious, and there are others, no less serious, which flow from the existing conditions under which the trade of the Empire is distributed.

12. Assuming that the preference aimed at by the Resolutions is given in the way most favourable to trade, namely, by the partial remission of existing duties in favour of British and Colonial goods, rather than by an increase of duties on foreign goods (coupled with the imposition of duties on goods of foreign origin now admitted free which compete with British and Colonial produce), it is obvious that, as the total trade of the Empire with foreign countries far exceeds the trade between the various members constituting the Empire, the volume of trade upon which taxation is to be placed exceeds the volume

which would be partially relieved. The result would not only necessitate increased taxation but would involve a serious net loss of trade, the burden of which in both cases would fall with greatest severity on those parts of the Empire which have the largest proportion of foreign trade, and the loss to these parts would more than outweigh the gain to the other parts.

13. On closer examination it would appear that the material results of the proposal would be even more prejudicial than appears from the general statement of its more obvious results. In the case of this country, the bulk of the imports from foreign countries and almost the whole of our imports from the Colonies consists of food or raw materials for manufacture.

14. To impose a duty on food means at once a diminution of the real wages of the workman. If, in addition to this, a duty were imposed on raw materials, a further encroachment would have to be made on wages to enable the manufacturer to compete with his rivals in countries where there are no such duties.

15. The Honourable Mr. Foster, in his speech introducing the motion now under review, drew a vivid picture of the vigorous and unrelenting competition which the British manufacturer has to meet in the markets of the world; and, if he somewhat over-estimated the results of that competition, there can be no question as to the fact that in many branches of trade in which Great Britain once held a distinct superiority other nations now compete on equal terms. In so far, then, as the British manufacturer failed to shift the burden of any duty on food and raw materials on to wages he would be at a disadvantage in the open markets of the world, and the remission in the Colonies of part of the duty in his favour would scarcely place him on level terms with his foreign competitor even there.

16. It must not be forgotten, moreover, that at present about one-fourth of the export trade of this country consists of foreign and Colonial produce, and that the imposition of duties on foreign produce would involve an enormous immediate outlay for the extension of bonding facilities, and the necessary charges for their use and maintenance. The result would be to place such obstacles in the way of this trade that its transference elsewhere would speedily take place, goods which this country now receives for re-export being sent direct to their market, or through some other entrepôt where they would not be subjected to such disabilities. Thus the position of this country as the great market of the world, already threatened, would be destroyed.

17. These changes could not fail to seriously injure our important

carrying trade and to react injuriously on every industry in the United Kingdom.

18. On the other hand the gain to the Colonies, whatever it might be, would, even at first, be altogether incommensurate with the loss to the Mother Country. And it is improbable that there would be any permanent gain, for, apart from the general loss of purchasing power due to the fall in wages and profits resulting from the imposition of duties, it is obvious that the reduction of our imports from foreign countries would be followed by a reduction in our exports to them, no inconsiderable part of which consists of Colonial produce imported in a crude state and more or less manufactured in this country. The demand, therefore, for Colonial produce, even with the preferential advantage proposed to be allowed to it, would not be likely to increase, and the price obtained for it would, therefore, not be ultimately enhanced.

19. If the differentiation is to be confined to some specified articles, the difficulties of arriving at an equitable arrangement would be in no way diminished. Some of these difficulties were clearly pointed out by the representatives of New South Wales, Queensland, and New Zealand, in the course of the discussion, and no practical standard was suggested by which the value of the concessions to be made on each side could be tried or adjusted. These would obviously vary according to the number of Colonies sharing in the arrangement and many other circumstances, and, as the people of this country and those of the Colonies would approach the consideration of the question from entirely different points of view, a satisfactory agreement would seem almost impossible. To this country it would mean a possible increase of revenue for a period, but at the same time a serious curtailment of trade, with loss of employment and enhanced price of food and other necessaries, and it would, in the main, be judged by its effect on our commerce and on the condition of the people.

20. To the Colonies, on the other hand, it would in the first instance mainly present itself as a question of revenue. A remission of duty on the bulk of their imports would involve an entire readjustment of their fiscal system, requiring the resort to increased direct taxation or other means, and though there might be at first an increase in the price of their produce imported into this country, the revenue difficulty would probably appeal to them most strongly.

21. A consideration of these practical difficulties, and of the more immediate results above indicated, of a system of mutual tariff discrimination, has convinced Her Majesty's Government that, even if its consequences were confined to the limits of the Empire, and even

if it were not followed by changes of fiscal policy on the part of foreign Powers unfavourable to this country, its general economic results would not be beneficial to the Empire. Such duties are really a weapon of commercial war, used as a means of retaliation, and inflicting possibly more loss on the country employing it than on the country against which it is directed, and which would not be likely to view them with indifference.

22. Foreign countries are well aware that the Colonies differ in their fiscal policies and systems from the Mother Country and each other, and if a policy of the kind advocated were adopted, our foreign rivals would not improbably retaliate, with results injurious to the trade of the whole Empire.

23. In the course of the discussion at the Conference the opinion was generally expressed that, although in present circumstances, while so large a proportion of the trade of Great Britain is with foreign countries, the arrangement might scarcely be acceptable to this country, the Colonial trade of Great Britain increases so much faster than the foreign that the conditions and proportions would be reversed at no very distant date, and the arguments now urged against the policy of the Resolution would no longer be regarded as valid.

24. As a matter of fact, however, the proportion of the Colonial trade of this country to its foreign trade is very nearly the same now as it was forty years ago.* The development of external trade does not always keep pace with the growth of population, more especially when it is subject to tariff restrictions either avowedly or incidentally protective, and although the Colonies have much room for expansion in the matter of population, and English capital has flowed into them, perhaps more freely than into foreign countries, there is at present no appearance of any sustained alteration in the relative proportions of foreign and Colonial trade. But even if those proportions were reversed, Her Majesty's Government are convinced that the evil results of a preferential policy would be mitigated only slightly,

---

* Comparisons are only possible since 1854. For the five years, 1854–58, the total imports into this country were £820,904,330; the imports from British possessions being £195,556,090, or 23·8 per cent. of the whole. During the five years, 1889–93, the total imports were £2,112,252,916, and the imports from British possessions were £482,427,761, or 22·8 per cent. of the whole. The total exports during 1854–58 were £657,699,825, and the exports to British possessions £186,056,817, or 28·3 per cent. of the whole. During the period 1889–93 the total exports from this country were £1,521,736,951, of which the exports to British possessions were £438,491,512, or 28·8 per cent. Taking imports and exports together, the trade of this country with British possessions in the earlier of the two periods formed 25·8 per cent. of the total, and in the later 25·3 per cent.

although they might fall with less severity on this country and with greater severity on the Colonies than would be the case under existing circumstances.

25. I have dealt with this question at some length, because the strong support which the proposal met with from the majority of the representatives at the Conference entitles it to the fullest consideration, and renders it desirable to set forth the reasons which have satisfied Her Majesty's Government that it would fail to secure the object aimed at—namely, the stability and progress of the Empire.

26. I now pass to the second part of the Resolution, which urges "That until the Mother Country can see her way to enter into Customs arrangements with the Colonies, the Colonies should take steps to place each other's products in whole or in part on a more favoured Customs basis than is accorded to the like products of foreign countries."

This Resolution raises somewhat different issues from the preceding one. At first sight it would appear that this was a matter in which only the Colonies making such arrangements are themselves concerned, and that as Her Majesty's Government have allowed the Colonies full liberty to frame their fiscal systems with the view, if they think fit, of protecting their local industries, there can be no objection to their making arrangements to extend a somewhat similar protection or preference to those of a sister Colony.

27. It must be remembered, however, that the primary object of a differential duty is a diversion rather than an increase of trade, and that as the proportion of the external trade of most of the Colonies which is carried on with foreign countries is insignificant compared with that carried on with the Mother Country and other parts of Her Majesty's dominions, it will be difficult for one Colony to give a preference in its markets to the trade of another solely at the expense of the foreigner, and without at the same time diverting trade from the Mother Country or from sister Colonies which may not be parties to the arrangement.

28. Serious injury might thus be inflicted on the commerce of a neighbouring Colony, and unfriendly feelings generated, which might provoke retaliation, and would in any case estrange the Colonies concerned in a manner which would not conduce to the great aim which the Conference had in view throughout.

29. Any agreement for reciprocal preferential treatment between two Colonies will, therefore, require careful consideration in regard to its probable effect on the commerce of the rest of the Empire, and although Her Majesty's Government have the fullest confidence that the

loyalty and good feeling happily prevailing between the various parts of the Empire would prevent one Colony seeking an advantage to itself which could only be gained at the serious prejudice of other parts of Her Majesty's dominions, it is impossible for them to relieve themselves of their responsibility in regard to the general interests of the Empire in such a matter.

30. The last part of the Resolution, which urges "That for the purposes of this Resolution the South African Customs Union be considered as part of the territory capable of being brought within the scope of the contemplated trade arrangements," opens, as Lord Jersey has remarked in his Report, a prospect of additional complication.

31. The Orange Free State is a party to that arrangement, and if a Colony outside South Africa were to extend to the produce of that State preferential terms granted to the produce of the Cape Colony, Her Majesty's Government might, unless the same terms were extended to all countries entitled to most-favoured-nation treatment in that Colony, be involved in a serious controversy with those countries.

32. Having now indicated generally the views of Her Majesty's Government on the policy advocated by the Conference, I turn to the Resolutions which urge the removal of such obstacles, arising from legislation or Treaty, as impede the carrying out of that policy.

The only legislative obstacle to such arrangements as are contemplated by the Resolutions is the clause in the Constitution Acts of the Australian Colonies prohibiting the imposition of differential duties. After full consideration Her Majesty's Government decided that, however much such duties might be inconsistent with the fiscal policy of this country, they should not, in so far as such duties can be imposed without breach of Her Majesty's Treaty obligations and without detriment to the unity of the Empire, interfere with the discretion of the Colonies in the matter. Parliament has, therefore, on the initiative of Her Majesty's Government, agreed to relieve the Australian Colonies of the special disabilities under which they were placed by the operation of their Constitution Acts, and, in consequence, has passed the Act of which copies are enclosed,* repealing the provisions referred to, and that Act has now received Her Majesty's assent.

33. In the case of the Colonies of New South Wales and Victoria, section 45 of the Constitution Act of the former and section 43 of the

---

* Australian Colonies Duties Act, 1895, 58 & 59 Vict. cap. 3.

APPENDIX A. 309

Constitution Act of the latter also prohibit the imposition of differential duties, but as the repeal of these provisions is now a matter within the competence of the local Legislatures, Her Majesty's Government leave it to them to take the necessary action.

34. While, however, Parliament has thus removed all legislative restrictions on the Colonies, so far as Imperial legislation is concerned, it will be necessary, in order that Her Majesty's Government may be in a position to give effect to their responsibility for the international obligations of the Empire, and for the protection of its general interests, that any Bill passed by a Colonial Legislature providing for the imposition of differential duties should be reserved for the signification of Her Majesty's pleasure, so as to allow full opportunity for its consideration from these points of view.

35. For this reason and in order to prevent inconvenience it will be desirable, if such duties are included in a General Tariff Bill, that a proviso should be added that they are not to come into force until Her Majesty's pleasure has been signified.

36. I may here point out that any Act such as that passed by the Legislature of New Zealand in 1870, which proposed to enable the Governor of the Colony in Council to suspend or modify any of the duties imposed by the Customs Duties Acts of the Colony, in accordance with any inter-colonial agreement, besides being open to grave objection on constitutional grounds, would deprive Her Majesty's Government of any opportunity of considering such agreements, and unless, therefore, the articles to which the power should apply and the extent to which remission might be granted were specified, Her Majesty's Government would have grave doubts as to the propriety of advising Her Majesty to assent to such an Act. They trust, therefore, that the Colonial Legislatures will not seek to divest themselves in any measure of their power to fix the amount of their taxation, nor to confer on the Executive a power the exercise of which without the fullest deliberation might inadvertently give rise to serious complications, not only with other Colonies but with foreign Powers.

37. The second Resolution states "That this Conference is of opinion that any provisions in existing Treaties between Great Britain and any foreign Power, which prevent the self-governing dependencies of the Empire from entering into agreements of commercial reciprocity with each other or with Great Britain, should be removed." The Treaties aimed at by this Resolution are the Commercial Treaties between this country and Germany and Belgium.

38. The particular Articles of these Treaties which might give

rise to difficulties in regard to preferential arrangements between the various portions of the British Empire are as follows:

BELGIUM, ARTICLE XV.

"Articles the produce or manufactures of Belgium shall not be subject in the British Colonies to other or higher duties than those which are or may be imposed upon similar articles of British origin."

"Les produits d'origine ou de manufacture belge ne seront pas grevés dans les Colonies Britanniques d'autres ou de plus forts droits que ceux qui frappent ou frapperont les produits similaires originaires de la Grande-Bretagne."

The English and French texts are both given, as there is a shade of distinction in the translation of the word "British."

ZOLLVEREIN (German Empire).

ARTICLE VII.

"The stipulations of the preceding Articles I. to VI." (they contain the whole Treaty) "shall also be applied to the Colonies and Foreign Possessions of Her Britannic Majesty. In those Colonies and Possessions the produce of the States of the Zollverein shall not be subject to any higher or other import duties than the produce of the United Kingdom of Great Britain and Ireland, or of any other country of the like kind; nor shall the exportation from those Colonies or Possessions to the Zollverein be subject to any higher or other duties than the exportation to the United Kingdom of Great Britain and Ireland."

39. It is to be observed that any advantages which might be granted by Great Britain to either Belgium or Germany in virtue of these particular stipulations must also be extended to various other countries under the ordinary most-favoured-nation clauses in existing Treaties. If, however, Article XV. of the Belgium Treaty and Article VII. of the Zollverein Treaty were no longer in force, there are no stipulations of a similar character in any other Treaty concluded by this country and now in force which could give rise to the same difficulties.

40. The general effect of these stipulations in regard to import duties, as understood by Her Majesty's Government, is stated in the note on page 5 of Lord Jersey's Report as follows:

1. They do not prevent differential treatment by the United Kingdom in favour of British Colonies.

2. They do not prevent differential treatment by British Colonies in favour of each other.

3. They do prevent differential treatment by British Colonies in favour of the United Kingdom.

41. In regard to the first of the foregoing propositions, I may observe that, as will be gathered from what has been said above, the question of admitting Colonial produce into the United Kingdom on more favourable terms than the produce of foreign countries is a question which Her Majesty's Government are not at present prepared to take into consideration; and if, at any future time, it were to come into practical discussion, it could be approached with equal freedom whether the Treaties with Belgium and the Zollverein were in force or not.

42. As regards the second proposition, the opinion formed by Her Majesty's Government as to the interpretation of Article XV. of the Treaty with Belgium is in conformity with an opinion expressed by the Law Officers of the Crown, to the effect that the words "Similar articles of British origin," or in the French text "produits similaires originaires de la Grande-Bretagne," relate to the produce of the United Kingdom alone.

43. It must, however, be recollected that in the construction of any Treaty the interpretation of one of the parties alone does not necessarily prevail.

44. In regard to the third proposition, it seems clear that under the terms of Article XV. of the Belgian Treaty, and of Article VII. in the Treaty with the Zollverein, the British Colonies cannot grant to the produce of the United Kingdom any preferential treatment as to Customs duties without such treatment being also extended to Belgium and Germany, and through them to other countries which have ordinary most-favoured-nation clauses with Great Britain.

In these circumstances the question arises whether it is desirable:

(a) To endeavour to obtain the abrogation of Article XV. of the Belgian Treaty and of Article VII. of the Zollverein Treaty separately, without the denunciation of the entire Treaties; or

(b) Failing the abrogation of these particular clauses alone, to denounce the Treaties themselves, which can be done by giving twelve months' notice.

45. In regard to the separate denunciation of these Articles, it may be stated that both the Belgian and German Governments have been asked whether they would consent to the abrogation of these particular clauses without the rest of the Treaties being terminated,

and the reply in both cases was to the effect that the clauses could not be denounced apart from the rest of the Treaty.

46. Her Majesty's Government have no Treaty right to demand the abrogation of these Articles separately, and in view of these replies, there would evidently be no use in further approaching either Government in this direction; and the only method of getting rid of these clauses would be the denunciation of the Treaties themselves.

47. Such denunciation would be a step of the greatest gravity, and whilst Her Majesty's Government are fully alive to the desirability of removing any Treaty stipulations which may hamper the action of the Colonies in regard to trade relations, they consider the advantages to be derived from such a step should be very clearly shown to outweigh the disadvantages before it could properly be resorted to.

48. It has been shown above that the United Kingdom could, if it were at any time judged proper, grant preferential terms to Colonial produce without infringing the particular articles in question, and further that the British Colonies could also grant preferential treatment to each other without infringing them as they are interpreted by Her Majesty's Government. The only point, therefore, which remains for consideration is, whether the advantages to be derived from permitting the United Kingdom to enjoy preferential treatment in the British Colonies is sufficient to outweigh the disadvantages to the Empire of the denunciation of the entire Belgian and Zollverein Treaties.

49. The following figures may serve to indicate generally how the interests of the United Kingdom are affected.

The annual value of the exports from the United Kingdom, according to the Statistical Abstract, may be roughly estimated as having been in 1893 :

To Germany	£28,000,000
To Belgium	£13,000,000
Total	£41,000,000

The value of exports from the United Kingdom to all the self-governing Colonies for the same year may be roughly estimated at £35,000,000 (India not included).

The comparison would not be quite the same if account were taken of the exports of British and Irish produce only. Here it would seem that the exports from the United Kingdom to British

APPENDIX A. 313

self-governing Colonies exceed the exports to Belgium and Germany. The self-governing Colonies, moreover, being geographically distant, the exports to them give proportionately more employment to shipping than do exports to adjacent countries like Belgium and Germany. But the exports to Belgium and Germany are undoubtedly important in themselves.

50. The denunciation of the Treaties with Belgium and Germany would thus expose the trade of the United Kingdom to some risks, and might possibly be followed by a loss of some part of the export trade to those countries; probably of some portion of it, which consists in the distribution of foreign and Colonial produce. With the denunciation of the Treaties the commerce of the Empire with these countries would have to be carried on under fiscal conditions subject to constant changes and fluctuations, or at all events without that permanence and security which is of primary importance to successful and profitable interchange. It would be extremely difficult, in existing circumstances, to negotiate new Treaties of a satisfactory character at an early date, and the loss which might in the meantime result to a trade of forty-one millions sterling would, perhaps, prove to be irreparable. On the other hand, no scheme has been proposed which foreshadows any precise advantages to be secured to the export trade, amounting to thirty-five millions sterling, from the United Kingdom to the British Colonies, in the event of the termination of these Treaties.

51. I may further observe that the self-governing Colonies themselves would lose any advantage they now derive from their inclusion in the German and Belgian Treaties; since, if those Treaties were denounced, both countries would, in view of the circumstances attending the passing of the Resolutions of the Colonial Conference and in view of the high tariffs existing in many of the Colonies, no doubt decline to include the British Colonies in any new Treaty that might be negotiated, and considering the small amount of their trade, it would be very difficult for them, if in an isolated position, to secure advantageous terms except by very heavy concessions. In this connection it might be expedient for the self-governing Colonies themselves to consider how much their interests are involved. A large item in the exports from the United Kingdom to Belgium and Germany is "wool," about £8,000,000 in value, largely, there is no doubt, Colonial wool. Other articles of Colonial export also find a market in Belgium and Germany.

52. In these circumstances, as preferential arrangements in which this country should be included cannot, under present conditions, be

considered a matter of practical politics, and as the clauses in the Treaties do not, in the view of Her Majesty's Government, prevent inter-colonial preferential arrangements, Her Majesty's Government consider that it would not be prudent to contemplate the denunciation of the Treaties at the present moment, bearing in mind that this could always be done on twelve months' notice, if circumstances should hereafter show it to be desirable.

53. In conclusion, it only remains for me to state that in the consideration of these questions the discussions at the Conference have been of the greatest service to Her Majesty's Government. The discussion throughout was maintained at a high level, and the speeches were eminently practical and to the point, and I have observed with pleasure the unanimity which prevailed as to the importance and desirability in principle, not only of preserving but of strengthening the bonds of sentiment, sympathy, and mutual benefit which now unite the Empire. This was one of the main objects for which the Conference was summoned, and Her Majesty's Government are convinced that the result has been a substantial and permanent contribution to the establishment and maintenance of that mutual understanding and sympathy without which that Imperial union which we prize so highly can scarcely hope to be permanent.

I have, etc.,
RIPON.

No. 2.

The Marquess of Ripon to the Governor-General of Canada, the Governors of the Australasian Colonies (except Western Australia), and the Governor of the Cape.

My Lord,

Sir,

Downing Street, June 28, 1895.

In my despatch of even date,* I communicated to you an expression of the views of Her Majesty's Government on the Resolutions passed by the Colonial Conference at Ottawa in regard to the trade relations of the Empire.

2. In the course of the discussions there, a question of considerable importance was more than once alluded to, namely, the question of commercial agreements between Her Majesty's Government and foreign Powers in regard to their trade with the Colonies.

* No. 1.

APPENDIX A. 315

Such Conventions have already been made on more than one occasion in regard to the trade of Her Majesty's Dominions in North America with the United States of America, and recently with the Government of France in regard to the trade between that country and Canada; and the Cape Colony has also entered into a Customs Union with the neighbouring Independent Republic, the Orange Free State.

3. Although the area within which such agreements are possible is now but limited, owing to the network of commercial Treaties by which the nations are bound together, there are still some Powers, such as France, with which agreements of the kind could be made, either because no commercial Treaty exists between them and this country, or because some of the Colonies have not adhered to the existing Treaty. It appears desirable, now that the same liberty of tariff legislation has been accorded to the Australian Colonies as has been enjoyed by Canada, the Cape Colony, and New Zealand, and that the Colonies generally are considering the question of extending and increasing their external commerce, that the views of Her Majesty's Government on this question should be generally known.

4. In the first instance it is advisable that the international position of such agreements and the procedure to be followed in regard to them should be made clear, and in this connexion I desire to quote from the able speech delivered by Sir Henry Wrixon at the meeting of the Conference on the 10th of June.

5. Referring to this question, he said:

"I do not know that I have ever thoroughly understood the position which the Imperial Government takes with regard to the power which they have already allowed to Canada and the Cape, because we all know that nations can only know one another through the supreme head. Each nation is an entity as regards any other nation, and I have no knowledge of how you could recognise a part of an Empire making arrangements for itself. If you look at the thing in the last resort, supposing conflicts arose, or cause of war, the foreign Power that had cause to complain of the breach of a commercial Treaty must naturally look to the head of an Empire, and they could not be put off by telling them to look for satisfaction to the dependency. If any foreign Power made an arrangement with the Cape, and had cause to complain, and wanted to enforce any proviso, they must go to the Empire of Great Britain; and, therefore, as far as I can understand it, I am quite against any attempt to recognise the right of a dependency of the Empire to act on its own behalf. Everything must be done through the head of the Empire when we are dealing with foreign nations. One nation is one individual, and it can only deal with other nations on that basis; therefore I deliberately excluded any reference in my motion to that subject, and I may only add that I think it is quite unncessary to refer to it, because we can have no doubt that the Imperial Government will extend the same consideration to all the dependencies of the Empire that it has already extended to Canada and the Cape, if in any case any dependency of the Empire shows that it has good ground for entering into a commercial Treaty outside. I have not the slightest doubt that the Imperial Government would do for other dependencies what it has already done for the premier dependency of Canada and the Cape.

"Hon. Mr. FITZGERALD.—Do you wish it done by legislation?

"Sir HENRY WRIXON.—No. I do not understand how it can be done, because I have no idea of a nation as anything else than one complete unity with regard to an outside nation, and I cannot understand a dependency of the Empire arranging with an outside Power; and I presume, where the Imperial Government has allowed Canada and the Cape to make arrangements, the Imperial Government itself has contracted and would be prepared to vindicate the conduct of the dependency in the last resort. I understand that when occasion arises the dependency informs the Imperial Government of its desire to enter into certain arrangements. The Imperial Government authorises its Minister at the Court of the Power which is to be treated with to carry on that negotiation, and then, technically, it is the Empire which makes the Treaty. In our country some claimed more than this right. I repudiated any such position. I think it is not consistent with the unity of the Empire, and I added to that a reason why it was unnecessary—namely, because the Imperial Government will do for us what they have done for Canada and the Cape, and will help us to make a Treaty if we want to make a Treaty with any foreign Power."

6. This speech not only indicates the procedure to be followed in the case of such arrangements, but clearly explains the reasons for it. A foreign Power can only be approached through Her Majesty's Representative, and any agreement entered into with it, affecting any part of Her Majesty's dominions, is an agreement between Her Majesty and the Sovereign of a foreign State, and it is to Her Majesty's Government that the foreign State would apply in case of any question arising under it.

7. To give the Colonies the power of negotiating Treaties for

themselves without reference to Her Majesty's Government would be to give them an international status as separate and sovereign States, and would be equivalent to breaking up the Empire into a number of independent States, a result which Her Majesty's Government are satisfied would be injurious equally to the Colonies and to the Mother Country, and would be desired by neither.

The negotiation, then, being between Her Majesty and the Sovereign of the foreign State must be conducted by Her Majesty's Representative at the Court of the foreign Power, who would keep Her Majesty's Government informed of the progress of the discussion, and seek instructions from them as necessity arose.

It could hardly be expected, however, that he would be sufficiently cognisant of the circumstances and wishes of the Colony to enable him to conduct the negotiation satisfactorily alone, and it would be desirable generally, therefore, that he should have the assistance, either as a second Plenipotentiary or in a subordinate capacity, as Her Majesty's Government think the circumstances require, of a delegate appointed by the Colonial Government.

If, as a result of the negotiations, any arrangement is arrived at, it must be approved by Her Majesty's Government and by the Colonial Government, and also by the Colonial Legislature if it involves legislative action, before the ratifications can be exchanged.

8. The same considerations which dictate the procedure to be followed have also dictated the conditions under which, though never distinctly formulated, Her Majesty's Government have hitherto conducted such negotiations, and as to the propriety of which they are confident that no question can be raised.

9. These considerations are : the strict observance of existing international obligations, and the preservation of the unity of the Empire. The question, then, to be dealt with is how far these considerations necessarily limit the scope and application of any commercial arrangement dealing with the trade between one of Her Majesty's Colonies and a foreign Power, both in respect of the concessions which may be offered by the Colony and the concessions which it seeks in return.

10. It is obvious that a Colony could not offer a foreign Power tariff concessions which were not at the same time to be extended to all other Powers entitled by Treaty to most-favoured-nation treatment in the Colony. In the Constitution Acts of some Colonies such a course is specifically prohibited, but, even where that is not the case, it is obvious that Her Majesty could not properly enter into any engagements with a foreign Power incon-

sistent with her obligations to other Powers, and before any Convention or Treaty can be ratified, therefore, Her Majesty's Government must be satisfied that it fulfils this condition, and also that any legislation for giving effect to it makes full provision for enabling Her Majesty to fulfil her obligations, both to the Power immediately concerned, and to any other Powers whose rights under Treaty may be affected. To do otherwise would be a breach of public faith to which Her Majesty's Government could not lend themselves in any way.

Further, Her Majesty's Government regard it as essential that any tariff concessions proposed to be conceded by a Colony to a foreign Power should be extended to this country and to the rest of Her Majesty's dominions.

As I have already pointed out, there are but few nations with which Her Majesty's Government have not Treaties containing most-favoured-nation clauses, and to most of these Treaties all or some of the responsible Government Colonies have adhered. Any tariff advantages granted by a Colony, therefore, to a foreign Power would have to be extended to all Powers entitled by Treaty to most-favoured-nation treatment in the Colony, and Her Majesty's Government presume that no Colony would wish to afford to, practically, all foreign nations better treatment than it accorded to the rest of the Empire of which it forms a part.

11. This point has already arisen in connection with negotiations on behalf of Colonies with foreign States. When informal discussions with a view to a commercial arrangement between the United States of America and Canada took place in 1892, the delegates of the Dominion Government refused the demand of the United States that Canada should discriminate against the produce and manufactures of the United Kingdom, and the negotiations were broken off on this point. Similarly, when Newfoundland, in 1890, had made preliminary arrangements for a Convention with the United States under which preferential treatment might have been accorded to that Power, Her Majesty's Government acknowledged the force of the protest made by Canada, and when the Newfoundland Government proposed to pass legislation to grant the concessions stipulated for by the United States, my predecessor, in a despatch dated the 26th of March, 1892, informed the Dominion Government that they might rest assured "that Her Majesty will not be advised to assent to any legislation discriminating directly against the products of the Dominion."

12. It must not be forgotten that, as I have pointed out in my

other despatch of this date,* whilst the grant of preferential tariff treatment is a friendly act to the country receiving it, it is an unfriendly act to countries or places excluded from it, and Her Majesty's Government are satisfied that the bonds which unite the various parts of the Empire together require that every Colony should accord to the rest at least as favourable terms as it grants to any foreign country. If a Colony were to grant preferential treatment to the produce of a foreign country and were to refuse to extend the benefit of that treatment to the Mother Country and the other Colonies, or some of them, such a step could not fail to isolate and alienate that Colony from the rest of the Empire, and attract it politically as well as commercially towards the favoured Power. Her Majesty's Government are convinced that the Colonies will agree that such a result would be fraught with danger to the interests of the Empire as a whole, and that they will also agree that it would be impossible for Her Majesty's Government to assent to any such arrangement.

13. In regard to the other side of the question, namely as to the terms which a Colony seeks from a foreign Power, the considerations mentioned appear to require that a Colony should not endeavour in such a negotiation to obtain an advantage at the expense of other parts of Her Majesty's dominions. In the case, therefore, of preference being sought by or offered to the Colony in respect of any article in which it competed seriously with other Colonies or with the Mother Country, Her Majesty's Government would feel it to be their duty to use every effort to obtain the extension of the concession to the rest of the Empire, and in any case to ascertain as far as possible whether the other Colonies affected would wish to be made a party to the arrangement. In the event of this being impossible, and of the result to the trade of the excluded portions of the Empire being seriously prejudicial, it would be necessary to consider whether it was desirable, in the common interests, to proceed with the negotiation.

14. Her Majesty's Government recognise, of course, that in the present state of opinion among foreign Powers and many of the Colonies as to differential duties, and in a matter which, to some extent, would affect only a particular Colony, they would not feel justified in objecting to a proposal merely on the ground that it was inconsistent in this respect with the commercial and financial policy of this country.

But the guardianship of the common interests of the Empire

* No. 1.

rests with them, and they could not in any way be parties to, or assist in, any arrangements detrimental to these interests as a whole. In the performance of this duty it may sometimes be necessary to require apparent sacrifices on the part of a Colony, but Her Majesty's Government are confident that their general policy in regard to matters in which Colonial interests are involved is sufficient to satisfy the Colonies that they will not, without good reason, place difficulties in the way of any arrangements which a Colony may regard as likely to be beneficial to it.

I have, etc.,
RIPON.

APPENDIX B.

To illustrate the difference in the style of Parliamentary oratory that the changes of some seventy years have brought about, I give extracts from George Canning's speech in the House of Commons on Parliamentary Reform, in 1822, and from that of the member from Missouri in the House of Representatives, Washington, on the Cleveland-Wilson Tariff Bill, 1894. Of course the reader must bear in mind that Canning was one of the greatest rhetoricians that the House of Commons has produced, while the member from Missouri is only a successful speaker in Congress. Still the difference in style is one of kind, not merely degree; also it is a question which kind of eloquence would tell best in the House of Representatives to-day.

Mr. CANNING.—" If this House is adequate to the functions which really belong to it—which functions are not to exercise an undivided, supreme dominion in the name of the people, over the Crown and the other branch of the Legislature, but checking the one and balancing the other, to watch over the people's interests—if, I say, the House is adequate to the performance of these its legitimate functions, the mode of its composition appears to me a consideration of secondary importance. I am aware, that by stating this opinion so plainly I run the risk of exciting a cry against myself; but it is my deliberate opinion, and I am not afraid to declare it. Persons may look with a critical and microscopic eye into bodies physical or moral, until doubts arise whether it is possible for them to perform their assigned functions. Man himself is said by inspired authority to be 'fearfully' as well as 'wonderfully made.' The study of anatomy, while it leads to the most beneficial discoveries for the detection and cure of physical disease, has a tendency, in some minds, rather to degrade than to exalt the opinion of human nature. It appears surprising to the contemplation of a skeleton of the human form, that the eyeless skull, the sapless bones, the assemblage of sinews and cartilages in which intellect and volition have ceased to reside, that this piece of mechanism should constitute a creature so noble in reason, so infinite in faculties, in apprehension so like a god; a creature formed after the image of the Divinity, to whom Providence

> Os—sublime dedit; cœlumque tueri
> Jussit, et erectos ad sidera tollere vultus.

So in considering too curiously the composition of this House, and the different processes through which it is composed, not those processes alone which are emphatically considered as pollution and corruption, but those also which rank among the noblest exercises of personal freedom, the canvasses, the conflicts, the controversies, and (what is inseparable from these) the vituperations and excesses of popular election, a dissector of political constitutions might well be surprised to behold the product of such elements in an assembly, of which, whatever may be other characteristics, no man will seriously deny that it comprehends as much of intellectual ability and of moral integrity as was ever brought together in the civilised world. . . . Let it not be thought that this is an unfriendly or disheartening counsel to those who are either struggling under the pressure of harsh government or exulting in the novelty of sudden emancipation. It is addressed much rather to those who, though cradled and educated amidst the sober blessings of the British Constitution, pant for other schemes of liberty than those which that Constitution sanctions— other than are compatible with a just equality of civil rights or with the necessary restraints of social obligation; of some of whom it may be said, in the language which Dryden puts into the mouth of one of the most extravagant of his heroes, that

> They would be free as nature first made man,
> Ere the base laws of servitude began,
> When wild in the woods the noble savage ran.

Noble and swelling sentiments! but such as cannot be reduced into practice. Grand ideas! but which must be qualified and adjusted by a compromise between the aspiring of individuals and a due concern for the general tranquillity; must be subdued and chastened by reason and experience before they can be directed to any useful end. A search after abstract perfection in government may produce, in generous minds, an enterprise and enthusiasm to be recorded by the historian and to be celebrated by the poet: but such perfection is not an object of reasonable pursuit, because it is not one of possible attainment; and never yet did a passionate struggle after an absolutely unattainable object fail to be productive of misery to an individual, of madness and confusion to a people. As the inhabitants of those burning climates, which lie beneath a tropical sun, sigh for the coolness of the mountain and the grove, so (all history instructs us) do nations which have basked for a time in the torrent blaze of an unmitigated liberty, too often call upon the shades of despotism, even of military despotism, to cover them.

> O quis me gelidis in vallibus Haemi
> Sistat, et ingenti ramorum protegat umbra—

a protection which blights while it shelters; which dwarfs the intellect, and stunts the energies of man, but to which a wearied nation willingly resorts from intolerable heats and from perpetual danger of convulsion. Our lot is happily cast in the temperate zone of freedom, the clime best suited to the development of the moral qualities of the human race; to the cultivation of their faculties, and to the security as well as the improvement of their virtues—a clime not exempt, indeed, from variations of the elements, but variations which purify, while they agitate, the atmosphere that we breathe. Let us be sensible of the advantages which it is our happiness to enjoy. Let us guard with pious gratitude the flame of genuine liberty, that fire from heaven, of which our Constitution is the holy depository; and let us not, for the chance of rendering it more intense and more radiant, impair its purity or hazard its extinction."

The MEMBER FROM MISSOURI.—"Farmers are not natural born fools. No tariff can add to the price of things that are exported, and the farmers know it. They know that the M'Kinley Bill is a fraud and a shame. Being exporters they know that it adds nothing to the prices they receive, and being importers they know it adds much to the prices they pay. The authors of that Bill went to the country on it, and did you ever know any one get such a beautiful trouncing before? (Laughter.) Down in Brother Cannon's district, an old fellow who had been voting for him and Republicanism for forty years heard the news that Cannon was beaten. 'Pack up, Sal,' he said. 'You and me's got to move to somewhere where Republicans live.' Then he went to town, and heard more news, and pretty soon came back and said: 'Unpack, Sal; there is no place on God's earth left to move to.' (Laughter.) Any industry that depends upon the tariff is a pauper industry. It's contrary to nature. (Applause.) God Almighty never intended us to hog everything. If He had, He'd have made us with snouts. (Wild laughter.) God could have made this world, if He had wanted to, with exactly the same climate and soil all over it, so that each nation would have been entirely independent of every other nation. But He didn't do that. He made this world so that every nation in it has got to depend for something upon some other nations. He did that to promote kinship among the different people. Let us drop this unnatural business, and return to the rules of sanity. There is no end to the ingenuity of man. You can fix up a scheme, if you want to, for raising oranges in Maine, but a barrel of those oranges would make William Waldorf Astor's pocket-book sick. (Laughter.) You can raise elephants in the jungles of Vermont, but it would take all the inheritance-tax on the Gould estate to pay the cost. (Laughter.) You can raise Polar bears on the equator if you spend money enough, but it would take a king's ransom to do it. (Laughter.) Whom the gods destroy they first make mad; and that's what's the matter with the Protectionists. Your greed grows by that on which it feeds. You refused the Morrison Bill, with its little reduction; you rejected the Mills Bill, with its small charges; and now you are kicking at the moderate Wilson Bill. You may beat this Bill by the help of the assistant Republicans. (Laughter.) But if you do, you will build a Free-trade party, and the men with brains, and hearts, and love of humanity will rend the temple of Protection till not one stone remains upon another in that robbers' roost. (Applause.) You want to know what a tariff reformer really is. I'll tell you. A tariff reformer is a rudimentary Free-trader. (Laughter.) He is the germ of a Free-trader; the egg from which a Free-trader is hatched. (Laughter.) And you Protectionists are acting simply as incubators—(laughter)—hatching out Radical Free-traders so fast that it takes a lightning calculator to keep count of the chicks. (Laughter and applause.) What the brook is to the river, what the young colt is to the war-horse, that the tariff reformer is to the Free-trader. You can misrepresent him, you can abuse him, you can call him names, you can make faces at him, but you cannot disturb his peace of mind, for he knows that the coming years are his. (Applause.) Those of you who don't want to be run over by the car of Juggernaut had better get out of the way of the procession. (Laughter.) This army is marching on, and where the advance halts to-day the rear-guard will camp to-morrow. You are breeding Free-traders faster than rabbits are bred in Australia. (Laughter.) If you reject this Bill you are preparing a club bigger than that of Hercules, and some day there'll be such a cracking of Protectionists' skulls as will startle the man in the moon when he goes sailing over Homestead and Johnstown and Sparrow Point. (Laughter.) In those days it will be worse for Protectionists than for the foxes in the days when Samson tied firebrands to their tails. (Laughter.) The waves would not recede for Canute; no more will this great wave of popular sentiment be stayed by the commands of the tariff barons. (Applause.)"

APPENDIX C.

Some of the remarks of Lord Chief Justice Kenyon in the case of the King against Waddington, tried in the year 1800, which I have referred to in the text, may be of interest; as, old-fashioned though they are, they show how the ancient principles of our law condemn the exploitation of the public by means of commercial monopoly. We can imagine how surprised this old judge would have been at the practices of the Rings, Trusts, and Combinations that I have referred to in my notes.

He says, in giving judgment:

"So far as the policy of this system of laws that has been lately called in question, I have endeavoured to inform myself as much as lay in my power, and for this purpose I have read Dr. Adam Smith's work, and various other publications upon the same subject. . . . But without attending to disputed points, let us state fairly what this case really is, and then see if it be possible to doubt whether the defendant has been guilty of any offence. Here is a person going into the market who deals in a certain commodity. If he went there for the purpose of making his purchases in the fair course of dealing, with a view of afterwards dispersing the commodity which he collected in proportion to the wants and convenience of the public, whatever profit accrues to him from the transaction, no blame is imputable to him. On the contrary, if the whole of his conduct shows plainly that he did not make his purchases in the market with this view, but that his traffic there was carried on with a view to enhance the price of his commodity; to deprive the people of their ordinary subsistence, or else to compel them to purchase it at an exorbitant price; who can deny that this is an offence of the greatest magnitude? It was the peculiar policy of this system of laws to provide for the wants of the poor labouring class of the country. If humanity alone cannot operate to this end, interest and policy must compel our attention to it. Now this defendant went into the market for the very purpose of tempting the dealers in hops to raise the price of the article, offering them higher terms than they themselves proposed and were contented to take, and urging them to withhold their hops from the market in order to compel the public to pay a higher price. What defence can be made for such conduct? And how is it possible to impute an innocent intention to him? We must judge of a man's motives from his overt acts; and by that rule it cannot be said that the defendant's conduct was fair and honest to the public. It is our duty to take care that persons in pursuing their own particular interests do not transgress those laws which were made for the benefit of the whole community."

APPENDIX D.

I HAVE alluded to the danger threatening Australia of being swamped by an influx of Chinese. It is surprising how soon they make themselves at home in a country, and seek to get their share of the best that is going. Years ago, when an advance in Protective duties was proposed in Victoria, a Chinaman, who had married a European wife, got his wife to address to a Royal Commission this statement of his claim for a duty:

"Possum Gully, September, 1882.

"My husband, who is a good Chinaman, wants to know if you will put a big duty on the birds' nests that his people bring to this country, *as it is only the rich boss Chinamen that use them.* He has found out how to make them from sparrows' nests, so if you put about five shillings on each nest he will make them,

"Yours respectfully,
"ANNIE A."

APPENDIX E.

It may amuse the reader who is interested in studying the social conditions of the United States, to call to mind some of Sydney Smith's comments upon that subject in the early part of the century.

"One of the great advantages of the American Government is its cheapness. The American king has about £5,000 per annum; the vice-king £1,000. They hire their Lord Liverpool at about £1,000 per annum, and their Lord Sidmouth (a good bargain) at the same sum. Their Mr. Crokers are inexpressibly cheap—somewhere about the price of an English doorkeeper or bearer of a mace. Life, however, seems to go on very well, in spite of these low salaries. . . . A judge administers justice without calorific wig and particoloured gown, in a coat and pantaloons. He is obeyed, however, and life and property are not badly protected in the United States.

"Literature the Americans have none—no native literature we mean. It is all imported. They had a Franklin, indeed, and may afford to live for half a century on his fame. There is, or was, a Mr. Dwight, who wrote some poems, and his baptismal name was Timothy. There is also a small account of Virginia by Jefferson, and an epic by Joel Barlow, and some pieces of pleasantry by Mr. Irving. But why should the Americans write books, when a six weeks' passage brings them, in their own tongue, our sense, science, and genius, in bales and hogsheads? Prairies, steamboats, grist-mills, are their natural objects for centuries to come. Then, when they have got to the Pacific Ocean—epic poems, plays, pleasures of memory, and all the elegant gratifications of an ancient people who have tamed the wild earth, and set down to amuse themselves,—this is the natural march of human affairs.

"We are terribly afraid that some Americans spit upon the floor, even when the floor is covered by good carpets. Now all claims to civilisation are suspended till this secretion is otherwise disposed of. No English gentleman has spit upon the floor since the Heptarchy.

"Unitarians are increasing very fast in the United States, not being kept down by charges from bishops and archdeacons, their natural enemies.

"America seems, on the whole, to be a country possessing vast advantages and little inconveniences. They have a cheap Government and bad roads; they pay no tithes and have stage-coaches without springs. They have no poor laws and no monopolies, but their inns are inconvenient and travellers are teased with questions. They have no collections in the fine arts, but they have no Lord Chancellor, and they can go to law without absolute ruin. They cannot make Latin verses, but they expend immense sums in the education of the poor."

THE END.

www.ingramcontent.com/pod-product-compliance
Lightning Source LLC
Chambersburg PA
CBHW031853220426
43663CB00006B/602